# CORESELF POSITIONING
## to Get on the Same Page, *Literally*

TIM PRESTON &
JONATHAN THOMAS

# CORESELF POSITIONING

## TO GET ON THE SAME PAGE, LITERALLY

**8 Steps That Refine Our Current Position and Identify Our Best Action Plan**

amplify
an imprint of Amplify Publishing Group

amplify
an imprint of Amplify Publishing Group

**www.amplifypublishinggroup.com**

***CoreSelf Positioning to Get on the Same Page, Literally: 8 Steps That Refine Our Current Position and Identify Our Best Action Plan***



**For more information, please contact:**
Amplify Publishing, an imprint of Amplify Publishing Group
620 Herndon Parkway, Suite 220
Herndon, VA 20170
info@amplifypublishing.com

Library of Congress Control Number: 2024910327

CPSIA Code: PRV0125A

ISBN-13: 979-8-89138-286-2

Printed in the United States

Simple. Not Easy., LLC 337 Bridge Street
Northampton, MA 01060 www.SimpleNotEasy.org

*To Tim for bringing the wisdom, organization, and energy needed to move this project from wishful possibility to actuality.*

*To Jonathan for sharing the words that bookmarked in my mind, "Everything I am going to teach you is Simple, Not Easy."*

*To the countless individuals who have contributed their time and energy to review and make this material better. To everyone who has completed a CoreSelf Map or participated in a CoreSelf Workshop. To our family and friends who have been patient with our time commitment. Lastly, to those who will enhance and bring this material to the next level.*

"Your beliefs become your thoughts,
your thoughts become your words,
your words become your habits,
your habits become your values,
your values become your destiny."

— **MAHATMA GANDHI**

"You, who are on the road
Must have a code you try to live by
And so become yourself
Because the past is just a goodbye …"

— **GRAHAM NASH**

# Contents

Foreword: **Stories of Observing: *Reimagined*** xi

**Suggestions for How to Use this Book** xv

Preface: **Plan to Be Surprised and a Promise** xxiii

**YOUR Story Is What Makes This Work** xxxiii

Part 1: **CoreSelf Mapping** 1
**Getting on the Same Page** *with oneself*

**STEP 1:** TRIANGLES and Others Involved 17

**STEP 2:** ENERGY and Where I Am vs. Where I Want to Be 31

**STEP 3:** VALUES and How We Practice Them 61

**STEP 4:** PLANS and Thoughts 85

**STEP 5:** SITUATION and Emerging Details 103

**STEP 6:** STRENGTHS and Resources Available 111

**STEP 7:** STRUGGLES and Receiving Credit for Past Efforts 119

**STEP 8:** STRATEGIES and Real Questions 127

Part 2: **CoreSelf Guidelines** 141
That Reveal *Real Questions and a Best Next Step*

**Action:** Identifying Sustainable Plans or
Unpacking Real Questions

**Guideline 1:** SLOW DOWN to Get There Faster 145

**Guideline 2:** TRUST THE MAP As You Engage 151

**Guideline 3:** QUESTION RESPECTFULLY and Actively Listen 157

Part 3: **CoreSelf Positioning** 163

**Getting on the Same Page** *with others*

**Action:** Same Page Partnership *literally*

Part 4: **CoreSelf Journaling** 205

**Action:** Daily 4**S** Journaling combined with 1505 to Maintain Focus on What Matters Most

Part 5: **Mastering CoreSelf Agility** 247

**Action: Putting—Pulling It All Together**

Epilogue: **Work to Be Done and an Invitation** 250

Appendix: **Glossary of Terms** 252

About the Authors 256

Notes 258

FOREWORD

# Stories of Observing: *Reimagined*

"We cannot create observers by saying 'observe,'
but by giving them the power and the means for this observation
and these means are procured through education of the senses."

— MARIA MONTESSORI

*Maria Montessori (Italian physician and educator. 1870 - 1952) developed the Montessori Method in 1907. She believed that the first duty of the educator was to recognize the human personality of the individual, and to observe and respect it; moreover, she was emphatic that through education and senses an individual can observe and understand their surroundings. Over a century later, there still remains much work to be done in K-12 to teach our children the important skills of self-observation and regulation.*

---

William James, now known as the "founder of psychology in America," used hypnosis as a primary research tool in the 1880s when he wrote about the "hidden self."

Dr. Ernest Hilgard's research in the 1950s also included the use of hypnosis; with participants relaxed and in a trance, Dr. Hilgard asked them this question:

**Q: "Is there a part of you that sees yourself differently?"**

Some participants responded affirmatively and invited Dr. Hilgard to speak with that part of him or her. Dr. Hilgard wrote extensively about this phenomenon that he called the "Hidden Observer." Here are excerpts of participants describing their Hidden Observer[1]:

**A: "... doesn't deal with pain. It looks at what is, and doesn't judge it"**

**A: "... is watching, mature, logical, has more information."**

**A: "... an extra, all-knowing part of me."**

**A: "... is analytical, unemotional, business-like."**

**A: "He seems more mature than the rest of me. More logical, an amused by me that couldn't hear because of course you can hear."** She explained that she used the masculine pronoun for the hidden observer because she thinks of males as more logical and females as more intuitive.

When asked to explain, she indicated that, ***"The observing part, corresponding to what would ordinarily have been a hidden observer, was not hidden, was instead at the top of her hierarchy, observing everything with curiosity."***

Jonathan's clinical work followed both James and Hilgard in developing what we call the *Internal Observer and Navigator* (I/ON). Jonathan's most significant contribution is the ability to access and activate one's I/ON without hypnosis—by utilizing a simple single page CoreSelf Mapping (CSM) worksheet and asking two observing questions:

1. **Where am I?**
2. **Where do I want to be?**

These two simple questions ignite the pilot light of one's Internal Observer. With ongoing CoreSelf practice, participants are able to more extensively engage their Observer/Navigator function. They are often able to gain and explore new insights and possible best next steps in challenging situations.

## Simple. Not Easy.

Paradox *(noun)* 1. a statement or proposition that seems self-contradictory or absurd but in reality expresses a possible truth.

Very early in our acquaintance, Jonathan said to Tim, "What I am going to tell you next is simple to say, but not easy to do." Exploring the *simple/not easy* paradox with regard to resolving complex situations has kept us well-occupied for many years and provided the name of our company.

It is best to approach the method described in this book as you would a ring of keys that open many safety deposit boxes: compartments containing valuable information that answers many questions and meets many needs.

Doing a CoreSelf Map (CSM) opens one of those boxes and gives you access to that information. You can complete a CSM on a single sheet of paper in a few minutes; that is the *simple* part. The *not easy* part is letting go of expectations and allowing the process to switch on an unfamiliar mind function that has much to offer in response to some of your deepest questions and concerns. Clearly stating your questions and wishes for going forward in your work and important relationships will allow the CoreSelf Mapping process to unfold most effectively.

Gaining proficiency in *Getting on the Same Page* with oneself via CSM is only part of the benefit. Building and maintaining strong relationships in a busy world can be challenging. The most important ongoing benefit is *Getting on the Same Page* with others, both personally and professionally. Part Three of this book expands on CSM with CoreSelf Positioning (CSP) to reframe these two important questions:

1. **Where are we?**
2. **Where do we want to be?**

# Suggestions for How to Use this Book

"If I had an hour to solve a problem,
I'd spend 55 minutes thinking about the problem
and five minutes thinking about solutions."

— ALBERT EINSTEIN

*Einstein (German-born physicist and mathematician. 1879 - 1955) believed the quality of the solution you generate is in direct proportion to your ability to identify the problem you hope to solve. He emphasized above with "and my life depended on the solution."*

---

No aspect of solving challenges or reducing uncertainty can offer more perspective than proper awareness and reflection. The very process of identifying and articulating our situation, resources available, and giving ourselves credit for past efforts allows us to discover where we are, then decide where we want to go and how to get there. It prompts questions, leads to answers, and creates roadmaps to best next steps.

This book is intended for individuals that are new to the CoreSelf Framework as well as those who have already experienced CoreSelf Mapping™ or CoreSelf Positioning.™ Each chapter is structured to improve the reader's confidence in utilizing the material to Get on the Same Page with oneself and others.

## Layout and Structure of this Book

In the spirit of Simon Sinek's "Golden Circle," introduced in his well-received 2006 TED Talk and expanded on in his bestselling book, *Start with Why* (2009), we offer our:

**WHY:** Help others **Get on the Same Page**

HOW: by accessing and paying attention to their Internal Observer & Navigator

WHAT: with CoreSelf Mapping (CSM), CoreSelf Positioning (CSP), CoreSelf Journaling (CSJ) tools, workshops, Speaking with an Advisor, CSM App and this book.

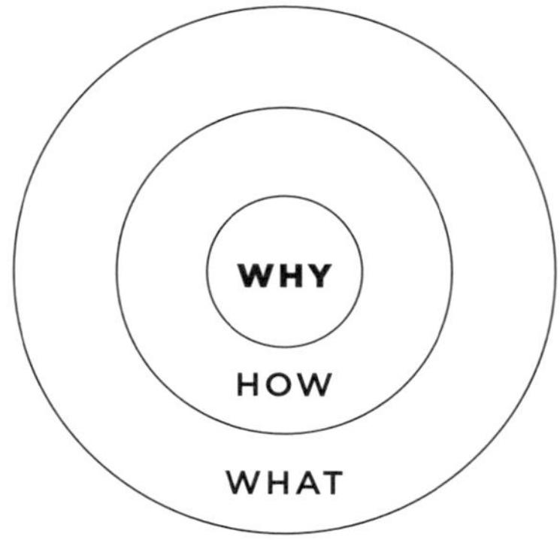


Stephen Covey often used basic geometry to elaborate on his most important topics. We will be doing the same to expand on our CoreSelf Framework. For example, Covey used a triangle to depict his definition of "habit: found at the intersection of: knowledge, skill, and desire." Knowledge is the theoretical paradigm, the WHAT to do and the why. Skill is the HOW to do. Desire is the motivation, the WANT to do. *In order to make something a Habit in our lives, he suggests that we must have all three.*

In these pages you will find that combining a few basic geometric symbols—triangles, circles, arrows—can have a significant and powerful impact when combined with two important questions:

1. **Where am I?** and
2. **Where do I want to be?**

Our intention is to present the CoreSelf Framework in a simple, accessible format that the reader can productively use on a daily basis.

## *Overview*

This *Overview* is for readers new to CoreSelf Mapping (CSM). For maximum benefit, we recommend reading the chapters in order and returning later to the expanded material contained in the *User Guide*. Readers will be introduced to fundamental concepts and illustrations, which will sequentially build upon each other.

Once one becomes proficient with CSM, each chapter contains a *User Guide* that can be referenced as a resource for increased understanding and clarification of details.

***For those preferring a fast-track approach, it is possible to immediately start at "Step 1: Triangles," and only read each overview until you see the marks below this paragraph (proceed to pages 17-21). In our studies, this approach can be completed in less than 90 minutes.***

+ + +

Regardless of which approach the reader takes, we have deliberately chosen a method that is "hands-on." Our research has repeatedly shown that experiencing the CoreSelf Mapping first and then exploring its components in more detail is conducive to learning the CSM method. Readers benefit from experiencing the Mapping exercise in a real-life context while considering a situation of some interest to themselves.

## *User Guide*

The *User Guide* has been created for readers familiar with CoreSelf Mapping (CSM) or CoreSelf Positioning (CSP), who are looking to expand their knowledge and proficiency with the tools; moreover, the *User Guide* chapters sharpen focus on specific skills that are relevant to a particular stage within the CoreSelf Mapping or Positioning process (e.g., Step 2 - Emotions & Sensations, Step 4 - Values & Practices).

While the *Overview* portions are intended to explain overall concepts and their sequence, the *User Guide* expands on these concepts and encourages the reader to reflect on important CSM elements that can greatly enhance one's professional and personal journey in Mastering CoreSelf Agility.

This book can function as a *User Manual*, like those you receive with a new appliance or computer. Give yourself time to gradually take in the descriptions, diagrams, and directions that are involved in practicing CoreSelf Mapping. This section provides behind-the-scenes understanding of CSM's workings. While the CSM can provide rapid results, we suggest absorbing and practicing with one section of the CSM at a time. Working with a certified CoreSelf Advisor can provide enhanced progress and faster results. Additional resources are available on our website, SimpleNotEasy.org.

## The Book's Building Blocks

Once the reader feels proficient in *Getting on the Same Page* with themselves utilizing the CoreSelf Framework, these new skills can be leveraged in many ways. All of the skills learned in CSM directly transfer to *Getting on the Same Page* with others.

We will provide supplemental material with step-by-step instructions for applications involving partnerships and larger relationship networks in Part Three. We have found that building and maintaining personal and professional relationships using these methods to be a successful comprehensive strategy.

In Part Four we will show that a subset of CSM can be used as a daily *CoreSelf Journaling* practice for additional benefit.

## The Relationship Effect

Each of us participates in a complicated field of relationships. These constellations may appear to be like a branch of a family tree or the "star chart" of an organization. It turns out that working on making our star (our self) burn a little brighter makes the whole constellation shine brighter.

We are not talking about *Looking Out for #1.*[2] In fact, we are talking about the opposite: becoming one's best self by practicing compassion that leads to understanding and providing nurturance while also setting constructive limits. Research has shown that others will take notice of your thoughtful efforts and seek to match your example. Some will even ask you to teach them what you have learned.

### Road Maps

In Joseph Deitch's exciting book, *ELEVATE: An Essential Guide to Life*,[3] he tells the story of the intellectual re-awakening he experienced after many years as a business owner:

> *"I started exploring voraciously… I turned to both Eastern and Western philosophies, as well as to modern science. I essentially became my own lab rat, learning from my successes and even more from my failures.*
>
> *[…]*
>
> *But oh, what I would have given for a road map! Time and time again, I found myself yearning for answers… And it wasn't just about me: How could I help the other people in my life, those I lived with and worked with and cared so much about?"*

Deitch has succeeded in making his book a "manual of powerful insights and practical answers," particularly for his colleagues and students in the business community. He refers to "road maps" as theoretically desirable goals.

The CoreSelf Framework allows *you* to map the dynamics of your current situation with a few strokes of your pen; it also empowers you, with practice, to generate practical Best Next Steps and sustainable plans. A sequence of CoreSelf Maps in your journal can provide reliable guidance to move you in the right direction down the right road.

## The Rising Tide Effect

The phrase, "A rising tide lifts all boats," has its origin in ancient Chinese texts. Recently it has been adapted for use as a slogan in commercial and political advertising. Dr. Murray Bowen, one of the pioneers of family therapy, alluded to it as a way of understanding how members of family units influence each other.

"According to Bowen, changes in behavior of one family member are likely to have an influence on the way the family functions over time.[4]" In essence, he believed that working on "differentiation of self" was a valuable skill for understanding relationships. The ability to separate our own emotions and thoughts from those of others can be learned and practiced in all of life's relationships.[5]

Both the "IKEA Effect[6]" and "Betty Crocker Effect[7]" espouse the value associated with actively participating in assembling a product or mixing ingredients in a cake mix.

In this book, we assembled all the ingredients needed to *Get on the Same Page* and all you have to do is add the final ingredient: yourself. We have done the research, and we know it works. First, we will share with you a step-by-step process to let you experience "CoreSelf magic." Afterwards we will share with you why and how it works, for those who want to know more.

## Three Books in One

This volume contains three books in one, with the first divided into an *Overview* and *User Guide*. It is intended to be accessible to *everyone who practices these skills:*

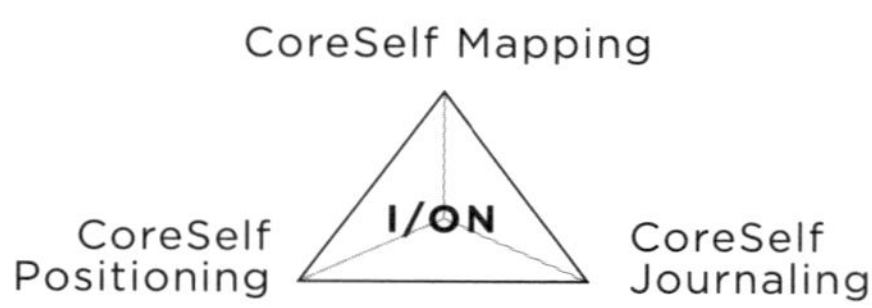

PREFACE

# Plan to Be Surprised and a Promise

"It is our attitude at the beginning of a difficult task which, more than anything else, will affect its successful outcome."

— WILLIAM JAMES

*William James (American philosopher and psychologist. 1842 - 1910) was the first educator to offer a psychology course in the United States. He knew it was the beginning of a difficult task that ultimately led to a successful outcome.*

*This book is not about taking a self-centered, help-yourself approach to getting ahead or simply getting by with strategies that are good enough. It is about getting on the same page with yourself, then with others—those relationships in our lives that matter most.*

*What if you could train your mind to observe each situation differently, not in terms of how to do what but in terms of where to move next (to fulfill your life goals)?*

*Our response to that wish has led us to ask three simple, actionable, and repeatable questions that work every time, regardless of one's uncertainty or apprehension in any situation.*

*Curious? Read on and plan to be surprised.*

---

## *Overview*

Our collective attitude since starting this project in 2017 has been one of humble optimism. We are extending a route first explored by two of the most admired scholars in the field of psychology in the nineteenth and twentieth centuries. Although their research on this particular topic has been largely overlooked for many decades, we are certain that they would welcome further study and development of the concept they pioneered.

James wrote in his article in Scribner's Magazine, "The Hidden Self:[8]"

> "It often happens that scattered facts of a certain kind float around for a long time, but that nothing scientific or solid comes of them until someone writes just enough of a book to give them a possible body and meaning. Then they shoot together, as it were, from all directions, and that book becomes the center of crystallization of a rapid accumulation of new knowledge."

William James, a forefather in the field of psychology, and Ernest Hilgard, a distinguished professor at Stanford University, confirmed through their research the existence of a "conscious observer" hidden away behind a barrier in the mind. Their work planted seeds for understanding and documenting how the human mind can experience events both from the *outside-in* through normal cognition and from the *inside-out* from the perspective of the *Observer* function of the mind. Their initial discoveries have been confirmed in recent years by neuroscience research that provides us with materials to create much more detailed and functional maps of human relationships.[9]

We all have multiple, meaningful dimensions of our lives that are not limited by the usual measures of success in the academic world or the marketplace. This book's framework for working on oneself will introduce you to new perspectives from which to observe your multifaceted life. We each possess a unique combination of the emotional energy we experience, the values we hold, and our potential to take meaningful action. Together these elements create a powerful set of lenses for us to observe where we are now, the distance forward that we can travel, and the new levels of certainty we can achieve.

*"Between stimulus and response there is a space.*
*In that space is our power to choose our response.*
*In our response lies our growth and our freedom."*

- VIKTOR E. FRANKL

**The Benefit of Best Next Steps** (leading to Small Wins)

In this book, we share a process that can move you forward in your situation immediately without delay of additional discussion or feedback from others. This eight-step worksheet allows you to accomplish three important things: 1) pick an important specific situation that is top-of-mind; 2) explore the situation by completing the steps in the worksheet; and 3) arrive at a key *Best Next Step*—bringing you closer to where you want to be—or presenting you with a *Real Question*. A Real Question is characterized by: I don't know the answer; I want to know the answer; I'm willing to consider the answer that will come next. Both results can provide insightful clarity, perspective, and direction.

External situations can create stress and internal dynamics tension. This pushing and pulling of a situation makes us feel stuck and unable to move forward.

Think about the commonly heard remark, "I am of two minds about that issue." If that statement is true, we need to ask if those states of mind are an indication of positive progress or troublesome tension. Most of the time being "single-minded" (i.e., extremely focused) is considered positive; a person in that state is more likely to get important things done and is less likely to become distracted. At other times, seeing a situation from multiple perspectives can fuel uncertainty.

Charlie Mackey, in his wonderfully illustrated book, *The Boy, the Mole, the Fox, and the Horse*, comments:

> *"Isn't it odd. We can only see our outsides, but nearly everything happens on the inside."*

Jonathan has long espoused that people in excellent mental health can indeed be understood to have *one brain, but four minds*. They have a mind that processes emotional energy, whose function it is to keep them safe. They have a mind that clarifies priorities and preferences, managing their decisions about what is most important to know or to do at any given time. Also, they have a mind that can choose and implement a strategy to move them closer to where they want to be. These three minds all track day-to-day and moment-to-moment events.

**Q: How can it be that these three important minds don't get in each other's way or, worse, battle with each other?**

**A: We each have a unique Internal Observer and Navigator mind that communicates with all three and can suggest best next steps.**

Many have never heard of the fourth mind, which William James called "The Hidden Self." Ernest Hilgard called it "The Hidden Observer," and we refer to it as the *Internal Observer and Navigator*. The original discovery of the fourth part of the mind by William James occurred in the 1870s, meaning that it preceded Freud's and Jung's earliest writings about "the unconscious" by several decades. As you will see in the unfolding chapters of this book, one need not engage in debates about the value of exploring the unconscious to understand how the *Observer* plays the role of moving-conscious awareness closer to center and into better balance with regard to emotions, beliefs, and actions.

We will show how *CoreSelf Mapping*, *CoreSelf Positioning*, and *CoreSelf Journaling* strengthen conscious capabilities, just as physical exercise and mindfulness training benefit other dimensions of health.

The *Internal Observer and Navigator* function monitors how an individual undertakes physical challenges, contemplates aesthetic and ethical questions, and develops practical action plans requiring ongoing effort to complete. This book demonstrates that, at particular moments, one effective way to coordinate all four minds is to pause to work through an eight-step, two-dimensional map answering these questions in sequence:

1. **Where am I *now*?**
2. **Where do I *want* to be?**
3. **How shall I *get* there?**

Our research shows that the mental process of slowing down to complete a *CoreSelf Map* can be trusted to activate the mind's *Observer* function. Completing the short-answer part of the exercise activates the *Navigator* function, very much like a GPS processes location data and provides turn-by-turn directions to reach a destination.

Training your mind to observe situations differently can provide insight and perspective. Investing the time and energy to ponder the notion of *Self* can increase compassion and understanding. Practicing the skills involved in *Getting on the Same Page* with oneself will directly benefit relationships with others.

Slowing down to go faster can seem both paradoxical and contradictory. We have all experienced times when life has literally brought us to our knees, tested our reserves almost to the breaking point, triggered a part of us that erupted in uncontrollable anger, or made us wonder if it is possible to continue. These are moments that shatter our identity. Suddenly no longer knowing who we are and what we are supposed to be doing prompts us to ask what can possibly be our best next step.

Our personal experience is accurately captured in Roger Trapp's discussion of business leaders' challenges:

*"Such contradictions, dilemmas or challenges (call them what you will) plague our everyday personal lives. But so complex is the modern business environment that leaders are confronting their own paradoxes on a regular basis. They want to protect their core business at the same time as innovating for the future; they are looking at new territories while seeking to consolidate their presence in existing ones; and, particularly lately, they are expected to meet various environmental, social and governance (ESG) goals at the same time as meeting financial targets."*[10]

We will share a single page, step-by-step worksheet that will allow you to have an insightful—personal or professional—conversation with yourself resulting in:

- **Slowing Down** to Engage your Observer/Navigator
- **Acknowledging** your Current (Emotional Energy) Position
- **Determining** your Desired (Emotional Energy) Position
- **Providing** Alignment with your most important Values
- **Identifying** your Best Next Steps Leading to Small Wins
- **Building** on Small Wins (Steps) that lead to Big Gains

With the plethora of self-help books, *where* do we begin? *What* will work for us every time? How will we move important relationships from good to great?

Life is, and always will be, full of contradictions. We will always be able to count on plenty of expert suggestions about possibilities to consider: fixed mindset versus growth mindset, criticism versus curiosity, reacting versus pausing, urgent versus important execution. We are confident that the CoreSelf Framework and material will resonate with you regarding these choices. The *Complete Your CoreSelf Map first* approach will allow all readers to experience the power of their Internal Observer in a real-life situation. This approach has been tested and validated.

*Getting on the Same Page with oneself* can reap significant benefits in aligning emotional energy, values, and best next steps to navigate quickly and efficiently toward your goals. The foundation you build will result in being a more centered self in three key areas: ***CoreSelf-Trust, CoreSelf-Respect,*** and ***CoreSelf-Certainty.***

## The Promise of This Book

Many of the best things in life are *simple* and the choices/decisions that were best for us, in hindsight often seem obvious. However, operating in fast-paced environments and a results-driven economy can make it seem *not at all easy.*

The exercises in the book will show you how to slow down to access an unfamiliar brain function. Once activated, it can provide sustainable Best Next Steps and Real Questions to move you toward a better place in any challenging situation.

This is a book that will help everyone to improve their performance in their most important personal and professional roles. It is a concise, actionable, and repeatable process. It acknowledges current emotional energy levels and big-picture values to clarify confusing situations and identify viable best next steps.

Your investment of time to learn, reflect on, and practice this material will pay huge dividends in the quality of your most important relationships and provide positive and precise direction as you navigate through life's various challenges.

## Plan to be Surprised

In the 2007 movie, *Dan in Real Life,* widower Dan Burns gives family advice in his newspaper column at the same time that he is struggling mightily to raise his three daughters as a single parent. His efforts to succeed as a parent lead to a greatly increased capability to be present and flexible. This experience is powerfully captured in his advice to readers at the end of the movie, which provides a simple reminder for us all:

> *Dear Readers, for most of you, this is my first column in your paper. In the future, I will be answering your questions, but today I want to break from my usual format and talk to you about the subject of plans. Not so much my plan for this column, but life plans, and how we all make them. And how we hope that our kids make good, smart, safe plans of their own. But if we're really honest with ourselves, our plans usually don't work out as we had hoped. So instead of asking young people, "What are you plans? What do you plan to do with your life?" maybe we should tell them this: "Plan to be surprised."*

This book is about relationships that matter most: with oneself, with family and friends, and with colleagues in the workplace. *CoreSelf Mapping* provides an effective framework with which to navigate through many arenas of daily life— emotional energy and sensations, values and practices, thoughts and plans—in effectively *Getting on the Same Page with oneself and others.*

***There are plenty of self-help books;***
***we suggest becoming a student of self,***
***so you can ultimately help others.***

Enjoy and plan to be surprised by what you learn about yourself and how simple it is to craft better relationships. Spend a few minutes each day observing the situations in which you find yourself and asking *Real Questions* of yourself and those who are most important to you.

## YOUR Story Is What Makes This Work

When we were very young, we communicated through gestures and pictures before we learned language. We were curious to experience all that life had to offer. Along the way, at times, we **feel confused and stuck**. On the outside everything may look fine, but internally we may struggle to find certainty at the center our being.

As adults, we are drawn to others who encounter and navigate through life situations similar to our own.

In very good times our stories can, amazingly, look and work like this:

Stories are how we create meaning and connection. All human stories eventually include many levels of emotional energy, many types of relationships and many complex situations. In difficult times, our stories can look and feel like this:

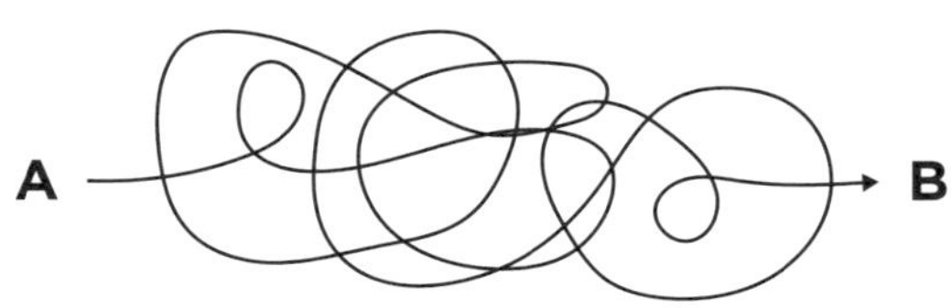


At those times, we would all be comforted if our stories could even look more like this:

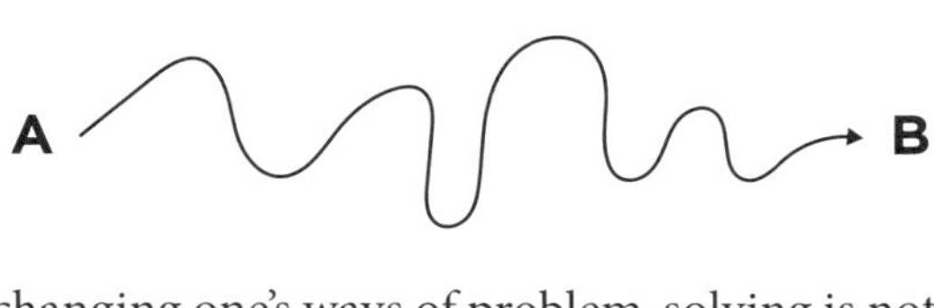


Even though changing one's ways of problem-solving is not easy, a tool explained in this book called The CoreSelf *Framework*™ simplifies the pathway.

Learning to activate a part of you called the Internal Observer/Navigator allows this to happen.

This book provides you with an eight-step CoreSelf *Mapping Worksheet* that demonstrates how the process works. We provide you an easy-to-use tool first, then help you add facts from your own story to explore and navigate best next steps or questions.

**Q: Why would we provide a tool first and explain it later?**

**A: Using the tool quickly demonstrates its value. You are able to get important feedback about challenging real-life situations by spending time now. "Getting on the Same Page with oneself" is an important first step that makes this experience work.**

It turns out that our approach was right. And wrong.

We were right to simply share something that we know works without prior explanation. We know that your story will have the most impact and value for you.

However, we were wrong not to share more stories that you are likely to identify with, stories that others also can relate to and that will pique your interest. When we are ready to grow, get unstuck, or improve relationships that matter most to us—we crave more stories that illustrate how humans connect most effectively.

## Tripods, Pyramids, and Our Minds

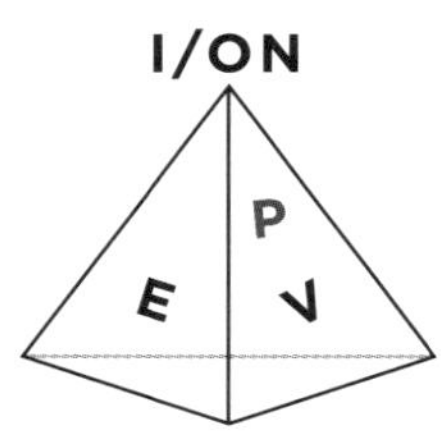


Surveying is said to be one of the oldest professions in the world with roots that trace back to ancient times, with a recorded land register in Egypt in 3000BC that included construction of the Great Pyramid of Giza.

Traditional surveyors utilized some basic tools (tripod, compass, plum-bob, theodolite) to examine and record maps and descriptions of uncharted territories with uneven terrain that often contained obstacles.

The American Congress for Surveying and Mapping's definition is:

> **"Surveying is the science and art of making all essential measurements to determine the relative position of points or physical and cultural details above, on, or beneath the surface of the earth, and to depict them in a usable form, or to establish the position of points or details."**

*The metaphor of a surveyor can be useful to describe how our minds work.* The mindset of a surveyor can offer helpful hints on how to observe uncharted terrain and record challenges in our daily lives; how to steady ourselves in unbalanced situations, using tools to center ourselves in apprehensive times, embracing guiding principles (e.g., location of point by measurement from two points of reference), or figuring out how to traverse unnavigable obstacles. A survey represents a process of collecting, analyzing, and interpreting data to develop insights. Effective surveys often involve multiple forms of data collection and are considered more in-depth than questionnaires.

When we use a surveyor's tools to study a huge pyramid, we can determine the measurements of a triangle at its base and the three triangular sides that converge at its apex. The base represents our *whole* self, each side represents a different *part* of our CoreSelf, and the apex is our unique *Internal Observer/Navigator*™ (**I/ON**) that centers our emotional energy (**E**), important values (**V**), and thoughtful plans (**P**).

When we are able to balance each side of this pyramid, each triangle will be equal in size (or surface area); if we were to hang a plum-bob from the apex, it would hang over the direct center of the bottom triangle, representing our balanced and centered self.

Without the right tools or mindset, it is easy to feel overwhelmed or stuck in the kaleidoscope of life. Each situation can represent a separate lens, each vying for the light source to project its particular image. Each turn of the tube changes our view of these situations, including their size and color.

Returning to our original metaphor, the three sides (facets) of our CoreSelf pyramid include:

1. Emotional Energy and Sensations (**E**)
2. Values and Practices (**V**)
3. Thoughts and Plans (**P**)

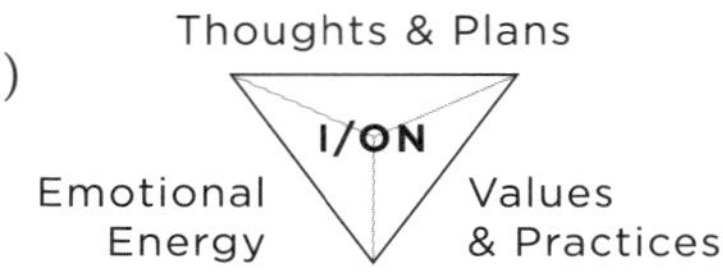


It is common in times of stress or feeling overwhelmed to focus all of our attention on the (E) side of, "How I am feeling." Significant events (e.g., work, health, divorce, death) can deplete our spirit and leave us asking, "What will I do now?" or "Why me?"

The size of our Emotional Energy and Sensations (E) facet can seem so large that it completely unbalances the other two facets of our pyramid. It can feel impossible to remember what values (V) are important to us, never mind considering practices that center us. Our thoughts and plans (P) can become impulsive or completely ignored. Stress changes our Focus. Focus redirects our Attention.

> Stress changes our Focus.
> Focus redirects our Attention.
> Attention drives our Experience.

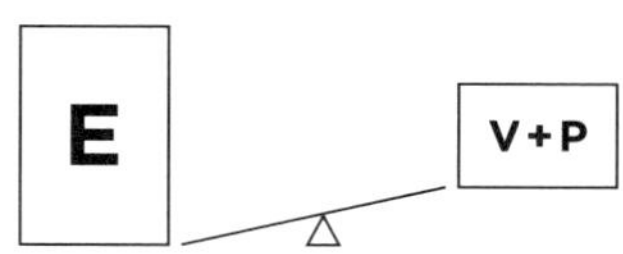


The CoreSelf Framework represents a simple, accessible tool that can help us observe and succinctly record our emotional energy, step back and remind ourselves of what values are most important to us, then navigate to a safer place and space where we can find balance. ***"How can a book, a framework, a pyramid help me get unstuck?"***

We each have a unique Internal Observer/Navigator that sits at the top of our pyramid of self that can observe each side separately and collectively. This part of you knows your entire history; it knows what you are capable of; it knows what you will and will not do; it has your best interests at heart; it is a part of you that wants to help and is available any time you want to talk (24/7). It works the way your brain does at its best!

### Start, Stop, Continue

We will share a way to stop over-focusing on the Emotional stress of challenging situations, start balancing Values and practices, and continue working to determine viable Best Next Steps (Plans).

### Tell me a story of how you know CoreSelf Mapping works.

Stories are how we communicate meaning, emotion, and energy. The CoreSelf stories we can share are countless. They come from the young and old, children and parents, relationships and partnerships, personal and professional. Here are some personal examples:

I met Jonathan as a result of a relationship in crisis. Jonathan was my partner's consultant and I agreed to meet with him. Professionally I was in a good place and owned a growing business; personally, I was divorced, had two young teenagers, and had not worked through growing up too fast in a poor, divorced, troubled, alcoholic family. While I have never spent time with a therapist, both of my children spent time with a child psychologist following my divorce.

Jonathan started out asking about my family and sketching a small family tree (being in sales, I could read what he was writing upside down); I thought, "Here we go, he's going to blame my family for all my faults." But this never happened!

Next he said, ***"Everything I am going to teach you is simple and not easy."*** We finished with him sharing a graphic illustration of how each of us were acting and reacting to each other's actions and reactions. His visual explanation provided insight and understanding. The personal relationship did not remedy itself; however, I came to believe that there is a tremendous opportunity for others to learn to practice his CoreSelf approach to mapping and navigating our most important relationships.

Nine years later (after selling my company in 2016) I reached out to Jonathan; you are holding in your hands one of the many results of our years of working together.

Serendipitously, working with Jonathan and understanding this material has allowed me to "do the work." It has made me a better human being. I had spent the majority of my younger years efficiently "compartmentalizing" stressful situations and was determined to "overcome the influences of my childhood." I conveniently found no time to express my emotions or let anyone pierce my armor. My three younger sisters can attest to my ardent desire to overcome the embarrassment of growing up on welfare in a dysfunctional family. Constantly chiding them, "Having a pity party? No one cares and the world expects nothing of you." I was hard, driven, and not going to let any of us use excuses or buckle under the pressure.

Even having spent a lifetime focusing on overcoming my past, I still find this difficult to write. While I did not like the way I grew up, it prepared me well. My sisters and I broke the proverbial mold and statistical barriers. I hope this is enough about my story (phew).

Jonathan has ten times my experience with the CoreSelf Framework; he invented it and our work with others has made it even more accessible. He has used this material personally to get through countless physical challenges and surgeries. His early work with parents and children is fascinating and spans decades. His curiosity and ability to observe and help children work through their dysfunctional families is a gift. Step 2 of 8 (more about this later) encompasses ten years of this gift.

The following slide is an excerpt from our CoreSelf *Connections*[11] deck:

### Most of the time we are fine … until we're not.

*CoreSelf Mapping* can be a useful tool for getting centered anytime, but it is often most helpful when we are under stress. Here's why:

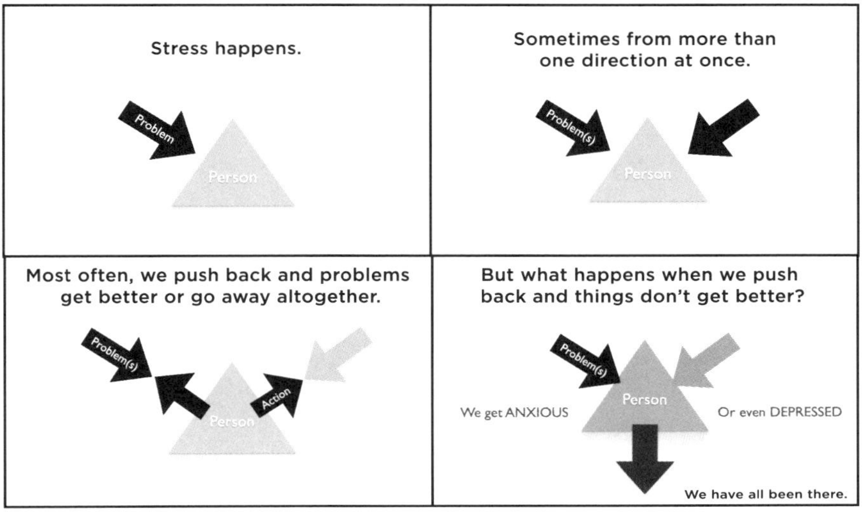


When we become stressed or overwhelmed, we often lose the ability to think clearly or take effective action. It becomes difficult to remember what is important to us. We are driven by our feelings, or cling blindly to beliefs and hope that things will get better. But this isn't the only option.

## The Circle—and Vicissitudes—of Life

All of us have been a child and some of us have children. Each of us has an inner child that shapes us and we all have others watching us navigate the vicissitudes of life. How we play the cards we are dealt has significant impact on those watching us—especially those silently observing us.

We will share the magic of the CoreSelf experience and power of asking Real Questions. One of Jonathan's stories represents the epitome of a *Real Question*:

Two parents are completing a CoreSelf *Map* together and the Situation revolves around their child, who has been psychiatrically hospitalized for an extended period and is returning home. It remains unclear if this difficult transition will change their course for the better or leave all parties in grief. As both are completing their long-hand portion of the CoreSelf Map, the mother writes her Real Question,

**"How do I raise the child I have, instead of the child I wanted?"**

*Getting on the Same Page* with oneself or others is not always about a challenging crisis or unresolved childhood experiences. Sometimes it is about growth or weighing our options in a structured way. It is about slowing down and realizing that the best course of action is to avoid making an impulsive decision. There are times that being true to our unique values represents a better approach than yielding to the expectations of others.

We have worked with partners who have been faced with a difficult decision to proceed with or pass on an opportunity; some of these choices appeared opportunistic and others have felt obligational. Slowing down to complete a CoreSelf Map provided alternate perspectives and best next steps, which are options that did not occur in the heat of the moment. Some of the best decisions we make are the ones we choose not to make. Deciding to not pursue an obvious path can be difficult, but it can make all the difference in the future.

Our roles and responsibilities—leader, manager, parent—can paint an external picture of success and of having our life in order, even when our internal picture is blurred and in disarray. No one else may see the conflict or tension; however, we feel it pulling at our core. Without aligning our internal self, this tension can negatively impact both our physical and mental health.

## Common Narratives and Difficult Courses of Action

We utilize three different narratives (starting on page 22): a young college student faced with a difficult family tragedy and perceived obligation to halt all studies to return home to remedy the situation; a troubled couple with children who have grown apart and unsure what the best course of action is for their family or marriage; and a profitable, midsize business that has grown rapidly to benefit its shareholders but finds its dispersed organization misaligned and not on the same page.

Each of the above narratives contains tremendous emotional energy that include: heightened emotions, tension, apprehension, confusion, and multiple perspectives. Effective discussion and resolution of any of them could easily result in a stalemate or silence, when different parties may feel unheard or overrun by an overbearing individual.

We will share with you how two Real Questions answered on a scale of 1-10 can contain all of the emotional energy of a difficult situation without stifling ongoing communication:

**Q:** "Where Am I?" (Mark with an **X**)

**Q:** "Where Do I Want To Be?" (**O**)

Exploring each of these unique situations and graphically answering the above questions, *might* look like this (granted, each individual *will* answer differently):

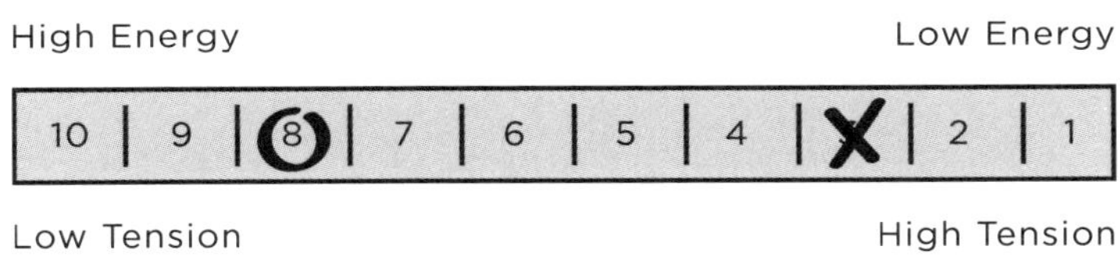


Once each party has answered the above questions, we will show you how to answer:

**Q: "How Do I/We Get There?"**

This book provides tools for Getting on the Same Page with oneself first, then building on that understanding with others. This framework allows you to "do the work" behind the scenes while watching internal and external forces align. If you already have a coach or therapist, this material will add pertinent color to future sessions— color in the form of insights, strategies, and questions that can be unpacked.

### Keeping Time and Score Works in Sports, Never in Relationships

We live in a fast-paced world filled with obligations and expectations—a world that professionally tends to keep score and time. While we all have the same amount of time, there never seems to be enough time to get everything done.

*Tension changes our Focus.*
*Focus redirects our Attention.*
*Attention drives our Experience.*

This book is about creating great relationships with people who matter most (including yourself ). It is about slowing down to go faster. Keeping score and time will never work in great relationships. Let us share with you a simple, accessible CoreSelf Framework that you can use immediately by yourself, then with others. Give yourself permission to try it first; then allow us to share with you why it worked!

The framework and approach of this material is about asking Real Questions, observing and simplifying (seemingly) complex situations, counterbalancing heightened emotions to channel valued energy into a positive force that can help us navigate to a better (sometimes safer) place. It is about getting on the same page with ourselves and others in a positive way. It is about accessible constructs delivered in a repeatable format.

Just Map It.

***Jonathan and Tim***

## PS Sequence of Getting on the Same Page

Other people's stories often focus on emotional energy pertaining to (urgent) situations and sharing the intention of "How bad they are feeling" (where they are).

If we want to get on the same page with another, we must *first* slow down to take inventory of our own emotional energy, long-term values, and possible actions.

Once we have clarified our own position, the process of getting on the same page with others becomes simpler and more straightforward. Practicing this new CoreSelf skill brings significant benefit to our most important relationships.

## Importance of Getting on the Same Page with oneself, before adding others

We often hear, "We need to Get on the Same Page." It is often phrased as a directive:

**Problem** A ⟶ B **Discussion**

Often the person speaking (left) wants to resolve a complex situation and may be combining multiple situations at the same time while the person receiving (right) is perceiving different complexities and also combining multiple situations (below):

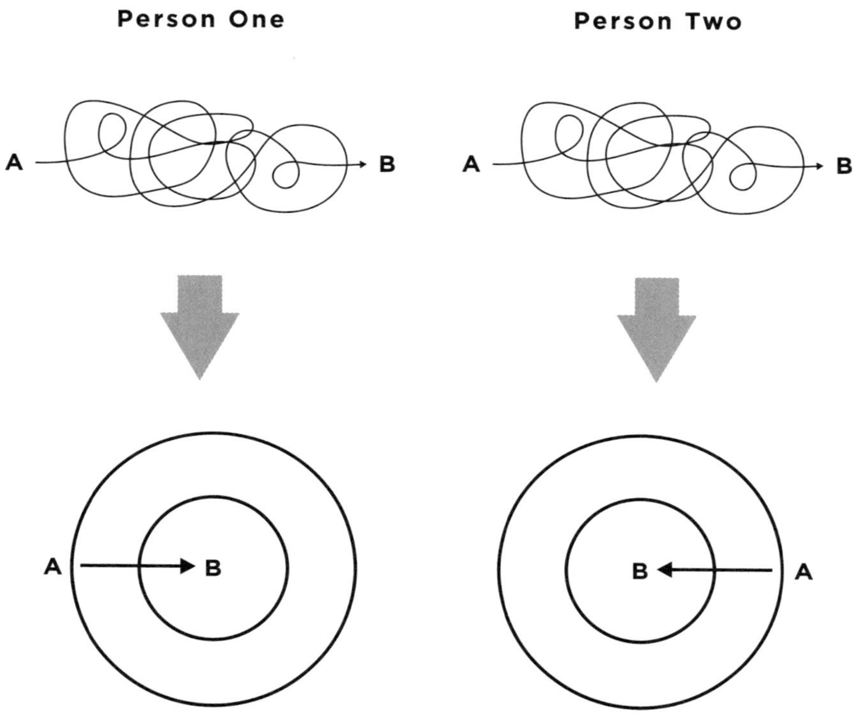


Taking the time to understand our individual positions—using the same process— regarding a *single, specific situation,* and centering ourselves, might look like this.

It is possible for both parties to describe and then share their individual position and then collaborate to create a common position/direction—and get on the same page!

**Partnership** B ←——————→ B **Agreement**

Changing "We *need* to Get on the Same Page" to "We *want* to Get on the Same Page" allows space to have a collaborative and safe conversation.

*If we just keep going over and over*
*the story in our mind,*
*we don't get anywhere.*

*Taking time to understand*
*Where we are and*
*Where we want to be,*
*helps us all get there.*

# PART ONE

# *CoreSelf Mapping*

# CoreSelf Mapping:
## Getting on the Same Page *with oneself*

"... one of the things this research shows is that a key in motivating change is recognizing the difference between where we are and where we want to be. Defining these two states creates a kind of potential energy that helps us to take that first difficult step."

— ROBERT WALDINGER AND MARC SCHULZ

*In "The Good Life: Lessons from the World's Longest Scientific Study on Happiness," Robert Waldinger, MD (American psychiatrist, author, and Zen priest) and Marc Schulz, PhD (American professor, clinical psychologist, and author) share that strong relationships make for a good life. Good relationships keep us healthier and happier.*

---

## *Overview*

The CoreSelf Framework may at first glance appear to be *counterintuitive*. It makes dynamic forward progress possible by temporarily slowing down the executive function of the mind. In our daily routines we depend on our *executive function* to create and to put into operation detailed plans and effective decisions, sometimes on tight timelines.

**Q: Why de-emphasize our productive executive function skill set?**

**A: To gain unique insights and reveal questions only available through the monitoring function.**

Monitoring function includes the ability to access, collect, and interpret internally stored information about our emotional energy, values, and plans.

Each of our monitoring brains contains memories of our entire life history or narrative; CoreSelf Mapping (CSM) provides instant access to this personal knowledge base. It helps us retrieve important information to navigate challenging situations.

The CoreSelf Mapping (CSM) process specifically and reliably activates one's personal monitoring function. CoreSelf Mapping and its extension, CoreSelf Positioning (CSP), can be used to effectively *Get On The Same Page* with ourselves and others. Learning to ask and answer questions about one's current location on the CoreSelf Map can provide additional clarity when considering detailed questions about one's situation.

In developing this method, we are *standing on the shoulders* of one of the best known psychologists of the twentieth century. During his research and practice at Stanford University, beginning in the 1950s, Ernest Hilgard, PhD, recognized the difference between executive and monitoring functions, then attempted to specifically evoke *monitoring awareness* in individual subjects. His contributions to psychology spanned over 40 years and highlighted the importance of utilizing the conscious monitoring function. His method was hypnosis,[12] a research tool commonly used at the time. After putting his subjects in a hypnotic trance, he asked them this Real Question:

| ***"Is there a part of you that sees yourself differently?"*** |
|---|

The responses to this question were audio-taped and played back to the individual subjects after they came out of trance. They described their responses in trance as coming from a part of themselves that they recognized, but to which they did not always have access. They found that particular part of their awareness surprisingly insightful and often practically helpful. His hypnosis research led Dr. Hilgard to describe that function of the mind as a normal but elusive capability that he called the "Hidden Observer;" he published his detailed findings in *Divided Consciousness: Multiple Controls in Human Thought and Action.*[13]

We have spent the last number of years exploring and researching this question:

**Q: Can the monitoring function be called upon by ordinary individuals without the use of hypnosis?**

**A: Yes. The CoreSelf Mapping worksheet activates one's monitoring function.**

What follows in this volume is our story of following in Dr. Hilgard's footsteps. CoreSelf Mapping provides the benefits of asking *Real Questions* and *Getting On The Same Page* with oneself and others. The structure of the CoreSelf Map uses both of these techniques as a source of direction to identify *Best Next Steps.*

Improving our relationships can be achieved by studying and applying the *CoreSelf Framework,* defined as a predetermined sequence that identifies actions that need to be taken. Adding Real Questions can get us on the same page with ourselves and others.

Here are questions and answers that we hear used every day:

**Q: How are you?**

**A: Fine.**

**Q: Why did you ___________ ?**

Emotional energy is the motivation that comes from our most fundamental feelings. The word emotion originates from the Latin word *movere*, which means energy in motion. Different emotions vibrate at different frequencies and can negatively or positively affect our energy levels. Emotional energy can be measured and channeled to radiate outwardly.

Questions paint pictures. Answers paint pictures.

**Q: Where is your emotional energy?**

**A: My emotional energy is centrally located where both my hopes and fears reside.**

Changing the questions we ask ourselves can help us paint vivid solutions. This begins by slowing down and focusing our attention on a single specific situation at a time.

### Solving Important Challenges

Identify a challenge that is both meaningful and interesting that you are motivated to resolve. Picture having a good conversation with a mentor about your questions. Then, imagine their feedback includes an insight that provides helpful direction and reduces apprehension.

*CoreSelf Mapping is an effective and efficient tool for building trust, respect, and confidence in oneself to identify the Best Next Step.*

The *Best Next Step* is a specific action in a sequence that raises accountability. Take time using the CoreSelf Mapping exercise to record and reflect on your current position in the specific situation. Begin to gain new insights and articulate *Real Questions* that might show challenging life events from a new perspective. The CoreSelf Map helps to counterbalance heightened emotional energy with one's important long-term values. This balance can provide space to navigate to possible best next steps.

> **"Putting first things first means organizing and executing around your most important priorities. It is living and being driven by the principles you value most, not by the agendas and forces surrounding you."[14]**

Selecting a single specific situation puts it foremost in the mind. Real Questions allow each of us to start with the situation that is currently most important. The magic of CoreSelf Mapping is that it provides an efficient and effective framework to collect all of the best ideas about how to resolve Real Questions.

The *secret sauce* to identifying sustainable solutions is as simple as changing the questions we ask ourselves.

## The Power of Who and Where Questions

Starting with a specific situation and changing the questions we ask can yield effective new strategies. The structured CoreSelf Framework asks many of these questions:

**Q: "Who else is involved in the Challenge?"**

**Q: "Where Am I?"**

**Q: "Where Do I Want To Be?"**

The Internal Observer/Navigator (I/ON) is a part of one's mind that tracks all important activity in all of the key arenas of one's life. It is able to observe all facets of a challenge and navigate to the Best Next Steps.

Activating one's Internal Observer/Navigator (I/ON) represents the CoreSelf game changer. The I/ON knows our history and can provide coaching to help us navigate uncharted territory. It provides a CoreSelf Framework to have a productive conversation with oneself with no need to share the backstory.

## Outside-In and Inside-Out Process

The CoreSelf Mapping (CSM) approach provides a way to enlist positive comments from others to explore outside points of view that may add valuable perspective. Traditional coaching and consulting approaches shift who is asking and who is answering important *questions*:

| Communicator | Self | Coach | Consultant |
|---|---|---|---|
| | *I guess questions.* | *I ask questions.* | *You ask questions.* |
| | *You search for answers.* | *You figure out answers.* | *I give you answers.* |
| **Investment** | No cost | Low to Medium | Medium to Large |
| **Time to Value** | Depends | Medium to Long | Defined in Deliverables |
| **Approach** | Self-directed; Skill & Knowledge Dependent | Meet You Where You Are & Wait until Ready | Get You to Where You Need to be |
| **Variables** | Right Guesses & Time | Right Questions & Time | Right Problems & Time |
| **Style** | Personal <-> Curiousity | Suggest <-> Direct | Direct <-> Edict |
| **Repeatable** | If Figure Out/Taught | If Taught Process/Skill | If Integrated to Systems |
| **Sustainable** | If Correct & Practiced | If Valued & Practiced | If Delivered & Integrated |

Figure 1.1 - **Traditional Approaches**
Who's Asking & Who's Answering

Note: 1. "**Self**" no coach or consultant.
2. "**Coach**" or personal "Therapist."

There is a complementary approach that is more cost-effective and timely. Saving time and money is a direct result of integrating these two approaches. Once learned, this simple framework is repeatable and scalable without the need for additional expense.

CoreSelf Mapping increases one's well being, identifies and develops strengths, and improves performance by Getting on the Same Page with oneself and one's team. CSM identifies and sets value-driven goals. CSM uses the power of psychology and neuroscience to uncover and adopt new approaches for oneself and for teams. It is a strength-based approach that leverages prior successes to build confidence and prompts inside-out understanding.

The illustration below represents an overview of how the CoreSelf Framework balances the flow between basic (outside-in) questions and (inside-out) feedback from ones' Internal Observer (I/O). This gentle dance between outside and inside provides insights and Real Questions by viewing challenging situations from many different viewpoints.

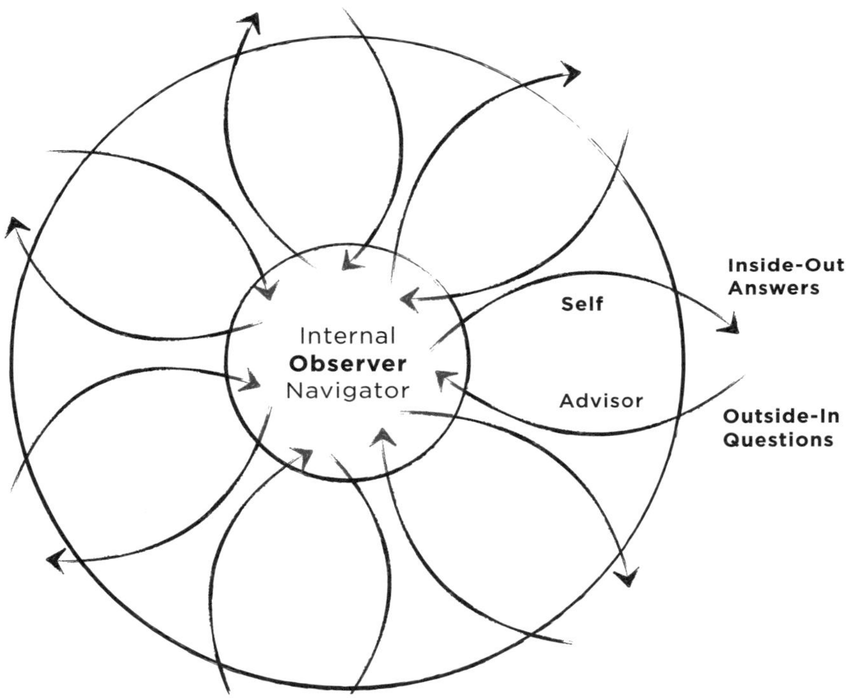


Figure 1.2 - **CoreSelf Advisor Approach**
Outside-In Questions and Inside-Out Answers

The CoreSelf Method delivers the advantages of both visual and narrative learning styles. Granting that we all learn differently, combining these styles reinforces and supports a wide range of applications.

## "A Walking Stick versus a Crutch"

In *The 7 Habits of Highly Effective People*[15], Covey wrote:

> **"As my study took me back through two hundred years of writing about success, I noticed a startling pattern emerging in the content of the literature. Because of our own pain, and because of similar pain I had seen in the lives and relationships of many people I had worked with through the years, I began to feel more and more that much of the success literature of the past fifty years was superficial. It was filled with social image consciousness, techniques, and quick fixes with social Band-Aids and aspirin ("Crutches") that addressed acute problems and sometimes even appeared to solve them temporarily, but left the underlying chronic problems untouched to fester and resurface time and again."**

Our "Step 4: Values and Practices" is one of several places where we revisit and expand on Covey's principle-centric work. Reflecting on values that matter most to us and how we practice those values can provide reinforcement and self-respect in our daily lives.

Serendipitously, in both the personal and professional arenas, the CoreSelf Framework reinforces many of Covey's 7 Habits;[16] when you engage with the CoreSelf Map (CSM) you are being proactive by asking and answering:

> **Q: "Where Am I?"**
>
> **Q: "Where Do I Want To Be?"**

The answer to the last question provides a desired destination and allows us to "begin with the end in mind."

A significant result of CoreSelf Mapping is identifying *Best Next Steps* or *Real Questions*, both of which provide supportive guidance. A walking stick in challenging situations can be instrumental in *Getting on the Same Page* with oneself.

CoreSelf Mapping is a process for observing and mapping the interrelationship of emotions, values, and plans. In Part One, completing a single-page mapping exercise leads the reader through eight steps that include observing points of awareness. Next participants write a **Situation, Strengths, Struggles, Strategies™ (4S)** entry consisting of four brief statements. Normally completed in fifteen minutes or less, this journaling process generates a set of thoughtful best next steps or an important Real Question. Making the time for contemplating an important issue can provide fresh viewpoints and new insights.

The result of mapping and journaling is that participants intentionally slow down their thinking and lower their emotional reactivity. This allows them to feel more integrated with their core self and better prepared to work toward a reliable plan to resolve the situation. Feedback from our unique Internal Observer/Navigator is always available.

CoreSelf Mapping and asking Real Questions with a broad spectrum of ages, personality types, and family/work situations has provided valuable data. This feedback has both simplified and added to the CoreSelf Map, making it more accessible for all users. Users quickly grasp the advantage of *visualizing* at any given moment where they are located on the map and where they want to be. Getting to a new position, closer to the Core, involves thoughtful consideration. Completing this eight-step process provides a clear Best Next Step or Real Question. Users report that their discoveries are more than worth their investment of time and energy.

Prior to co-founding 'Simple. Not Easy,' Jonathan spent over 40 years as a child and family-therapy clinician; after our first year together he summarized his thoughts:

> **Something about the process of the psychotherapy hour has been troubling me for a long time. Not during a session, but before or after, I have often felt that we, both clinicians and clients, are missing something. I worry that even when the sessions go well,**

**clients are at risk of becoming "hooked on therapy," waiting for the next session to get an outside infusion of something they feel they still need. I have been looking for a way to step back and survey the process to see how it could be structured differently. My wish is two- pronged: I hope that my clients can feel better informed and empowered to do more of the work of changing their mood or their negative situation on their own; I also hope to feel less depended upon, more like a walking stick than a crutch …**

**What in the past was an occasional benefit of the mapping process has become a predictable positive result in a very diverse group of clients. It is emerging as a coaching tool from which almost every client can benefit. I have become more convinced of that fact as the message about how to use CoreSelf Maps has become more refined over time. During the past several years, refinements in the map have led to a significant increase in client excitement about the process and their positive results …**

**The other thing that I've become more and more convinced about, through the process of doing this with so many people, is that everyone can do it. It's not just for people who are good writers, it's not just for people who are intellectually sophisticated; it's an accessible skill that can be developed through practice, but the capability is already there.**

---

## Generalist versus Specialist

In *The Earned Life*[17] Marshall Goldman discusses "one of the perennial choices we face in adulthood: Is it better to be a generalist or a specialist?" Reading his perspective on this topic reminded me of Dale Carnegie's desire and dilemma to teach public-speaking classes at the YMCA. in the 1900's.[18] Carnegie believed that the best speeches are given by people who know a topic very well; he said,

*"Talk about something that you know and know that you know."*

His initial dilemma in teaching a class for everyone: What can each attendee be an expert on? **What topic can everyone know and know that they know?**

The fact that we all are experts on ourself and that there is a part of our brain that knows everything about ourselves allows each of us to leverage the CoreSelf Map for significant (dare we say, huge) gain.

Whether you are a generalist or specialist, a teenager or an adult, inexperienced or very experienced—*CoreSelf Mapping* allows you to pick a front-of-mind situation without any delay or explanation to another.

When we observe where we are and where we want to be, and then we begin navigating our situation in writing—we become cognizant that *we know that we know.*

Once again, ***Your Story Is What Makes This Work.***

## Oneself and CoreSelf

We will use *oneself* (e.g., myself, ourself, yourself ) when referring to traditional ways we describe our everyday experience. This description includes all aspects of our reactions to internal and external stress, our wishes and intentions, our beliefs and actions, and any consequences of those actions. It's trying to deal with everything at once, day after day.

> CoreSelf will refer to the key components of ***self*** that generate and increase:
> CoreSelf-Trust, CoreSelf-Respect and CoreSelf-Certainty.

Each of the CoreSelf components are represented by the three circles on the left side of the CoreSelf Mapping worksheet labelled Emotional Energy and Sensations, Values and Practices, and Thoughts and Plans.

CoreSelf™ is defined as your most authentic or true self. It is graphically represented within the dashed line of the CoreSelf Mapping worksheet (see Appendix A on page 20) that represents important areas of our life—self-trust, self-respect, and self-certainty—being centered. Centering our CoreSelf in any one of these circles helps to center oneself in other areas. One's Internal Observer/Navigator provides insightful feedback and direction in each of these areas.

On the next page are a few samples of CoreSelf Maps completed by others; any personal components or names have been masked, as the intent is to share with the reader an overall view of where we will be going during the next eight steps of your own CoreSelf Map.

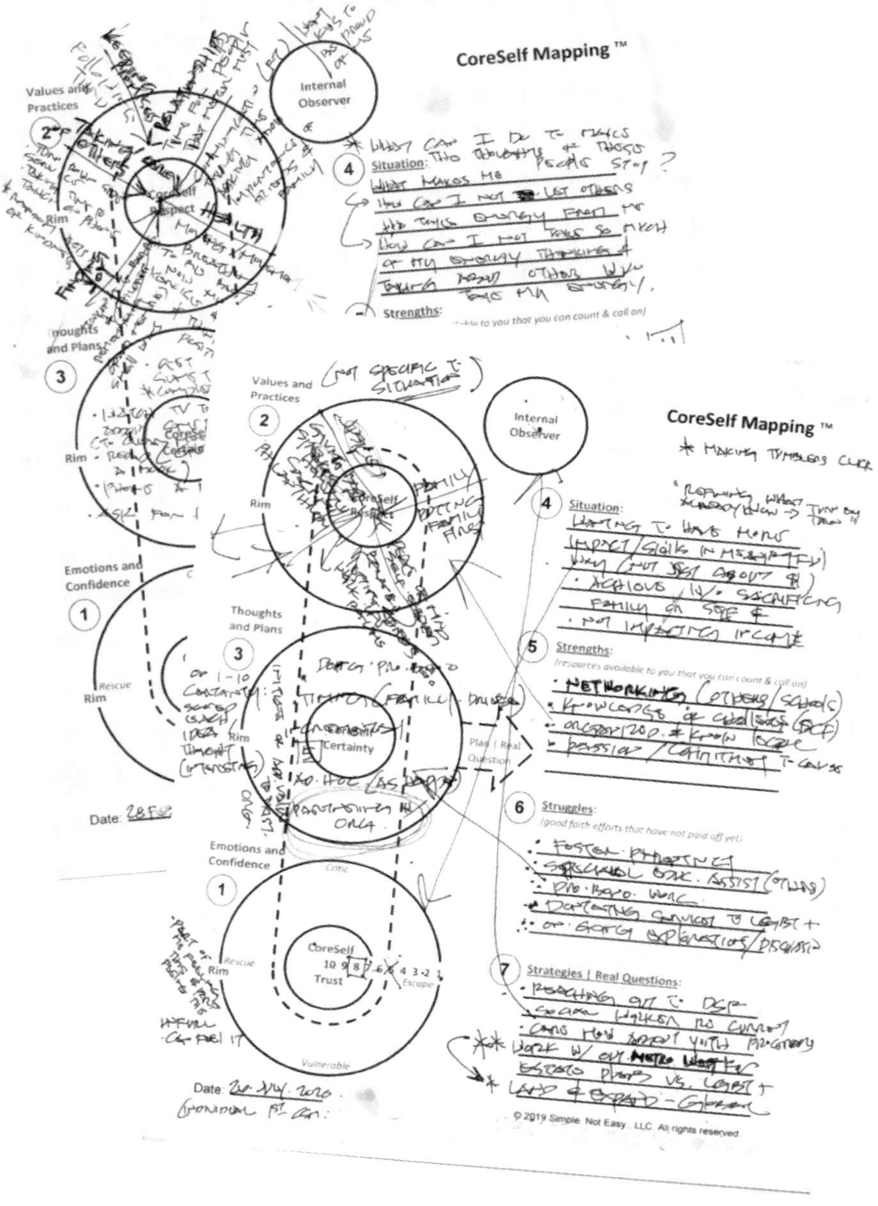


Figure 1.3 - **CoreSelf Map Samples**

# **CoreSelf Mapping:**
## Getting on the Same Page *with oneself*

"In our complex, fast changing knowledge economy, ability to manage one's thoughts and feelings is essential to business success."

— SUSAN DAVID

*The ability to manage one's thoughts and feelings is just as important in business as it is in our personal lives. In her book "Emotional Agility," Susan David (South African psychologist, speaker, and author) emphasizes the importance of labelling your thoughts and emotions, accepting them, and taking actions that are based on your values.*

*Susan David is a founder of the Harvard/McLean Institute of Coaching, is on the faculty at Harvard Medical School, and is recognized as one of the world's leading management thinkers.*

---

## *User Guide*

*CoreSelf Mapping* (CSM) is a tool that empowers individuals to navigate through difficult or challenging situations. It is a process that clearly and concisely locates where one is in a complex situation; it helps them find where they want to be, then reveals sustainable pathways to get there. CSM provides a step-by-step framework to assess your emotional energy level at a given moment in time. It counter-balances emotional energy with one's most important values and practices to develop strategies that sustain progress toward key goals.

*By learning how to activate and strengthen one's own Internal Observer—which operates in the conscious, monitoring function of our brain—one can gain valuable insight leading to practical and sustainable Best Next Steps.*

If needed, the *Overview* is a helpful refresher for those already familiar with completing CSMs.

| Situation | Confusion | Curiosity |
|---|---|---|
| Where Am I? | creates a **gap** which is good for us | peaks and creates **interest** to know more |
| Where Do I Want to Be? | desire to **resolve** confusion creates curiosity to learn | desire to **learn** to satisfy curiosity |

CoreSelf Mapping's eight-step process leverages Hilgard's psychological theory of the conscious Hidden Observer[19] and work by neuroscientists John O'Keefe, Edward Moser, and May-Britt Moser[20] that describes in detail the brain's ability to build navigational maps.

As with any other skill or muscle, this ability can strengthen with practice and intentional daily journaling. We will share additional background and some detailed suggestions in Part Four: **CoreSelf Journaling.**

# **TRIANGLES** and Others Involved

"You can't connect the dots looking forward; you can only connect them looking backward. So you have to trust the dots will somehow connect in your future. You have to trust in something - your gut, destiny, life, karma, whatever. This approach has never let me down, and it has made all the difference in my life."[21]

— STEVE JOBS

*Jobs (American business magnate, inventor, and investor. 1955 - 2011) explains that you cannot predict with certainty how far the pattern of positive and negative life events will extend into the future; instead of pondering what might happen, it is more effective to look more deeply and systematically at the connections between important recent occurrences.*

---

## *Overview*

Sustaining secure personal and professional connections is sometimes *challenging*, especially when we are facing complex or *conflicting* situations.

Another perspective on Steve Jobs' ideas for achieving greater certainty is to discover patterns in past events that are being recreated in the present and may possibly extend into the future. Fortunately, there is a well-researched approach to understanding triangular relationships in everyday human behavior. In its simplest form, a triangle can be thought of as three dots connected by three lines. Triangles appear in many areas of life: mathematics, art and architecture, navigation, education, and business. Examples include: Buckminster Fuller's use of triangular elements in his geodesic domes and Stephen Covey's triangle illustration to depict how habits are at the intersection of knowledge, skill, and desire.

A simple triangle can be used to understand the intricate dynamics of human relationships. Murray Bowen, MD, pioneered the use of triangles to study multi- generational family units and developed the Bowen Family

Systems Theory[22]. Many of his students discovered that Bowen's work not only benefits clinical work with families; it also effectively improves communication within organizations and their teams. The ability to closely observe and document personal and professional relationships over time can be instrumental in effecting positive change.

*If one takes the structure of a "family tree" and inverts it, the shape resembles the triangular flow of an organizational chart … and all of Dr. Bowen's principles of relationship dynamics still apply.* Many professional business consultants use these principles to great advantage.

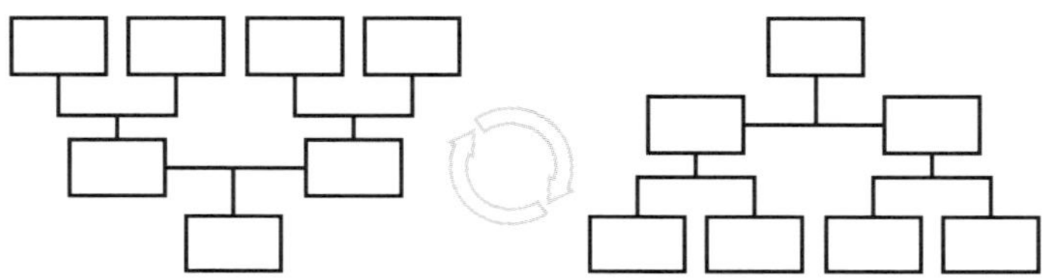

## A Sports Metaphor

The 6-4-3 double play in baseball can be represented by a triangle: the shortstop (6), the second baseman (4), and the first baseman (3). Granted, the ability to execute this difficult play requires practice, timing, and accuracy, and happens very quickly. We are fortunate to have instant replay to allow us to *slow down* the sequence to appreciate the speed and complexity of a perfectly executed double play.

Bowen's Family Systems Theory[23] demonstrates how highlighting relationship triangles slows down executive functioning and activates monitoring function. Once activated, similar to instant replay, this visual exercise slows us down to explore alternative best next steps based on our values. Moreover, including in the triangle two other individuals involved in the situation allows for pauses in the intensity of emotions while alternative vantage points are considered. The overall triangle exercise clarifies where we are in the current situation and also considers where we would prefer to be. (More about Bowen's work in the next chapter.)

## Identifying a Situation or Question in Life

When learning to *Get on the Same Page* with one's CoreSelf, it is important to choose a specific situation that is important and interesting to you. This strategy does not apply if there are several similar situations in mind, or one that is almost resolved. Select a puzzling and as yet unresolved situation that evokes intense curiosity.

Perhaps it feels like a piece of the puzzle is missing, but it is clear that identifying a best next step is important because the outcome *matters.*

Consider bringing a digital camera to document an action scene. To create a time-lapse image, the camera would take a series of snapshots that you could page through later. If while taking this sequence of photos, the camera is quickly moved back and forth, it would record many situations. But the result would be an unhelpful *blur*!

Selecting a *single, specific situation* can establish focus on one of the best images of the series. After reviewing that image, go to other parts of the scene and explore other possibilities around it. Specifically choosing the *best image* and noting the first few feelings or thoughts about the situation that it brings to mind are the basis of the next few steps of this exercise. As you continue, it will become more about noticing who or what else is there and what else you want to consider or pursue. Focusing on a specific image from a particular moment provides something from which to "push off."

Take a moment to think of your specific important or challenging situation … Got one? Excellent, let us continue.

# CoreSelf Mapping ™

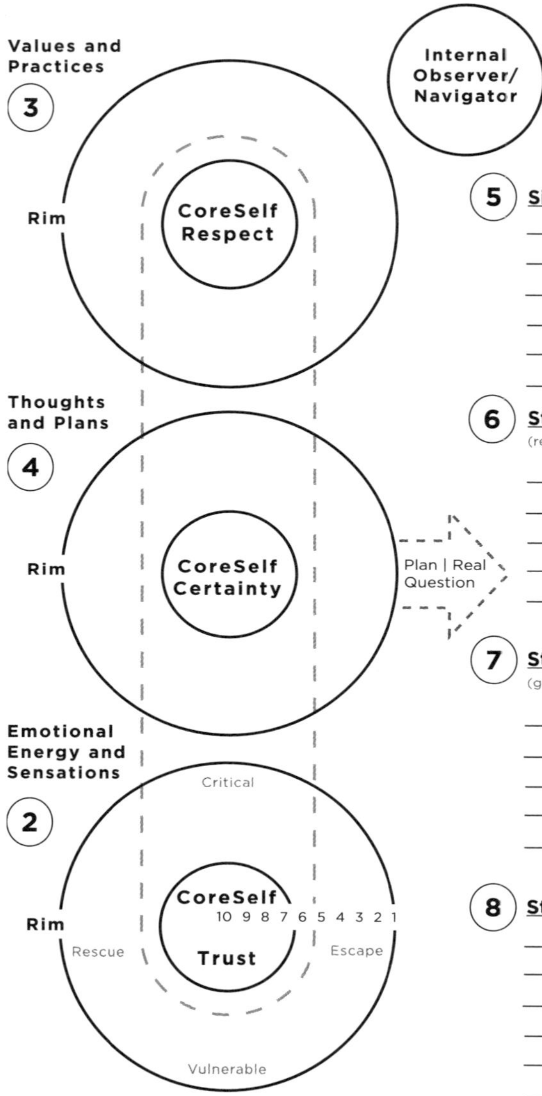


5 **Situation:**

____________________________

6 **Strengths:**
(resources available to you that you can count & call on)

____________________________

7 **Struggles:**
(good faith efforts that have not paid off yet)

____________________________

8 **Strategies | Real Questions:**

____________________________



**Date:** __________

**Appendix A: CoreSelf Map Worksheet** (scan and print)

Draw a triangle on the blank back of the CoreSelf Mapping worksheet. Label the top point (vertex) of the triangle with your initials or first name. Next, consider *who* else, besides yourself, is involved in this situation. Identify two other people that play key parts in the situation that you are studying. Put their initials or first name on each of the remaining two points (vertices). Now, consider the legs (lines) between each of the vertices as symbolic of the relationship between yourself and each of these two people. How would you subjectively describe the relationship at this moment in time?

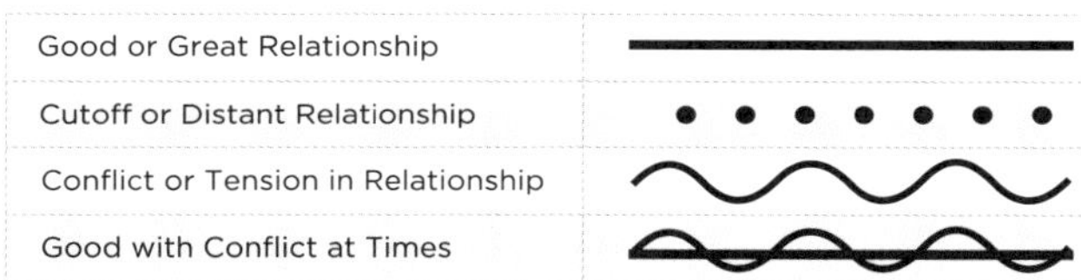


Figure 2.1 - **Observing Relationships**
(a.k.a. Closeness and Distance)

Go ahead and graphically label how you perceive these relationships, in real time. For example:

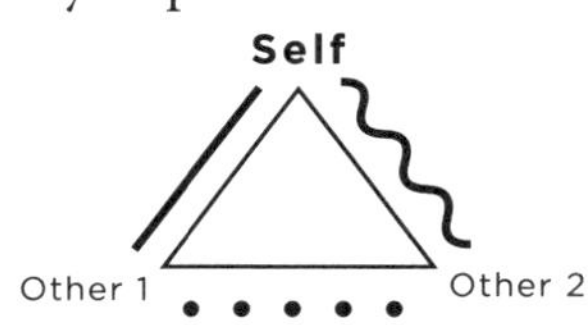


Figure 2.2 - **Sample Triangles**
(current Relationships depicted)

Lastly, please make your best guess about the relationship between the two other people in the triangle (bottom left and right) and label it as well.

Note: *At this point, it may be helpful for future reference to jot down the situation you are considering somewhere on this piece of paper with your triangle. Based on your comfort level, you can describe it in detail or utilize a short-hand that only you can understand, similar to using initials or first names of individuals labeled on your situation triangle. Either way, you will want to be specific enough that you can recall this situation later in its entirety, as you progress through this material.*

+ + +

## Mapping Our Narratives

Consider the next few narratives and take note if any component resonates. Have you heard a backstory similar to any of them? If you tweak a line or character here or there, does it resemble a story you can relate to? Do you have a story of your own?

> **A young adult** who is a serious student, develops strong friendships, and volunteers in the community, goes on to college and then secures a good job in an area of interest. Their future seems quite promising and their persistent efforts are being rewarded appropriately. However, a close family member then experiences an unexpected tragedy. This young adult **feels an overwhelming obligation to interrupt their own plans completely to come to the rescue of that family member,** even though it is unclear if any of their efforts will have a positive outcome.
>
> **A working couple with children** are both doing the best they can to "make ends meet," balance individual work responsibilities and the needs of growing children that never seem to tire, leaving little to no time to attend to each other's needs. Time passes with each playing their respective part as years go by and the children become more independent. Eventually, each partner **finds that they are feeling increasingly distant from the other.** Communication is not effective and planning becomes exclusively based on individual needs.
>
> **A small company** spends its early entrepreneurial years just trying to survive. Through years of persistence and shear grit they succeed in becoming a sustainable, midsize company, balancing profits with expanding costs and staff. More time passes and the company starts to grow by acquiring other small companies; this organic growth continues and the shareholders are pleased. One day management **notices that all these disparate acquired companies came with their own cultures** and ways of doing things, and no one seems to be concerned about a common plan.

What should happen next?

We will refer back to these three narratives—individual, partners, and professionals—to illustrate how this material can be used to **get on the same page** with self and others.

Below is another way to view these three narratives. If one of these narratives resonates with you more than another (circle or mark that relationship column).

| Stage | **Individual** | **Partners** | **Professionals** |
|---|---|---|---|
| *Current* | | *Where Am I?* | |
| **Executive** | | | |
| **Emotions** | Overwhelmed & Uncertain | Vulnerable & Unfair | Surprised & Critical |
| **Beliefs** | Responsible & Obligated | Partnership & Children | Profits & Growth |
| **Reactions** | Why me? | What happened? | How do I . . . ? |
| **Monitoring** | | | |
| **Energy** | | Will this get me closer to where I want to be? | |
| **Values** | | What values matter most to me? What will I actually do? | |
| **Plan** | | Is this decision in alignment with my values? | |
| *Destination* | | *Where do I want to be?* | |

Figure 2.3 - **Mapping Our Narratives**
Getting on the Same Page with our Self (CSM)

The situational benefits of getting on the same page with our *self* start with:

- Awareness of Who Else is Involved (closeness and distance)

In the following steps we will fill in many of the boxes above and explore many Real Questions—Real Questions (RQ) that strengthen self-trust, self-respect, and self-certainty.

# **TRIANGLES** and Others Involved

"Maybe stories are just data with a soul."

— **BRENÉ BROWN**

*Brené Brown (American professor, author, and speaker) is a researcher and storyteller who's spent two decades studying courage, vulnerability, shame, and empathy. She's known for her widely viewed Tedx Talk in 2010[24]. In her words, "I believe that you have to walk through vulnerability to get to courage, therefore … embrace the suck. I try to be grateful every day, and my motto right now is "Courage over comfort."[25]*

---

## *User Guide*

Dr. Murray Bowen's Family Systems Theory explores how relationships shape individual behavior and functioning in family, work, and social systems. The goal of Bowen-based Family Therapy is to apply Bowen's principles in order to develop more effective options for decreasing chronic anxiety, increasing effective self-management skills in relationship to important others, and increasing flexibility and resiliency to meet life's challenges.

Bowen's method for identifying the repeating patterns in family, social, and business relationships has been utilized by medical and mental health professionals with great success since the 1960s. While Bowen continued to do family research and teaching at the Georgetown University School of Medicine's Department of Psychiatry until his death in October, 1990, he had stopped identifying himself as a psychotherapist years before and wanted to be known as a systems theorist, saying often that good clinical work "*is about being able to observe a system at work.*"

*The significance of starting with a simple triangle in Getting on the Same Page with oneself is that it initiates questions about "**Who**" is involved and "**Where**" we are focusing to learn more in a specific situation of interest.*

The concept of Triangles, while fundamental to Bowen's family systems theory,[26] was not part of our original CoreSelf Map worksheet; it was added as the framework was utilized with high-performing professionals. It turned out that often the most highly effective performers (those with high executive brain function) were so quickly accessing and processing information, it was difficult for them to consider the wider and more personal context of that challenging situation. They had become so adept at rapidly analyzing disparate data, events, and markets, that they found it difficult to turn that skill off, regardless of the task. It was not unusual for them to fast-forward with rapid-fire questions, like:

**Q: "Why is this sequence out of order?"**

**Q: "Can you just tell me what we are trying to achieve?"**

Characteristics of individuals with high executive-functioning brains include:

- trying to immediately figure out the: Why, What, When, and How
- needing to simplify complex systems and processes
- having an incessant need to accomplish things; being focused on to-do lists and not always aware of surrounding events or their own or others' states of mind.

In the early years of researching CoreSelf Mapping's (CSM) usefulness in organizations, entire teams would experience the benefits and insights that CSM delivers; it was not unusual for a manager to respond, *"Can you share this map-thing that my team is talking about with me?"* Imagine our frustration when we shared it with them and they did not have a similar experience … after much frustration and discussion, we decided to start with a blank page with nothing for the executive function to figure out, nothing to access, nothing to resolve. We then asked,

**Q: What if we start with a triangle and diagram who else is involved?**

It turns out that if you ask anyone—including highly performing or high executive functioning individuals—to start with a blank piece of paper, to think of a specific situation that is front of mind for them, then draw a triangle, and consider two other people who are involved with the situation … this short task creates just enough space for them to pause their executive brain function and activate their monitoring function.

Benefits of leveraging our monitoring-function brain allows one to:

- *Slow down* and begin observing our self and the situation.
- Observe and then ask: What is my/our energy level? Am I seeing the Big Picture? Am I moving toward growth mode or just avoiding decline?
- Activate our Internal Observer/Navigator to discover a *Best Next Step* or ask a *RQ*.

Today, the triangle exercise is integral to and the first step of completing a CoreSelf Map. It encourages that individuals slow down, allowing them to respond to the simplicity of a blank page and a simple triangle, and activates their Internal Observer. Working through the CSM exercise spurs a longer conversation about relationship triangles. The *triangle lens* provides startling clarity and insight, especially when observing a field of familiar relationships.

For example: after completing a few CoreSelf Maps with Dave, he returned to the first step of the CSM when we created a triangle and labeled the vertices. He is a high-functioning executive who has an incredible knack for business and analyzing market data and leading indicators. He energetically expressed, *"I just used the metaphor of a triangle this morning with one of our vendors. I shared with them that my salesperson was given a direction to proceed, then given a very different directive from them that I didn't know about. None of us are in sync, which creates enormous confusion and reduces momentum for both of us."* This led to an additional hour of conversation about triangles and interlocking triangles. This conversation illustrates the benefits and momentum created by Getting on the Same Page™ with others, which will be covered later in this book. Let us begin here with *Getting on the Same Page™* with oneself.

> *"The concept of triangles provides a theoretical framework for understanding the micro-functioning of all emotional systems ...*
>
> ***A two-person emotional system is unstable in that it forms itself into a three-person system or triangle under stress."***
>
> \- MURRAY BOWEN, MD (1972)

Think about triangles in your personal and professional life:

- yourself, your mother, and father or sibling
- yourself, your significant other, and a child or best friend
- yourself, a potential employer, and the employer's customers
- yourself, your boss, and a helpful or distracting colleague
- yourself, a person on your team, and an outside vendor
- yourself, ______ and ______

Through his work at the Menninger Clinic and at the National Institute of Mental Health, Bowen ultimately came to understand triangles and interlocking triangles as basic building blocks of the social systems to which humans belong. These systems include the family and the workplace, as well as the larger society (Bowen 1978). Triangles and interlocking triangles reflect the proposition that to understand individual behavior and functioning, it is necessary to understand the context—the relationship system—in which the basic patterns of functioning are laid down.[27]

## Servant Leadership and Triangles

CoreSelf Mapping utilizes the triangle from a Bowen perspective to describe relationships between self and two others. Servant Leadership[28] is a philosophy introduced by Robert K. Greenleaf in the 1970s; some experts describe servant leadership as "the upside-down pyramid."

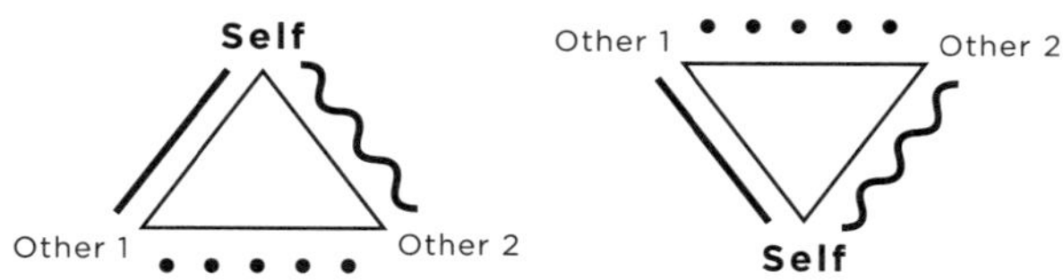


Figure 2.4 - **Triangle Orientation**
(Relationship Descriptions vs Structure)

In both CoreSelf Mapping (CSM) and later in CoreSelf Positioning (CSP) we will be using triangles to depict others involved in a situation and the current relationships (e.g., closeness and distance) between those parties.

The CoreSelf triangles do not represent the structure of the relationship or who serves whom; therefore the triangles can be inverted to whatever orientation suits the reader. Throughout the remainder of the book, we will adopt the first triangle with *self* at the top of the triangle, since we are focused on Getting on the Same Page with our self and others.

---

## The Eighth Step: Backstory of Adding the Triangle

Dr. Murray Bowen's family systems theory significantly influenced Jonathan's practice and work helping others for over 40 years. "Triangles" is one of the *Eight Concepts of Bowen's Theory.*[29] In Bowen's systems approach to understanding family relationships, the triangle is integral to an understanding of family dynamics, not only between individual members, but also to family related across distance and time.

Multi-generational family diagrams (also known as "family trees") help us to document emotional closeness and distance between family members and to track differences and similarities in levels of functioning over time.

As we were introducing CSM to professional organizations, an interesting, incredibly frustrating, and inconsistent experience was occurring. Entire teams would experience the *magic* of CSM and a manager would call to ask: "Can you show me this map thing that my team is talking about?" We would share it with the manger and… *nothing.*

I was debriefing and expressing my frustration with Jonathan about such a manager that did not experience the magic of the CSM. Doubting myself with "*What am I missing? Is it my delivery? What am I doing wrong?*" (Does this sound familiar?), I thought it might help if I explained his role in the company, which included managing a sales team that represented different vendors.

As I was explaining Dave's role in the company—ironically using triangles, Jonathan casually responded, **"Interlocking triangles."** What?

Well, knowing enough to be dangerous—I had read about Bowen's Concepts—and not enough to be accurate (love that phrase), I asked,

**Q: What if we simply turn the CSM worksheet over, so the participant starts with a blank piece of paper?**

With nothing to figure out yet (executive brain function), we ask the individual to think of a single, specific Situation, draw a triangle, and label the vertices with two others involved in the Situation.

**Q: Could this slow down the executive-function long enough to engage the monitoring-function of the individual?**

**A: A resounding YES!**

I had an opportunity a few months later to re-share the same CSM with same manager and he was able to experience the *magic* of the CoreSelf Map. Eureka! And our conversation continued for another two-hours discussing triangles inside and outside his organization.

# **ENERGY** and Where I Am vs. Where I Want to Be

"On a ten-point scale, if I am at level two in any field, and desire to move to level five, I must first take a step toward level three. A thousand-mile journey begins with the first step and can only be taken one step at a time."

— STEPHEN COVEY

*Covey (American educator, author and speaker. 1932 - 2012) illustrates the importance of order and priorities in his book "First Things First," in which he visualizes a glass canister to be filled with rocks and water. Big rocks symbolize one's most important priorities, followed by little rocks representing day-to-day responsibilities, then sand representing unimportant minor tasks, and concluding with water that represents distractions preventing one from getting work done. Covey points out that if we do not put the largest rocks in the jar first, there will be no room for them later—and the project will fail.*

*Following through on this analogy, consistently taking inventory of our current emotional energy—on a ten-point scale—and the distance to our desired location, can have similar benefits.*

---

## *Overview*

Our brains function very much like a digital GPS (Global Positioning System); that is, we are *neurologically wired* to answer two important questions at any moment:

1. **Where am I?**
2. **Where do I want to be?**

These questions are not just about physical location. They represent our safety and comfort level within a given situation.

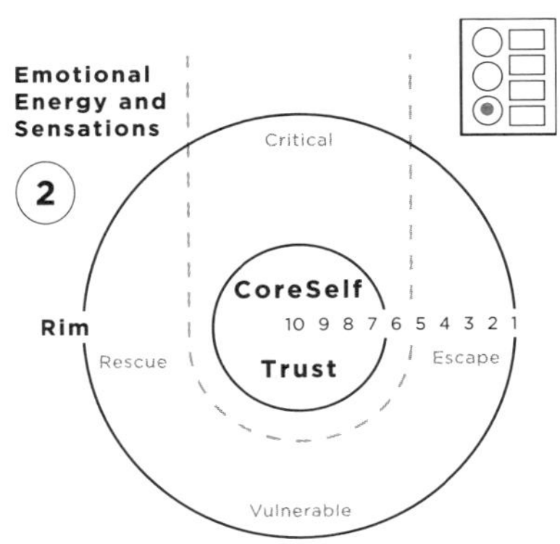


Figure 3.1 - **Bottom Circle**
(a.k.a. Emotional Energy and Sensations

Picture yourself on the radius of a circle with a 10-point scale:

| High Energy | | | | | | | | | Low Energy |
|---|---|---|---|---|---|---|---|---|---|
| 10 | 9 | 8 | 7 | 6 | 5 | 4 | 3 | 2 | 1 |
| Low Tension | | | | | | | | | High Tension |

You can demonstrate how this works by drawing an actual circle with a "10" at the center and a "1" on the rim that forms a line (like above). Where you are on that line at any moment gives you vital information about your level of energy or tension. Take a moment to think of your challenging situation (in Step 1) and mark an 'X' over the number indicating your current location on the radius, then circle the number that represents where you want to be.

*The space between one's position in the current situation and a future desired position is a space where a remarkable amount of learning and insight can happen.*

Most of us are aware that our brains are wired to protect us. Many of us are familiar with the brain's capability to shift into survival mode and to react with "freeze, fight, or flight," responses based on our assessment of immediate danger. This is called "Being on the Rim," which is our brain's most important way of protecting us from danger. Our emotional defenses serve a vital purpose, shielding us from injury and keeping us functioning until danger is less or past. What is most important is to acknowledge and name what we are feeling without becoming immobilized.

Susan David, MD, author of *Emotional Agility*, reminds us:

> **"Emotions are data, not directives. We get to choose who we want to be; our emotions don't."**

The bottom circle efficiently leverages and creates new awareness in the space between "where you are" and "where you want to be" by loading enormous meaning and energy into a numbered space that can be unpacked as one progresses through the remaining six steps of the CoreSelf Mapping worksheet.

+ + +

We will expand on this comment and provide more graphic examples of how your brain functions so effectively in this way later in this section ("Step 5: Situation," and in the article, "Certainty in Self-Positioning," on our website) But for now,

Asking ***"Where am I?"*** allows time for:

pausing to take inventory,
naming my emotions,
feeling important sensations,
noting my energy level,
asking essential questions,
taking time to slow myself down.

Asking ***"Where do I want to be?"*** allows space for:

creating movement,
considering and contemplating,
finding a new opportunity to connect,
exploring my core self,
identifying a best next step,
practicing that step to get there.

Seeing the difference between *now*, *not now*, or *not yet*, can create new connections and ultimately help us navigate to a better place to be. If *Where* and *Who* questions are asked, positive choices are more easily accessible. For example:

***"What am I going to do now?"***

and

***"How am I going to feel better?"***are much more difficult to answer than:

***"Where am I in a particular circle?"***

and

***"Who else is involved in this situation?"***

In simplest terms:

**"Where" and "Who" questions provide better responses than questions that ask "What" and "How."**

The Core region of the bottom circle is an important source of an enormous amount of emotional energy and confidence as we navigate from one situation to another. The experiences we encounter in our personal and professional lives can run the gamut from healthy and productive networks of family, colleagues, and friends, all the way to some strained and even broken relationships among that same network of people. We are inevitably going to be anxious at times not knowing what all the changes in our health, safety, or relationships will mean. We discuss a wider range of emotions in greater detail in the *User Guide*.

As we will see in a later section of the CoreSelf Mapping exercise, the prompt "How would you describe your Situation now?" allows us to write the story of these complexities more smoothly and clearly then we would imagine to be possible. The parts of the emotional-energy puzzle move closer into alignment with each other. Simply observing *the Situation* begins the process of stepping back from conflict and confusion. This allows other parts of the mind to bring more positive elements into play. Going forward with the CoreSelf Mapping process will demonstrate the mechanisms by which that happens. Dr. Seuss offered solace with,

*"When something bad happens you have three choices. You can either let it define you, let it destroy you, or you can let it strengthen you."*

We are reviewing the questions that we ask ourselves, the space that it can create, and the choices we have. This is only Step 2 of 8. Perhaps you are asking:

**Q: Why is it so important to focus on questions, space, and choices?**

**A: Because the questions we ask and space we create can directly impact the choices we identify and make.**

Research has shown that most of us care more about comfort than change[30]—the comfort of where we are versus the change that might be needed to get where we want to be. Add our propensity for immediate gratification (the infamous marshmallow study[31]) over delayed gratification, and the choices we make get even more clouded.

The eminent Swiss psychiatrist Carl Jung expressed it a bit differently:

*"People will do anything, no matter now absurd, to avoid facing their own souls."*

But he also said:

*"Who looks inside, awakes."*

---

## Origins of the Bottom Circle

Because this component of the CoreSelf Framework is incredibly significant and the result of over a decade of research, it makes sense to share—between the *Overview* and *User Guide*—my interview with *Simple. Not Easy* co-founder Jonathan Thomas, MSW (circa August 2021), which I believe will resonate with all:

I am curious to take another look at the origins of the Bottom Circle, the part of the CoreSelf Mapping process that focuses on motivation levels and degrees of trust and self-confidence.

> **Thanks for turning the page to the front of the CoreSelf Map. We are now looking at the lower left-hand corner of that page where Step 2 is placed. I sometimes think of the Bottom Circle as the booster rocket of the CSM vehicle where intense emotions, both positive and negative, make themselves known and are processed. The rim of the Bottom Circle vehicle is where the pressure goes when it needs to be released. The core of the Bottom Circle is the most secure place for motivational fuel to be kept. Understanding these dynamics is always a key factor when we are considering the questions that the CSM is designed to help resolve.**

When we talked before, you said that the workings of the Bottom Circle occurred to you over more than ten years of doing a specific type of clinical work. At the very beginning you were counseling children and their parents. I remember you describing the challenge of working with young kids who were struggling with powerful feelings; sometimes you were surprised to see these kids when they were obviously angry, sad, or in a lot of pain, having a mostly blank facial expression. They were working hard not to tell anyone what was wrong.

> **Looking back, I can see that working with those young children and their parents brought together all the important elements of what has ultimately made CoreSelf Mapping such an effective communication and planning tool. In the clinic, there was an urgent need to clearly understand why the child had been so upset or behaving so badly that a referral for therapy was being made. When meeting with the family, staff needed to put that reason into language that both the child and the child's caregivers could take in and speak about so that the family and the staff could sign off on the plan for going forward with counseling.**

Over time, it became clear that sharing a picture of the child's location in the Bottom Circle was a helpful way to begin. As parents were able to understand that their child was currently feeling close to the Rim, and that the child could imagine moving to another place on the Circle where they would be more comfortable, a growing sense of trust emerged in the working relationship of all the people involved. Parents were increasingly able to say another set of magic words: "We get it."

People often take note of the fact that the CoreSelf Map is constructed "upside down," beginning at the lower edge of the page. As we proceed through the remaining seven steps, we think the CSM's logic will become convincing, beginning with how the Bottom Circle demonstrates our respect for being both centered and grounded in our method.

When an upset child was unable or unwilling to speak, I asked myself, "Where did that emotion go? How does a child of that age keep such intense feelings under tight control? How and when will those feelings show up again?" Memories of those young faces, surprisingly not crying or yelling, were the basis for thinking about the Bottom Circle in the early days. Looking back, it was an advantage for me to watch the process unfold moment by moment, and to not take anything for granted.

In that very remarkable internship, I received basic training in family counseling and developmental psychology. I had expert teachers and supervisors who carefully watched over all the details of the counseling process. I quickly learned that kids, especially those who are upset, don't just sit down and tell a stranger what's wrong and how to fix it. I spent many hours watching carefully as they used toys, clay, and a sandbox to show me what they were worried or upset about. I learned to wait, sometimes for many hours, as the details of their stories became clearer. Gradually, I understood that what helped them most was attaching a name to a particular feeling.

Babysitters of all ages and first-time parents know what a major challenge it is to help calm a child who's having a tantrum. If the caregiver is clever, they may say: "Use your words. I can help you better if you use your words to tell me what's going on." What magic words can help a child in this situation to get calmer? My kid clients taught me that in fact there are words they can say that make them feel better. They acquainted me with four of them: "Hurt." "Scared." "Sad." "Lonely."

If I was extremely patient, the child might be able to say something like: "When I got in that fight and he hit me so hard, it hurt a lot!" Or, "I'm scared because something awful is going to happen and I can't stop it;" or "I'm sad because my best friend moved too far away to visit;" or, "I'm lonely in this new school. I've got no friends at all."

After witnessing many of these moments, it occurred to me that there was an umbrella term under which the hurt, scared, sad and lonely feelings all fit. It was Vulnerable.

As I was listening to their stories, whenever they used one of the words that meant "vulnerable," I could see the child relax a bit and begin to feel not better, but less bad. If I asked them directly about those feeling words, they might avoid the question. But if I ever heard, "I'm just so sad," I'd think to myself, "Okay, now we're getting somewhere." After seeing some children over a long period of time, that impression often turned out to be true. I became confident that hurt, scared, sad and lonely, were reliable signals that upset children could eventually become more confident about managing their own emotional experience if, for one moment, they could trust someone else to hear the names of their feelings.

Then I asked myself the question, "How does a child manage to keep powerfully negative feelings inside and get through a

**minute, or an hour, or a whole school day without falling apart? What contains those powerful feelings so that they can go ahead and do what they have to do?" Eventually I figured out that there's an equally powerful pressure inside them that's saying, "Shut up, keep quiet, don't let anyone know how much it hurts."**

**I mentioned emotional physics before, and this is an important example. What happens naturally is an internal balancing action, with an extreme feeling on one side countered by an equal and opposite feeling on the other: an impulse to give in to pain balanced by a warning from an internal critic that says, "Don't give in to showing weakness; someone may use it against you." Taken together, these opposites help the individual to not fly off in either direction, but to appear to be in control, which protects them in the short term. None of this action and response is necessarily an indication of weakness or illness. It's a coping mechanism that we all use instinctively. Children use it as a way of managing their most stressful moments, which works well in short-term emotional crises. Longer-term internal balancing is the subject of the CoreSelf Mapping project, as we will see.**

Did you have a word or umbrella for "shame, blame, don't tell them" like you did for "vulnerable?"

**It's critical, as opposed to vulnerable. When I admit I'm hurting, I become open to a shameful possibility: "I've only got myself to blame that I'm hurting because I got myself into all this trouble." Kids sometimes send themselves critical messages to try to control the pain. "Keep that feeling inside; no one wants to hear about it. Just shut up and do what you have to do." Which means sustain indefinitely that high level of internal pressure.**

For some of us, that was being a young kid trying to take care of parents who weren't, for lots of reasons, able to be great parents.

**Unfortunately, that's so true. Some kids have parents who are constantly overwhelmed or not even around, and some also have younger siblings who also need parenting. Sometimes the older kid, already in the vulnerable/critical predicament, goes way above and beyond what should be expected of a child of that age to manage family problems; then they become a substitute caretaker for the younger ones. Now we can see another polarity developing. Part of them is becoming a rescuer. If children are already struggling with their own difficult feelings, and then they see another person needing even more help than they do, they may try to figure out how to provide that help. Rescuing someone else can make the rescuer feel better about themselves for a time.**

**Some overwhelmed parents don't know that they have a child who is trying to be the most responsible person in the family. Some kids are smart enough to take care of some serious problems and feel good about doing it and getting praised for it. However, that choice of coping mechanisms can lead to a different predicament. Other people may begin to assume that the child in the rescuer role is always going to be there, being the responsible adult. After a long time of being super-responsible, the rescuer-child can end up feeling: "This plan is no good, because I'm putting out all this energy and I'm not getting anything back. Nobody's taking care of my stuff." Eventually, part of the child or teenager is going to feel, "I'm stupid to keep taking care of everything for everyone while I get nothing."**

**That's the equal and opposite reaction that I saw in kids. Sometimes the reason that they were getting in trouble in school was that they were doing the taking care of everything at home. The feeling was, "I'm so done with this routine; I'm out of here!" When you reviewed the back stories, there were two sets of opposite feelings common to many of these situations.**

What were the four words you ended up with?

> **Vulnerable versus critical and rescue versus escape were the four categories of words, with additional details within them. Vulnerable contains hurt, scared, sad and lonely. Critical, in its extreme version, is shame and blame. These words carry a lot of intensity when they are said to oneself and more so when said out loud.**
>
> **It comes down to a simple but hard to grasp truth: a feeling you are having is only a fraction of your whole self. A statement closer to the truth is: "Part of me is feeling vulnerable, part of me is feeling critical of me; part of me wants to make it better for somebody else, and then part of me says after I've been doing that forever, I want out of here." Understanding that emotional counterbalancing process helps us to figure out better ways to operate in challenging emotional situations. The foundation skill is to acknowledge: "Part of me is feeling this and part of me is feeling that," and to also know that still another part, operating outside the Bottom Circle, can help navigate closer to a more trustworthy approach. We will explore that part soon.**

So, I hear there have been evolutionary steps in understanding how the Bottom Circle works. When did you add, "Well, it's okay to feel this way and to feel that way. Let's put a number on it. How much do you feel this way?"

> **Great question! What came next was the realization that in "emotional physics," just as in the rest of nature, every action has an equal and opposite reaction. To the degree that I'm being a rescuer, there is another part of me managing a powerful impulse to escape all that responsibility.**
>
> **And you are correct that, if asked, we have a way to put a particular number or level on how far out toward the rim we are with a particular feeling. The intensity on opposite sides of the rim is always equal to keep the balance. If I am scared or sad at a level 5 out of 10,**

**then I am also a level 5 on the critical control. And the numbers go up and down in parallel, though most of the time we are aware of only one side of the Circle; "I know part of me is sad," but, "I'm less aware of being critical of myself for feeling that way."**

That's the action-reaction?

**Yes. Part of me is hurting; another part of me can counterbalance that. If I balance out my rescuing with some escaping, then I can stay in the game. I balance out the part of me that's hurting with a part of me that manages the pain so that it doesn't take me over and overwhelm me. One way people stay in control is by managing their feelings in such a way that they can get many tasks accomplished; we know, however, control can come at the cost of immense internal tension.**

So, you've got this understanding of the emotional extremes in delicate balance. When did you introduce the idea of the core of the Bottom Circle?

**Early in my career I had the advantage of learning in detail about how children experience intense emotions and also how they learn to use names for their feelings. Kids were able to tell me that their Vulnerable/Critical/ Rescue/Escape feelings happened when they felt close to the Rim. Every child that I asked was able to place their finger on the map in that specific zone. Of course it was also important to ask them where they were on the map when they were feeling safe, confident, and not worried about taking care of someone else or needing to get away. The answers to those questions involved moving their pointer finger or pencil much closer to the center of the circle that became labeled the Core.**

**As I spent time with the parents of those children explaining some of our work together, the parents quickly agreed that they could also know the difference between Core and Rim experiences. After more discussion and practice with the two-circle map,**

**adults pointed to mid-levels between the Core and Rim in their own emotional experience. They could also begin to talk about activities that pushed or pulled them or their kids to move closer to, or farther from, the Core.**

**(Adults can talk about the "radius" from 10 in the center to 1 on the Rim and pick a number to correspond with their location in a given moment. If someone chose to keep track every hour for a whole day, depending on their health and good or not so good fortune, the points would move frequently, documenting a normal mid-range, perhaps with spikes toward the Rim and drops toward the Core during peaceful moments.)**

**In recent years, I have written an article called "Certainty in Self-Positioning," which describes in detail the neuroscience work done by prominent researchers that confirms our ability to locate ourselves in space and in social relationships. It is available at www.simplenoteasy.org.**

The idea that there are levels of energy and confidence from the center of the Core all the way out to the Rim is important to understand. We have talked about "Compassion" being part way from "Vulnerable" on the Rim to "Trust" in the Core. Where does the term "limit-setting" fit with regard to "Escape?"

**It's time to look at the levels of the bottom circle of the CoreSelf Map. (See pages 54-55: Figure 3.5 or 3.6.)**

Now that we are looking at the more detailed map, we can see that there are some emotions that are mid-way toward the Core which provide potential pathways toward a higher degree of Self-Trust.

This diagram demonstrates that the CoreSelf Map is a tool for "literally becoming centered." One can use it to transfer from a Rim energy state to one closer to one's Core; for instance, moving from "Shame/Blame" to "Understanding," or from "Rescue" to "Generosity," and so on.

**Yes, that's what we refer to as CoreSelf Navigation.**

Wow. You began talking with children and their parents, many of them in troubled situations, emotionally and/or physically. As children, we had amazing childhoods or we didn't. I think that just about covers the spectrum. Then we wake up one day as adults and we have personal lives; we have opportunities to merely sustain ourselves or to grow to the next level. I'm intrigued by bringing this process to the workplace; I can think of two examples where this could apply.

I listened the other day to a woman who has functioned steadily as top manager describe how she was feeling vulnerable at work. Her standard of performance is 110-120% on a regular basis, both for herself and her team. She was feeling vulnerable because she hasn't been as focused at work lately because her mom has an operation coming up. Knowing that she has been distracted has been painful for her. The sad part to hear was that the critic in her was preventing her from telling her team why she was distracted.

**Right, the Critic's message is always: "Don't tell anyone how bad you are feeling."**

We talk often about the need in professional situations for a "psychological safety zone." In this case, her organization hadn't created that zone for her. It's difficult to listen to her not feeling comfortable enough to say to her team: "I'm being distracted by an illness in my family. I'm going to take care of 100% of my responsibilities, but you are going to notice that for now I am not performing at my usual level. This is a temporary situation; thanks for understanding."

Another example is a manager who loves his job and who has a very analytical style of operating. He shared that when he attends quarterly operation meetings, his internal critic goes into overdrive causing him to feel that he's not going to measure up compared to some of the other managers. At the conclusion of each of these meetings, he just wants to leave (vulnerable). He's caught in a cycle of critic and vulnerable. He explained, "I'm good at taking care of my team, I'm providing good data; I'm good at explaining why we will or won't hit our numbers for valid reasons. I know what the market's doing. However, when I go to that meeting, I expect to get 'beat up,' and I just want to get out of there."

I read a quote this morning and I am curious about your feedback. Dr. Susan David writes, "Emotions are data, not directives. We get to choose who we want to be. Our emotions don't." Now, what I thought was interesting about that is, if I take one word and I change it to: "We get to choose where we want to be; our emotions don't."

> **I could not agree more. In my experience of working with people in high intensity settings, their partnerships benefit greatly from including basic location information from the CoreSelf Map. If they begin by asking themselves: "In this tough situation, at this moment, am I closer to "Rescue," or to "Escape?" And then, if it's "Escape," they could ask, "Where am I now on the scale of one to ten?" They learn quickly that impulsive behaviors with low probability of success happen closest to the Rim in the one to three range. Knowing their location and their risk level, they can decide to pause or step back from the intensity of that moment. Pausing to check one's CoreSelf position before picking up the phone or pushing "Send" on the keyboard can prevent a lot of confusion from needing to be sorted out later.**

Yes, what you are saying demonstrates that Dr. David is spot on when she says "our emotions are data." You have said before that emotions are facts to the person having them. Emotions out on the rim: vulnerable, critic, rescue, and escape, provide motivation and direction, especially when there is potential danger. I've learned from you that it's important to tell people these are normal feelings, and this is your brain protecting you. "Emotions are data, not directives." And we get to choose moment to moment which facts to live by.

We have talked at other times about how children shouldn't have to wait until they are young adults or adults to learn about emotional intelligence, which includes the difference between feelings and thoughts. Emotions are data that can provide feedback as they come and go in our minds. In our better moments we have core energy along with our core beliefs and practices as a platform for creating best next steps right now.

**Exactly! Thank you. That summarizes our agreement with Dr. David perfectly and provides a couple of clues as to where we are going in our next chapter about The Big Picture.**

---

# **ENERGY** and Where I Am vs. Where I Want to Be

"What lies behind us and what lies before us are tiny matters compared to what lies within us."

— RALPH WALDO EMERSON

*Emerson (American essayist, poet, and philosopher. 1803 - 1882) understood that though our past history has already shaped us, it has been circumstantial and outside of our control; he ardently argued that one's past need not determine their present or future. He embraced the power of self-determination, of our ability to identify who we are and who we are to become.*

*There is no doubt that past experiences influence who we are, and our future course is not guaranteed. However, within each of us lies the ability to accurately observe where we are at the present moment—and where we would like to be in the future. While we may not always have step-by-step written directions, each of us possesses an innate ability to imagine and construct ways to achieve the previously unthinkable.*

---

## *User Guide*

Step 2: Emotional Energy and Sensations focuses on CoreSelf-Trust, a primary benefit of CSM. Navigating from the reactive Rim of the Self, when under intense outside pressure, towards a more centered state of mind, we effectively answer two key Real Questions on a 10-point scale:

**Q:** **"Where am I now?"** (on the CoreSelf Map)

**Q:** **"Where do I want to be?"**

Answering these two questions slows us down, creating space for curiosity and possibility. Importantly, answering these two questions fires up our Internal Observer—that monitoring, *legal stenographer of our life*, a unique part of us that is excited and waiting to share helpful insights that have been hidden.

A brief recap of "Step 1: **Triangles** and others involved" and its significance in the CoreSelf process:

Executive-functioning brain:

- Trying to figure out the "what, why, and when" of systems or data
- Satisfying a need to accomplish tasks
- Focusing on executing, often unaware of surrounding emotions in self and others

Monitoring-function brain:

- Asks, "Who else occupies positions in this Triangle?"
  Observes relationships with a "bigger-picture" perspective
- Can ascertain, "Are they close to or distant from me?"
- Asks "How are we all getting along?" (Better or worse?)

## Who becomes Where!

Who might I get closer to, to help resolve this situation?
Who am I potentially going to need to move farther away from?

Understanding the many functions of the bottom circle, labeled *Emotional Energy and Sensations* on the CoreSelf Mapping worksheet—has involved over a decade of research. Our ability to track its range and depth of involvement in emotional interactions has evolved after a review of many years of CoreSelf Mapping practice and study of its interaction with the other elements of the CSM.

In its simplest form, it appears as two concentric circles consisting of an outer circle labeled the *Rim*—a place of low energy or high uncertainty—and the *Core*—a place of high energy or low uncertainty. As you will recall, it allows one to efficiently and effectively answer two important Real Questions—regardless of one's level of stress or apprehension—at any moment in time:

1. Where Am I? *Anchor Point*
2. Where Do I Want to Be? *Destination*

We simplify the answers to these two questions by using a 10-point scale, where one is low or on the Rim, and 10 is high or towards the center Core.

High Energy — Low Energy

| 10 | 9 | 8 | 7 | 6 | 5 | 4 | 3 | 2 | 1 |
|---|---|---|---|---|---|---|---|---|---|

Low Tension — High Tension

The first Law of Thermodynamics states that **energy can neither be created nor destroyed, only altered in form**; the second Law of Thermodynamics says, in simple terms, **entropy always increases.**[32]

In Geoffrey Moore's wonderful book *The Infinite Staircase*,[33] he expands on these laws by pointing out "energy always flows from hot toward cool." He highlights the Paradox of Entropy: the tendency to wind down can be preceded by the tendency to wind up.

Each of the three CoreSelf circles on the left side of the CoreSelf Mapping worksheet has many layers of energy. The following will expand on each circle's energy levels and how it can alter its form based on one's level of comprehension; originating from its basic state to the counterbalancing state to a flow state that concludes with a practicing state. Each circle stands on its own at a particular level of understanding. We have the ability to change our state with increased practice and competence.

**How does one go about teaching emotions?** One of the most prominent school programs for teaching about emotions is RULER, developed in 2005 by Marc Brackett, David Caruso, and Robin Stern of the Yale Center for Emotional Intelligence[34]. The multiyear program is used in more than 1,000 schools, in the US and abroad, across grades K-8. The name, RULER, is an acronym for its five goals: pertaining to emotions.

**Scientists and educators agree on the need to teach emotions; they don't agree on how many there are and what they are.**[35]

## Four States of CoreSelf-Trust | Bottom Circle

### State 1 - The "Rim"

Take a moment to notice that the bottom circle, in Figure 3.2, has labels on the quadrants of the Rim, :

*Rescue* (west or left)
*Escape* (east or right)
*Critical* (north or top)
*Vulnerable* (south or bottom)

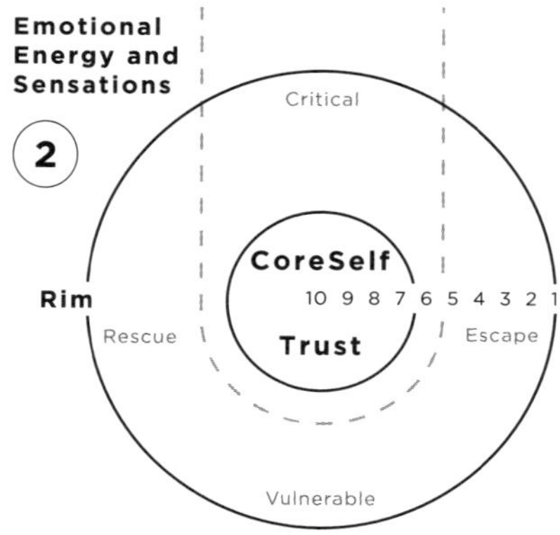


Figure 3.2 - **Bottom Circle - State 1** (a.k.a. Emotional Energy and Sensations)

Four basic categories that contain feelings of people when they are emotionally upset:

Worried About Others, Want To Help = RESCUE
Need Energy To Take Care of Self = ESCAPE
Shame, Blame, Don't Let Them Know = CRITICAL
Hurt, Scared, Sad, Lonely = VULNERABLE

These categories have a relationship to one other. While each contains different types of emotional energy and sensations, they also have an X-Y or opposite-pole relationship illustrated below:

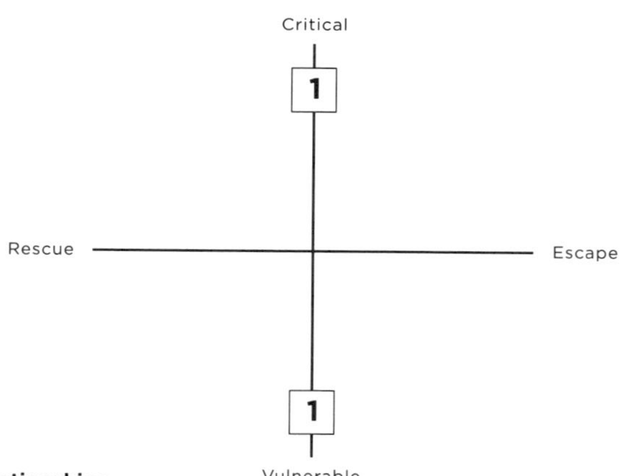


Figure 3.3 -
**Bottom Rim Relationships**

## The Paradox of Feelings

On the *Rim* of our experience, we may have contradictory—complementary— impulses:

*"I want to help (rescue)," and*
*"I want to run away (escape)."*

or

*"I am hurting (vulnerable)," and*
*"It's all my fault (critical)."*

All of these emotions on the Rim occur at the same time, but we become aware of them at different moments.

As we move closer to the *Core*, opportunities for positive resolution emerge.

Responding to the challenge of the COVID pandemic, millions of first responders and frontline medical providers experienced living through episodes of heightened emotions but managing to stay centered. They have been able to courageously perform for a limited time at the highest professional level as healers in difficult and dangerous situations, which are by definition "close to the Rim (Rescue)." They also inevitably felt the after-effects of their extraordinary efforts and needed to benefit from rest (Escape), free time, and an opportunity to draw upon a source of restorative Core energy for themselves and their families. (These patterns were confirmed through many years of counseling police, firefighter first responders, and frontline health professionals in hospital settings.)

Most of us do not put ourselves in difficult or dangerous situations voluntarily; however, when we find ourselves feeling overwhelmed with emotions that pull us simultaneously in what we experience as opposite directions—studying the image of the bottom circle can allow us to slow down by asking two important questions (on a scale of 1-10):

1. **Where am I?**

   *(then briefly, circle which feeling on the Rim resonates the most)*

2. **Where do I want to be?**

It is important to note that in a challenging situation our distance on the rim from one pole (X-Y) can tell us a lot about how far we are located from the opposite pole. *This often comes at first as a surprise, until one stops to check while completing a full* CoreSelf *Map. Once aware, we are able to further explore both feelings and thoughts and to use our resources to find a more sustainable and safer position closer to the Core.*

For example, if one is located near the rim at "1" of "10" on the *vulnerable* scale, then one is probably a '1' on the rim labeled *critical* (see Fig. 3.4).

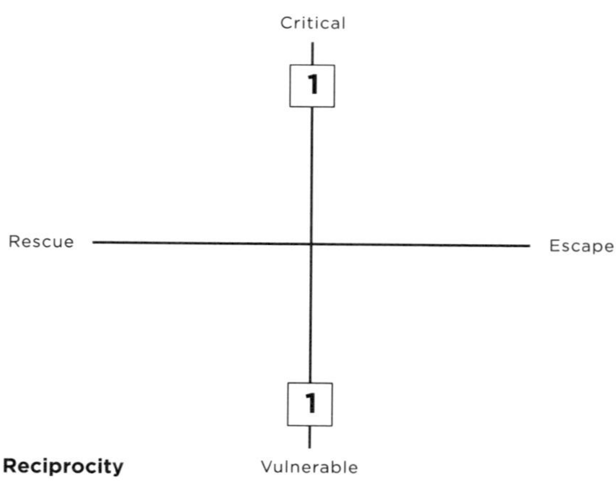


Figure 3.4 -
**Bottom Rim Reciprocity**

Traditionally, when practicing CoreSelf Mapping, if one asks and answers the questions about "Where am I?" and "Where do I want to be?" there is a natural tendency to move from the *Rim* (outside circle) towards the *Core* (inside circle). For instance, from a "1" close to the Vulnerable pole, to a "5" which is more centered and closer to one's Core of compassion (additional information on "Figure 3.6 - Bottom Circle" on page 55).

However, when we're *feeling stuck*, both vulnerable and critical at the same time, the tension between these two poles can erupt into a serious internal conflict. Then the implied arrow inward can abruptly and harshly point outward at others; for example,

> *"I am feeling hurt, because no one seems to understand the situation I find myself in, and—**it is all your fault**— you are to blame for all the hurt I am feeling."*

An ongoing CoreSelf Mapping practice keeps us better prepared to manage the urgent situations life throws at us. We can learn to pause before reacting and then take the time to look at the situation from a different vantage point. With practice, it can become natural to take a moment to look at a CoreSelf Map (many of us keep a 3x5 card in a purse or pocket) and ask, "Where am I?" immediately followed by "Where do I want to be at this moment?" closely followed by "How do I get there?" This sequence always initiates a journey of self-reflection, self-regulation, and self-centering.

Over time, the connection between these questions can become stronger and we may ask new questions, perhaps during the moment or at a later time and reflect while journaling: "How is this situation affecting me? What is triggering my reaction? What could I do to change this situation?"

Once we learn to create space and put in the time, we may uncover exciting questions and insights that can fundamentally restructure the situation—and allow us to course-correct.

Acknowledging vulnerability and self-criticism can provide essential information about ourself and outside pressures. Granted, we live in a time that favors instant gratification, living at the speed of thought and overnight delivery. Consequently, we often settle for a quick fix to solve a stubborn problem. Learning to slow down to take time to identify a Real Question might take practice, but the long-term benefits are significant.

We have already discussed the reciprocity relationship of opposing poles and the information they can provide. Now let us expand on the valuable core (center circle) of the bottom circle.

The outer layer of the bottom circle, the Rim, and its connection to the Core, form a relationship that can help counterbalance rim emotions with core actions. That shift can center us and provide space and time to navigate to where we want to be.

### State 2 - The "Core"

In this expanded version of the bottom circle (Figure 3.5), you will notice that each label on the quadrants of the rim: *rescue*, *escape*, *critical*, and *vulnerable*, have corresponding and counterbalancing categories close to the core.

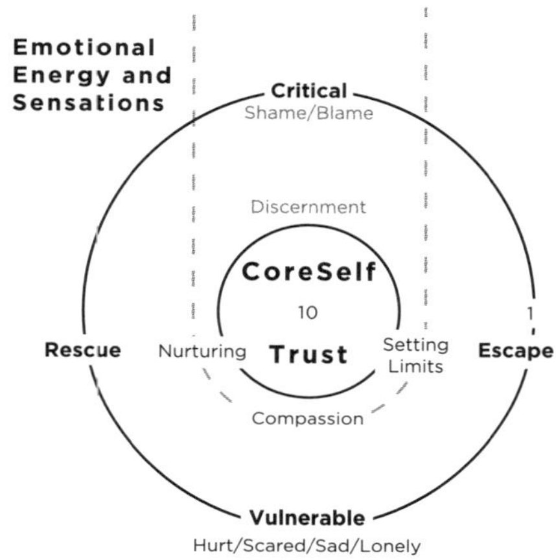


Figure 3.5 - **Bottom Circle - State 2** (Rim and Counterbalancing Core)

Next is an expanded view of Emotional Energy and Sensations in the bottom circle, with poles added for additional clarity; each of the *Rim* emotions has a corresponding action that can move one closer to their *Core*. For example, having compassion can alleviate vulnerable feelings of being hurt, sad, lonely, or scared.

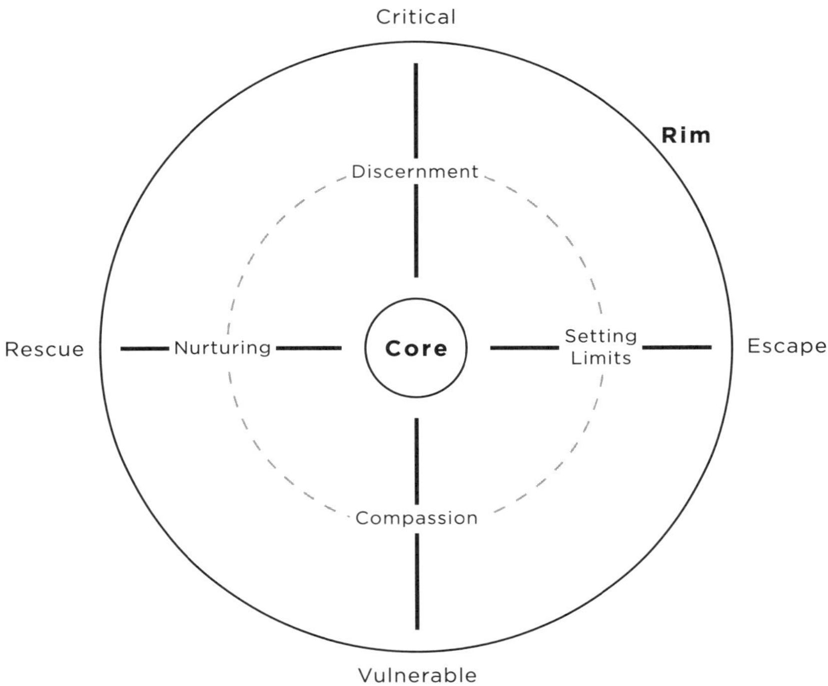


Figure 3.6 - **Bottom Circle**
(Core Counterbalancing Rim)

An alternate visual example of each of the four Rim categories having corresponding and counter-balancing Core categories might look like this:

Think of the fulcrum (triangle) as moving back and forth to represent the 1-10 scale from rim to core, being aware of one's position from the rim of *Escape* and closer to one's core of *Setting Limits*. For example: 'Where am I?' is answered with a '2' close to *Escape* and 'Where do I want to be?' is answered with a '6' towards *Setting Limits (*so I don't feel like I need to *Escape*). Reinforcing the prior state example, this illustration would represent the individual is also a '2' on the Rim of *Rescue* and might also want to consider a move closer to the core at *Nurturing* to mitigate feelings of wanting to *Rescue* (reference Fig. 3.6 to plot points).

The example of a child on the school playground noticing that another has no lunch today offers possible ways that this scenario could play out; the child can want to help (*rescue*) the hungry peer and give them their whole sandwich. However, that would leave the rescuer with no food now and hunger later. A choice to offer half of their sandwich to (*nurture*) the other child is a way to move them both closer to their core and a way to reduce pressure in the relationship. This solution proactively eliminates the need to escape now or in the future.

---

Note: Others have posited that the counterbalance to vulnerability is understanding and, correspondingly, the counterbalance of critical is compassion. We respectfully disagree and offer the following logic:

***If one is feeling vulnerable (i.e., hurt, sad, lonely, scared), showing compassion to oneself or to another opens the door for curiosity, which can lead to understanding as to why oneself or another is being critical (i.e., shaming, blaming); but this equation rarely works in the reverse.***

That is to say, if oneself or another shames or blames us and we show compassion for ourself or others, it is a long jump to assume we will seek understanding as to why we were feeling vulnerable (i.e., our, sad, lonely, scared) to criticism.

## State 3 - The "Flow"

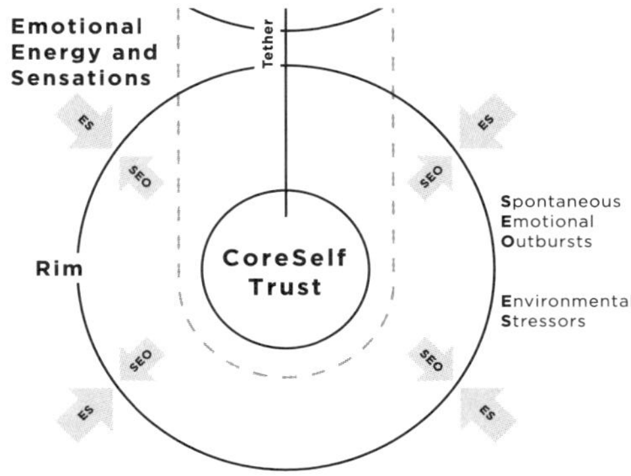


Figure 3.7 - **Bottom Circle - State 3**
(External and Internal Forces/Pressure)

In this state, we move from the energy of words to the energy of pre-verbal forces and the pressure those forces can exert— *this is where energy potentially changes its form.*

Life's outside forces—Environmental Stressors (ES)—can exert enormous pressure, heightening one's emotions and potentially eliciting feelings of being overwhelmed, uncertain, and filled with anxiety that can result in "Spontaneous Emotional Outbursts" (SEO).

External forces from outside the rim in any circle can exert undue pressure on an already difficult situation. Without space and time to filter our responses to these stressors, we may have emotionally reactive responses that are unavoidable at the moment and that create awkwardness professionally or personally. If focused upon by others, these moments can be much more difficult to remedy, leaving us with apologies to make and embarrassment to move beyond.

Abraham Lincoln is famous for writing the "hot letter."[36] Whenever he felt the urge to tell someone off, he would vent his anger into a letter, then put it aside until his emotions cooled down; later he would label it, "Never sent. Never signed."

Take a moment to consider how many times you wish you had acted like Lincoln. A good guess is that we all have already had our opportunities to use his excellent "hot letter" strategy, or we will at some future moment.

(Take notice of the tether to the middle circle above, which we will see again in the next step. After Step 3: Values and Practices, we will pull it all together in Step 4: Thoughts and Plans.)

## State 4 - The "Practice"

Effectively moving one's energy from the *rim*, a place of low energy and high tension, to our *core*, a place of positively charged energy—on a consistent basis—requires practice.

This graphic illustrates the reassurance from our Internal Observer/Navigator that there is a connection to our CoreSelf-Trust. Daily pressure can push or pull on us. Our reactions to this pressure will determine our experience.

Being aware of this flow can bring comfort. Learning how to center ourself is a skill that can be practiced. Practicing centering skills can help to counterbalance internal and external pressure.

Simply asking ourselves where we are and where we want to be can help us to center ourselves, with both CSM and CSJ.

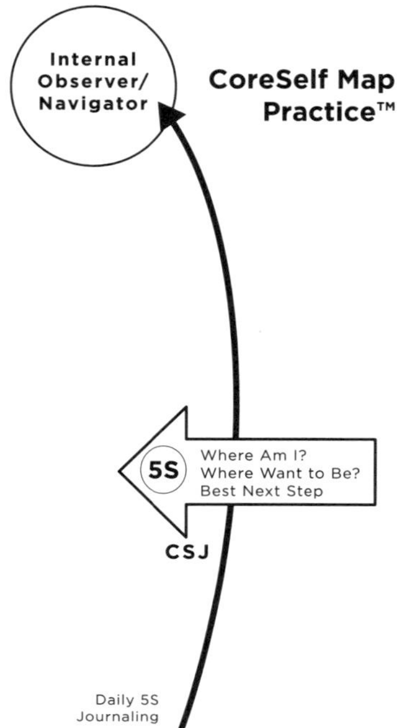


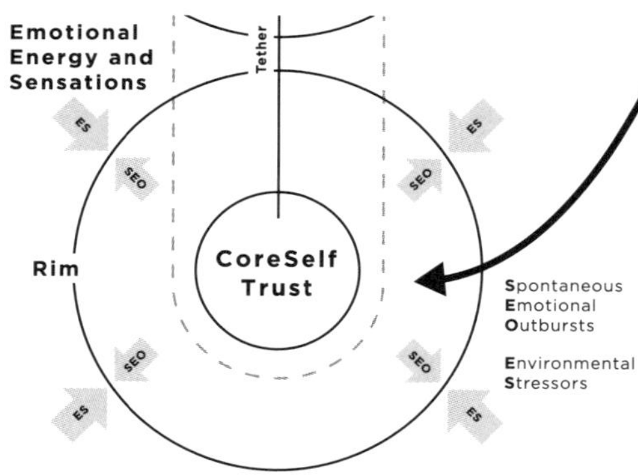


Figure 3.8 - **Bottom Circle - State 4** (Practicing Flow and Strengthening Self)

This last state provides a vantage point from which to observe the dynamic flow within the bottom circle's "tether" to the middle circle, and the bi-directional energy flow between one's Internal Observer and the core of each circle. Practicing 4S CoreSelf Journaling (CSJ) strengthens one's ability to observe, locate, and understand their emotional energy and sensations; mastering this component of CoreSelf Agility can help us change our energy state in positive ways to get on the same page with ourself and, ultimately, with important others.

# **VALUES** and How We Practice Them

"Personal leadership is the process of keeping your vision and values before you and aligning your life to be congruent with them."

— STEPHEN COVEY

*The importance of keeping things that matter most front of mind and aligning our life around them is a key theme in Covey's The 7 Habits of Highly Effective People,[37] specifically Habit 2—"Begin with the End in Mind." Such an alignment of vision and values directly correlates with top quality professional leadership.*

---

## *Overview*

The CoreSelf Mapping exercise strengthens one's ability to function well during difficult times. Awareness that an urgent situation is emerging at work or at home provides an excellent opportunity to put the CoreSelf Map exercise to use. Reminding ourselves of practices that center us can conserve valuable energy that can then help to ground us and build respect for self.

Make yourself into a detached instrument of observation, like a camera: the bottom circle lens zooms in to monitor the situation more closely allowing you to ask, "Where am I now with regard to this danger?" Having investigated the level of threat, the lens zooms back out, allowing you to determine, "Where do I want to be that would be safer?"

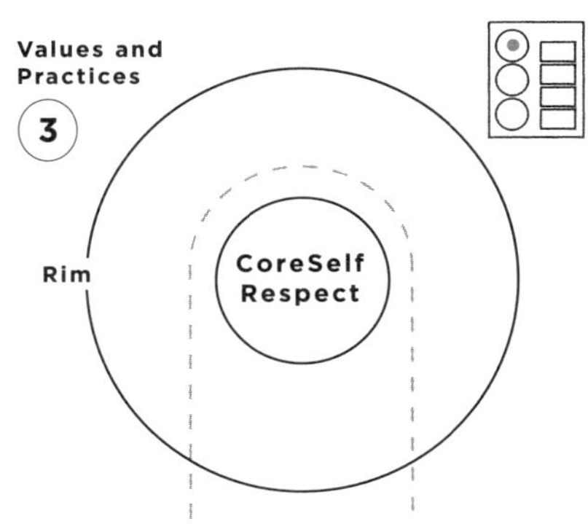


Figure 4.1 - **Top Circle**
(a.k.a Values and Practices)

For example, if I value "loyalty" but I am mistakenly given full credit for the success of a project that also depended on the efforts of others, clarifying which others made contributions lets me demonstrate loyalty in a way that is meaningful to them and to me.

*Respect generated by myself, for myself, powerfully compensates for intense outside pressures.*

As I discuss this later with my colleagues, I remember that another very important top circle value is creating close connections between myself and others.

Pause for a moment to consider these questions: "What is something you do regularly that brings you happiness or fulfillment? What activity can you count on to bring you closer to your Core Self, when it has been a challenging day or tough week?" It could be a workout at the gym or yoga class, time with family or close friends, a meditative walk alone in a favorite place or relaxation with a favorite book at the end of the day. Write down what comes to mind. Make a list of any other activities that you know will bring you closer to being your most centered self in both good times and bad.

***Practices are what you do to live your Values.***

For example, one's practice might be yoga or walking in nature; however, the name of the Value— health, spirit, joy, self-knowledge—may be quite different for each of us:

**Values** can be defined in many different ways, and *are not specific to this Situation*:

- Values are attributes of the person you are or want to be.
- Values are not goals, but rather guidelines for your actions.
- Values are the things you believe in at your Core.
- Values are qualities you find to be meaningful over the long-haul that contain interest and excitement when you practice them and help you recharge, get centered, and be your best self.

Makes sense?

Great.

Let us quickly review the Top Circle:

The center of this circle represents CoreSelf-Respect: a place where we have the highest level of self-esteem and respect for ourselves.

The outer circle or Rim represents a place where we're not sure we have all it takes; we might be feeling out of balance, or we are being heavily influenced by others.

## Visualizing "Values" That Matter Most and "Practices" That Center You

In this exercise, Step 3: Values and Practices:

1. Draw an arrow that starts on the *Rim* and points to the *Core*.
2. Above the line of the arrow, name one of your Values.
3. Below the line of the arrow, write specific ways you practice that Value. (Practices are generally many-to-one Value.)

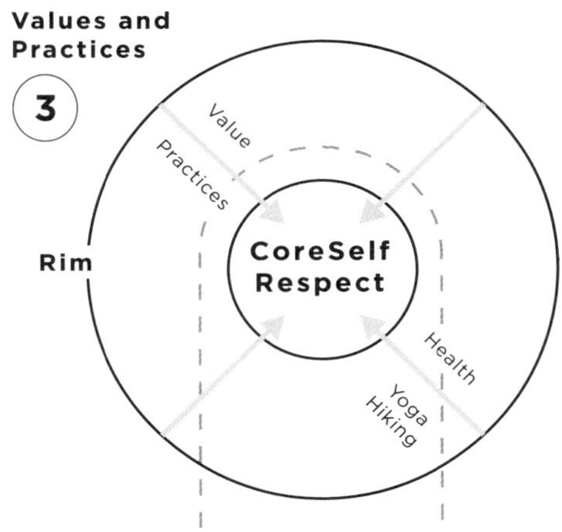


Figure 4.2 - **Values and Practices Example**

The illustration above is an example of how to draw the arrows and label your value and corresponding actions. Where you place your arrows is less important than recording 3-4 values that matter most to you.

+ + +

## Two Approaches to Expand on Your Values and Practices

Two different methods can be used to identify your values and practices. There is no right or wrong way, but you will probably find that one of these approaches will resonate with you more than the other.

## Practices to Values

For many it is helpful to begin with a list of activities, like those below, that one has done for many years. Many of us can close our eyes and re-experience any of those "peak moments." Meditation and mindfulness practices are examples of practices that increase the health benefits that result from deep relaxation.

Consider taking a few moments to brainstorm a list of these practices. Don't stop at one! Some of these practices work best when performed as a part of daily life: meditation, walking in nature, reading, or journaling. Other equally rewarding activities might require a bit more planning and investment of time: hiking up a mountain; road cycling; spending time with friends and family; traveling for pleasure.

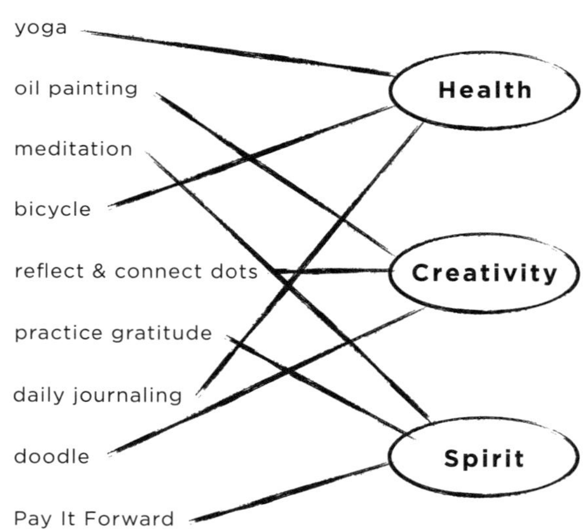


Once you have compiled a list of your *Practices*, we will shift to categorizing items as a parallel list of *Values*. Some of your values will immediately come to mind without much effort, like: Health (physical and emotional); Spirit (religious or any experience of joy); Loyalty (personal and professional); Compassion (for self and others); Community; etc.

Values have a one-to-many relationship with practices. List the values on the right-hand column and connect them to a practice, on the left that makes sense to you.

In sharing this material, we have found that many people know how to feel centered, but have not spent a great deal of time—or ever been asked—to consider the name of the value that over-arches, or could contain, these centering practices.

*It is not unusual to not know the exact name of a particular value, so we have included some possible choices for now. (see User Guide of this chapter for more resources).*

### Values to Practices

For others, especially those that have spent years writing down short- and long-term goals or lists, it is easier to jot down their values followed by all the ways they practice them.

For example:

**Health**

- yoga
- bicycle
- daily journaling

**Creativity**

- painting
- reflect and connect dots
- doodle

**Spirit**

- meditation
- practice gratitude
- pay it forward

## Non-Practiced = Aspirations

It is important to make note of new values we may choose to integrate into our core values. Values that may or may not become important in the future are referred to as "aspirations." They are important for two reasons. As:

1) *a reminder* and 2) *a placeholder.*

To "aspire" means to "ascend" or to "soar." Both definitions involve some dramatic movement and focused effort. An aspiration is not just a passing hope or wish. Adding a new value and its associated practices to your list requires dedication, meaning putting that practice in your schedule and not skipping it.

For instance valuing "the importance of family," but not actually spending regular time with family, can be an important *reminder* to make time to practice this value.

Another example might include wanting to write a book, but not making sufficient time to craft the necessary skills. Conversely, actively studying how to improve one's writing skills, creating an outline and writing on a regular basis all are ways to transform this aspiration into a practiced value.

Values not yet practiced are *placeholders* to be added at a later time in life.

A common placeholder value is: *Work-Life Balance*. In childhood, we learn mostly through play; except for chores or school, few activities feel like "work" to children. In young adulthood, following formal education, we find ourselves learning a trade, building a social network, and perhaps establishing our own family. As we prosper and age, many of us find ourselves ready to slow the pace down, to travel, to take better care of our health, and to spend more time with family and friends.

Our values and practices allow us to live a more centered life in both good and difficult times. Such activities and practices always, without fail, help us see the world from a CoreSelf perspective that drives decisions and behaviors while increasing our self-respect in several arenas: relationships (personal and professional); financial (security and charity); health (physical and emotional); spirit (religious practices or other activities that evoke joy).

## Expanding on Values

Much has been written about values, including both what they are and what they are not. A few favorites follow.

Susan David in *Emotional Agility* offers an exercise in values clarification:

## Seven Characteristics of Personal Values:[38]

1. They are freely chosen.
2. They are ongoing: not fixed, like goals.
3. They guide you rather than constrain you.
4. They are active, not static.
5. They foster self-acceptance.
6. They bring you freedom from social comparison.
7. They bring you closer to your personal style.

Stephen Covey in *The 7 Habits of Highly Effective People* reminds us that,

> "Principles are not Values.
> Principles are the territory.
> Values are the map."

Covey suggests, "Principles are like lighthouses." Let your "values be the buoys" of your life, keeping you in the safe channels of life; buoys that can be seen to the left and right of your vessel and aid in important navigation.

Values clarification is important enough that many excellent workshops are dedicated to this exercise. Hopefully, the examples we have provided reinforce your awareness of the transformative power of values and practices in all the many dimensions of your daily life.

When we realize the larger meaning or purpose that our actions serve (long-term values), we are more inspired and motivated, and we experience greater boosts to our self-esteem and self-respect. As Malcolm Gladwell says,

*"Practice is not the thing you do once you are good. It is the thing you do that makes you good."*

## Expanding One's CoreSelf-Respect

Many of us view our values in life as something that benefits only ourselves, not others.

Consider Angela Duckworth's definition of purpose:

> **"The intention to contribute to the well-being of others."**

While purpose can provide deeper meaning to our goals and aims, it can also help provide meaning to our work, increasing our drive and energy level to help others!

**Q: Does knowing that your values and practices matter to others increase your level of CoreSelf-Respect?**

# **VALUES** and How We Practice Them

"Our WHY is our purpose, cause or belief—the driving force behind everything we do. Our HOWs are the actions we take when we are at our natural best to bring our WHY to life. Our WHATs are the tangible manifestation of our WHY, the actual work we do every day."

— **SIMON SINEK**

*In 2009, Simon Sinek (British-born American author and motivational speaker) shared his "Golden Circle" with "Why" at its center in a TED Talk[39] that became the third most watched. At the time he was discussing business; however this same theme can be applied to one's personal Values and Practices. We would contend that one's Why is represented in their Values and How one Practices them. This ultimately determines What decisions one makes to get where they want to be.*

*This book is about Getting on the Same Page with one's self. These same skills can be used to get on the same page with others, which by default will strengthen relationships with important others. The authors cheer and agree wholeheartedly with Simon's comment, "There is an entire section in the bookshop called self-help, but there is no section called help others." Our intention is to contribute to the help-others section.*

---

## *User Guide*

Step 3: Values and Practices of our CoreSelf Mapping process provides opportunities to counterbalance difficult emotions and sensations that might deplete our energy by stepping back to look at the *Big Picture*. Taking a moment to zoom back from a potentially charged or difficult situation, let us reflect on our long-term values, practices, or activities that center us. These values and practices remind us what matters most in life. A recap of this exercise is in the *Overview*, if needed. In the *User Guide* we will expand on this important portion of the CoreSelf Map.

This top circle is titled CoreSelf-Respect, as practicing one's values can help us to refocus and reframe a particularly challenging situation within a broader context.

There are many elements of a person's narrative that highlight their values and what matters most to them. A key component of the Top Circle is that it is a place to clarify our personal values, the best foundation for our thoughts and plans.

*Values Help Us Define—and Practice—
what Matters Most to Us.*

As we move through life's stages, we will have opportunities to refine our values and practices. In younger years, we may aspire to values that we do not yet practice; later, we may finally choose to act on them, or add new ones. For example, consider the value of *work-life balance*. Early in one's career, it is wise to focus on developing a skill that earns enough income to support a developing lifestyle; after settling down, many may desire a better balance of work with quality of life.

Values and aspirations have important roles to play in our movement towards a sustainable style of living. Prioritizing the practice of values puts us in a unique position to assess current challenges, to measure the efficacy of proposed solutions, and to attend to realigning current strategies with our long-term values and aspirations.

**To Be or Not To Be a Value**

Nir Eyal in his *20 Common Values [and Why People Can't Agree On More]*[40] newsletter offers a compelling litmus test:

*"Here's a simple test: If someone can take it away from you, then it's not one of your values."*

He continues on with a personal example:

> "When we define values as attributes of the people we want to be, we can more clearly see our next steps, the actions we can take to move forward. My wife and I both "care about" our daughter, but that's in itself is not actionable.

> What's actionable is the desire to be attentive parents. Attentiveness is a value. And if we both want to be attentive parents, we can talk about what that means, and we can strive every day to live up to it. For us, it means being fully present when we're together, without getting distracted by our phones.
>
> There's a difference between the things you value and your actual values. The former come and go. But your actual values can guide you throughout your life, no matter the situation. In the end, you have a better measuring stick: real failure is failing to live by your values, and real success is taking action every day to embody them."

### Values Clarification

Sometimes we fall into practices because they make us feel good, without consciously connecting them to a specific value. Taking the time to specifically name the values connected to our most important practices deserves some time and effort. You may ask, "Why is it important to be specific in this area of life? What's wrong with giving our values generic categories, like the main areas of our life: financial, emotional, health, or spirit?"

Perhaps the answer is that it is not as important in our younger years. However, as we mature and begin the work of becoming our "best adult self," being specific about our values can yield insight into why we do what we do. That higher understanding is helpful in several arenas of self-development requiring focus and refinement in both normal and highly stressful situations.

This is how Sinek describes this process on an organizational level:

> **"Once you know WHY, the question of HOW you will bring your cause to life in accordance with your values and principles becomes the focus. The same guidelines for HOW we do things manifest themselves in the systems and processes within an organization. For a management team that prioritizes values, the most important component of HOW is having the discipline to hold**

> **the organization and all its employees accountable to those guiding principles, which enhances an organization's ability to sustain its cohesiveness when going through transitions of leadership and otherwise challenging times."**

A primary concern in this discussion of top-circle thinking happens in the context of individuals working out their best next steps. Sometimes having an outside point of view can be extremely helpful if the source of advice shares one's overall scheme of how the mind works best. Consider this *Top Circle* interchange between a CoreSelf Advisor and an **individual**:

> "You've mentioned that one of your ways to give back is fostering troubled kids. Kids that come from difficult backgrounds and consequently not the most desirable ones."
>
> **"Yes."**
>
> "You've mentioned that you hold them accountable with discipline and don't give up on them until they're where they need to be." What value would you attribute that practice to ...?"
>
> **"Being tenacious!"**
>
> "If we were to ask one of these troubled kids later—or another observing your tenacity—are there any other words that they might use?"
>
> **"... (silence and pause) ... Compassion!"**

Consider the impact of this self-reflection on learning about oneself. Being specific about values can have significant impact on insight. There is no doubt that one of this individual's key values is tenacity, and it has served them well in many other areas of life; however, it turns out that another key value of theirs is compassion, which they practice by making a difference in troubled kids' lives. It was the experience of tenacity being linked together with compassion that built self-trust and respect in the young peoples' minds. The adult individual's tenacious behavior became an even more effective *practice* when they consciously named their overarching value *compassion!*

*Integrity*

—

*Choosing courage over comfort; choosing what is right over what is fun, fast, or easy; and choosing to practice our values rather than simply professing them.*

- *BRENÉ BROWN*[41]

Another perspective is offered by Russ Harris, a physician, therapist, and author of *The Happiness Trap:*[42] "Values are how we want to be, what we want to stand for, and how we want to relate to the world around us." Values are attributes of the person we want to be. For example, our values may include being an honest person, being a loving parent, or being a valued member of a team. Naming our values does not achieve them, any more than writing down New Year's resolutions will make them happen. Values are not end goals but rather guidelines for actions and practice.

## Morphing Values: Expectations of Our Employers

In our experience, some employees believe that their personal values should become aligned with their employers' values. It is our experience that employees will benefit from avoiding making that shift. Here is how we discovered this phenomenon.

In our first year of sharing CoreSelf Mapping with professionals, we thought we could simply ask (on a scale of 1-10),

**Q:** **"How do the Company's Core Values resonate with you** (the employee)**?"**

Note: Employers would get direct feedback about this survey; if a Value did not resonate, the Company could clarify and reinforce its importance to the organization.

However, each time we pre-labeled a Company's Core Value outside the rim— expectations of others—employees would change their personal values to be more aligned with the company's values (expectations). How do we know this? Because each employee had completed a personal CoreSelf Map prior to doing a professional CoreSelf Map; a comparison demonstrated that they had changed *their Values.*

Today, we collect this valuable Company feedback in a different way that is effective but does not present a visual cue that can morph employees' unique values.

### Expectations of Self

Lying silently—and often unseen—in the space between the rim and core is *Expectations of Self*, (Fig. 4.7 Impulse to Conform) which can quietly surface. We can become so focused on 'Expectations of Others,' that we never see our own unspoken impulses to conform pulling on our self-esteem and enveloping or eclipsing respect for our self.

Not measuring up to or living up to *Expectations of Self* can be much more debilitating than grappling with *Expectations of Others*. Take a moment to slow down. Resist temptations to blame others or yourself during difficult situations. Instead, remind yourself of where you want to be and the practices that center you. Let your values counterbalance any excess emotional energy that you may be experiencing.

*CoreSelf Mapping can help us to distinguish others' expectations from our own*

### Comparing Self to Others (and Expanding on Expectations of Self)

A subtle derivative of *expectations of others* is *comparing oneself to others* Recent college grads, anxious about their finances, might comment:

> *"Many of my friends, who graduated when I did, all have jobs …."*

While a recent college graduate may feel frustrated, there are usually many other factors that may contribute to this equation: degrees obtained, market conditions, country location, work experience, network effects, and timing. Perhaps there are Real Questions lingering—waiting to be mapped:

**Q: "What skills are employers' customers wanting me to have?"**

This is a perfect opportunity to find out: spend time and energy working on a CSM to identify Best Next Steps. Consider a triangle of self, employers, and their customers.

## Four States of CoreSelf-Respect | Top Circle

### State 1 - Values and Practices

The center of the CSM's top circle labeled CoreSelf-Respect is the repository for our most important Values and actions we practice that center us. This equation always works: **Value x Practice = Self-Respect**. *Multiplying the left side always multiplies the right side equally.*

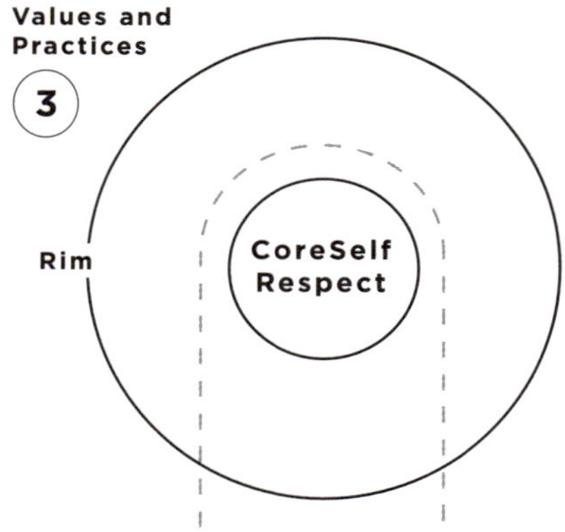


Figure 4.3 - **Top Circle - State 1**
(Rim and Counterbalancing Core)

Having already experienced the CoreSelf Map, the reader has already completed this step and it looks similar to Figure 4.2 in the *Overview*, with uniquely labeled arrows pointing from the *Rim* towards the *Core*.

During a traditional CoreSelf Mapping (CSM) experience, an advisor might expand on this section of the CSM by sharing that outside the *Rim* represents *Expectations of Others* and between the *Rim* and *Core* is an area known as *Expectations of Self (AKA Impulse to Conform)*.

*Many of our values and visions may not change; however, just being more aware of "what matters most" can result in being more committed to acting in a way that is more consistent with one's values and aspirations for a world that one wants to change.*

We have visited the outer layer of the top circle, the rim. Now let us look more closely at the inner layers, the states that help us create closer connections to our source of **CoreSelf-Respect**.

## State 2 - "Rim" and "Core" Expressions

In this expanded version of the top circle (Figure 4.4), you will notice that each label on the quadrants of the *rim* has corresponding and counterbalancing categories close to the *core*.

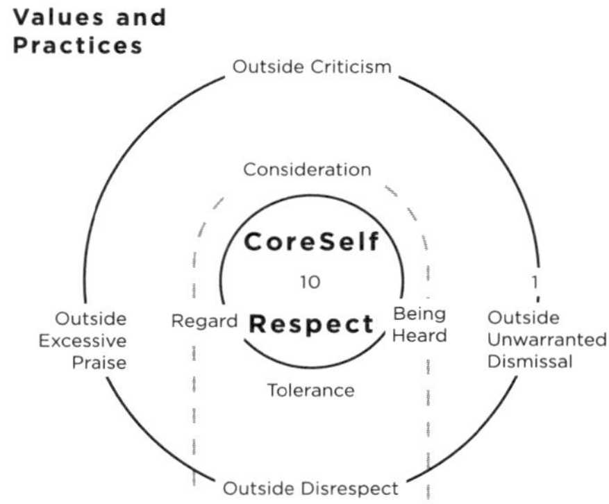


Figure 4.4 - **Top Circle - State 2**
(Rim and Counterbalancing Core)

Below is an expanded view of the *Values and Practices* top circle, with poles added for additional clarity; each of the *Rim* emotions has a corresponding action that can move one closer to one's *Core*. For example, having *Consideration* can alleviate stress from *Outside Criticism*.

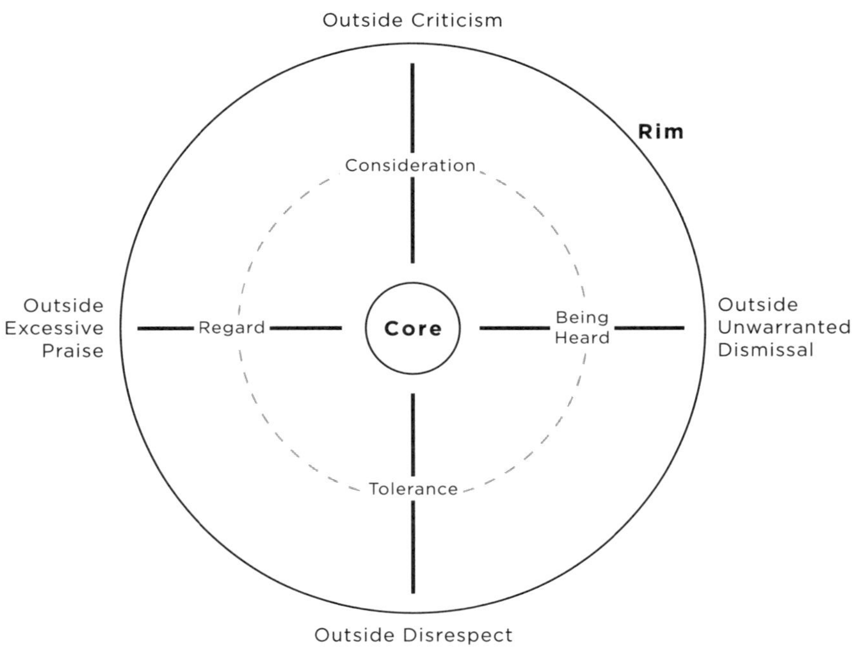


Figure 4.5 - **Top Circle**
(Core Counterbalancing Rim)

An alternate visual example shows how each of the four Rim categories has a corresponding and counter-balancing Core category that can look like this:

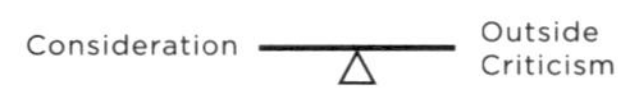


Think of the fulcrum (triangle) as moving back and forth to represent the 1-10 scale from rim to core. As the numbers rise, so does one's position from the rim of *Outside Criticism* to one's core of *Consideration*. For example: 'Where Am I?' is answered with a '1' close to *Outside Criticism* and 'Where do I want to be?' is answered with a '6' towards *Consideration*.

<u>Note:</u> Even though we are using the same two questions as we did in Step 2, there is no reciprocal information to be garnered; we are only referencing these questions for reinforcement of actions that can move one from rim to core. Unlike Step 2: Emotional Energy, there is no reciprocity between one pole and its opposite. That is, a value of "1" at *Outside Criticism* (Fig. 4.6) does not necessitate a "1" on the opposite pole named *Outside Disrespect*.

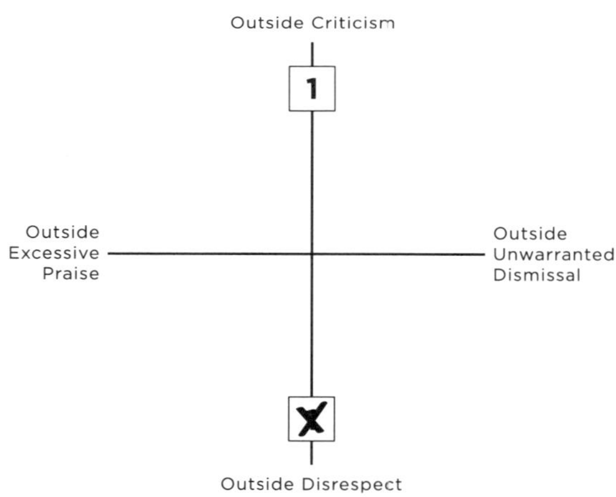


Figure 4.6 - **Top Circle is Not Reciprocal**
(unlike the Bottom Circle, which is reciprocal)

## State 3 - The "Flow"

Once again in this state, we move from the energy of words to the energy of forces and the pressure these forces can exert—*this is where energy potentially changes its form.*

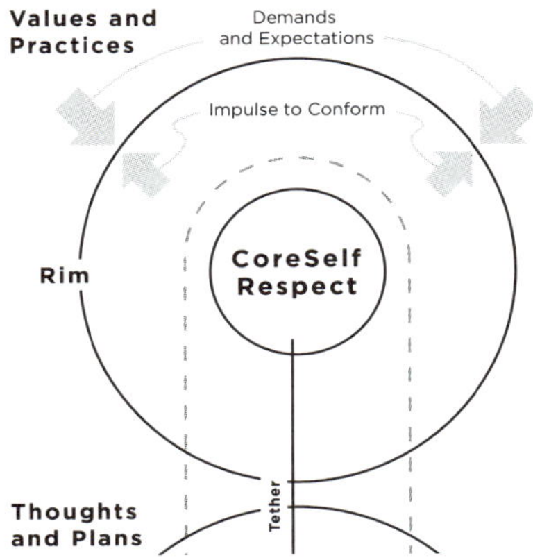


Figure 4.7 - **Top Circle - State 3**
(External and Internal Forces/Pressure)

Life's outside forces—*Demands and Expectations* of others—can exert enormous pressure heightening one's emotional responses and potentially eliciting feelings of being overwhelmed, uncertain, and filled with apprehension that can result in an *Impulse to Conform* to outside pressure.

## Expectations of Others

*Demands and Expectations* of others—a boss, parent, spouse, friend—can be debilitating when in major conflict with our values *or* can be invigorating when it reinforces our values.

> *"I did not think that my personal values would be appropriate for the professional CoreSelf Map; however, they still work and are appropriate."*

Take note of the **Tether** at the bottom of the Values circle, which we saw at the top center of the prior Step 2: Emotional Energy. Next, in Step 4: Thoughts and Plans, we will see how both of these circles are connected.

The tether between *Values and Practices*, is as important as the tethers between the *Top Circle* and *Bottom Circle* to the *Middle Circle*—and this may be one of the most important *counterbalancing* tethers.

## State 4 - The "Practice"

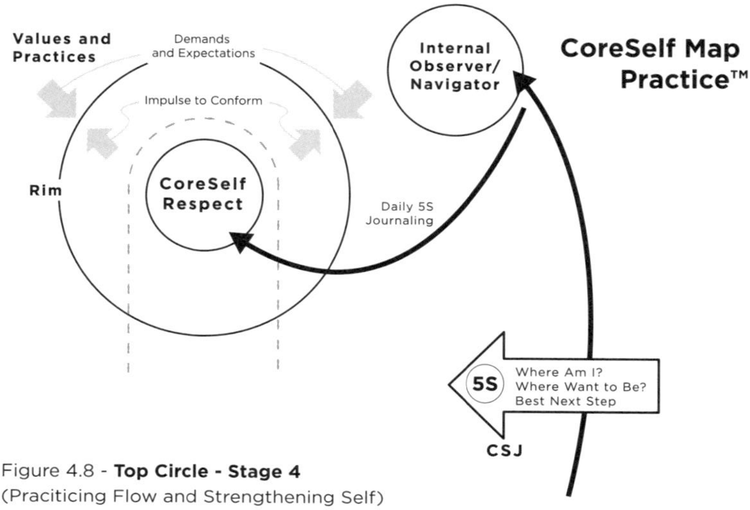


Figure 4.8 - **Top Circle - Stage 4**
(Praciticing Flow and Strengthening Self)

Effectively moving one's energy from the Rim (a place for the demands and expectations of others) to one's Core (a place for important values and practices that center one on a consistent basis) requires practice. This last state allows us to observe and appreciate how a daily journaling practice can focus and reinforce one's most important values. Practicing and strengthening these skills can provide insightful patterns and insights in our personal and professional journey.

This last state provides another vantage point to observe the dynamic flow of the top circle, its *tether* to the middle circle, and the bi-directional energy flow between one's Internal Observer. Practicing the 4**S** CoreSelf Journaling (CSJ) strengthens one's ability to observe, locate, and understand both the demands and expectations of others and self; mastering this component of CoreSelf Agility can help us appreciate how outside forces can pull—create tension—or can push—reinforce—on our values.

**My Thoughts, Notes, and Questions:**

*(if on Fast Track, please proceed)*

## Tim's Narrative Over Time

*Compartmentalizing and Insight*

As significant as the bottom circle is and the decades that Jonathan has invested in its creation and evolution, the top circle, labeled Values and Practices and named "CoreSelf-Respect" remains my favorite. As I write this I can hear him reminding me that they are both important, as they counterbalance each other—and both tether themselves to the middle circle, CoreSelf-Certainty, that we will visit in the next chapter.

Perhaps the top circle of the CoreSelf Map is my favorite because I grew up in what always felt like a highly charged divorced family. Mom was incredibly angry being left to raise four young children by herself as a waitress and bartender. Dad, a second-generation car mechanic, would spend the majority of his remaining decades trying to have another son, which left too many wives and a trail of daughters in his wake.

I share this story not for pity or as another sad story, but to illustrate that at a very young age, I was driven to break the mold—to not become a third-generation mechanic and perpetuate the embarrassment of divorce—which consequently made me incredibly goal-driven.

The top circle, for me, is all about heightened awareness and consistent practice of important values. I have had an affinity for this circle because for me it was a personal "game changer." In hindsight, focus on the top circle worked for me and allowed me to effectively "break the mold." Despite my own divorce with children, I have spent decades of my life intensely focused on achieving important business and personal goals.

Mission accomplished, right?

Well, not really. I spent very little energy sorting through my emotions and became an expert at what I thought was a great skill: *compartmentalizing.* Beleaguered by migraines, I became an expert at putting things in neat little lock boxes until it was time to open them. My younger sister refers to me as her *light-switch brother*.

Writing this book with Jonathan has allowed me to spend the last five years listening, learning, reflecting, and growing. Because of that effort, I have a tremendous new appreciation for both the simplicity and complexity of the bottom circle and its title: CoreSelf-Trust: *Emotional Energy & Sensations*.

When we started this book—before the COVID pandemic—and began sharing the CoreSelf Map with professionals, the business world had not yet openly begun to embrace discussion of emotions in the workplace. As a prior business owner, I contributed to this compartmentalizing, encouraging employees to "bring your passion, but please leave your emotions at the door." To remedy that concern in the workplace, the bottom circle was initially modified from just *Emotions and Sensations* to include *Energy and Confidence*.

Later, the bottom circle was revised to read: *Emotional Energy and Sensations*, accurately including Emotions, Energy, and Sensations that occur in all situations.

COVID highlighted the importance of "Psychological Safety," a term coined in 1999 by Amy Edmondson, as employers struggled with the epidemic's blurring of the boundaries of employees' professional and personal lives. At the end of 2020, business articles regularly included psychological safety as a key to team success. As COVID lingered, it increased the business community's conversations and concern for not just the professional welfare of their employees at work, but also for their personal health and emotional well-being.

I continue to enjoy the positive focus that the Values and Practices circle provides, and I am now aware of the counterbalancing energy it provides to the Emotional Energy of the bottom circle. The bottom circle contains so many amazing layers of information. After years of study, I am still discovering the layers of its value.

# **PLANS** and Thoughts

"We achieve inner peace when our schedules align with our values."

- STEPHEN COVEY

*Covey advocated growing from dependence to independence—and ultimately interdependence—under the Stephen Covey management theory. Stephen Covey believed that "all of our actions are the result of past conditioning and that we must change our habits, and who we are, in order to succeed in making large changes in our lives. We start with our lives dependent upon others."*[43]

*Stephen Covey's most popular book is "The 7 Habits of Highly Effective People." He published "The 8th Habit" fifteen years later.*

---

## *Overview*

Certainty about our best next step—and real questions—results from pausing to assess where we are and where we want to with be with regard to our emotional energy, our values and our current practical choices. Taking time to pay attention to our current locations in the Bottom and Top Circles activates one's unique Internal Observer which is always a reliable source of positive direction.

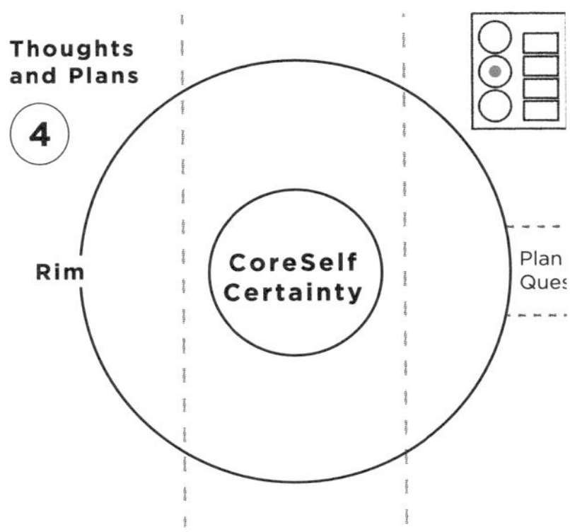


Figure 5.1 - **Middle Circle** (a.k.a. Thoughts and Plans)

The Middle Circle moves one towards CoreSelf-Certainty. First, let us refer back to (Step 1) "Who is involved in the Situation?" then, revisit (Step 2) "Where you are?" and "Where you want to be?" Next we review (Step 3) *Values* that center you and how you practice them. Having inventoried these positions, you are ready to consider (Step 4) *Thoughts and Plans* that get you to "Where you want to be."

Some of these thoughts might have occurred to you before—perhaps you were too busy to use or even make note of them. Occasionally thoughts surface that feel like *eureka moments*. Make a note of all of these. In this Middle Circle exercise, it may be helpful to jot down thoughts and plans in a bulleted or "to-do" list format.

## Don't Think—Just Write

Got it? Made a list?

Excellent.

**Q: What is my level of certainty that if I execute this plan it has the potential to get me where I want to be? What's my gut level of confidence?**

Before we complete our work in this circle, take a moment to reflect and rate your level of certainty of these plans collectively or individually.

Reminder: At this fourth step in the CoreSelf process, it is not uncommon to have a *eureka moment*, when you feel like you have an answer, a new direction, a best next step, or a question that had never occurred to you before. The process is working, but you are not done!

High Certainty / Low Certainty

| 10 | 9 | 8 | 7 | 6 | 5 | 4 | 3 | 2 | 1 |
|---|---|---|---|---|---|---|---|---|---|

High Confidence / Low Confidence

**Continue on.** The process has started and your results may already be exciting. Your Internal Observer is firing; however, it is common to arrive at an even more refined *Best Next Step* by Step 8: Strategies | Real Questions.

+ + +

## Thoughts and Plans - Level of Certainty

Below are a few illustrations of how potential thoughts and plans to resolve this situation might appear on your CSM worksheet:

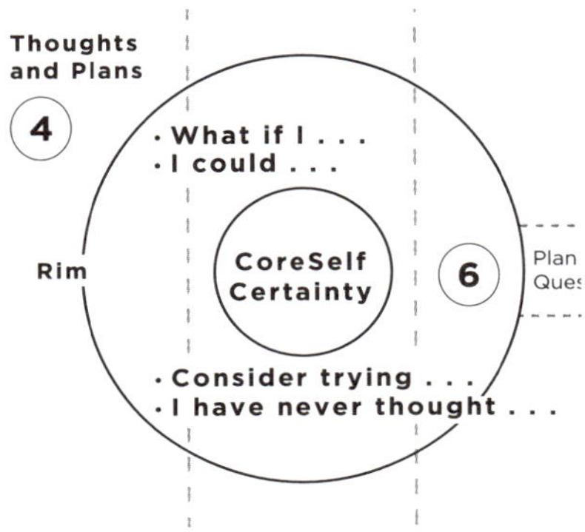


Figure 5.2 - **Thoughts and Plans Example**
Level of Certainty: Scaled Collectively

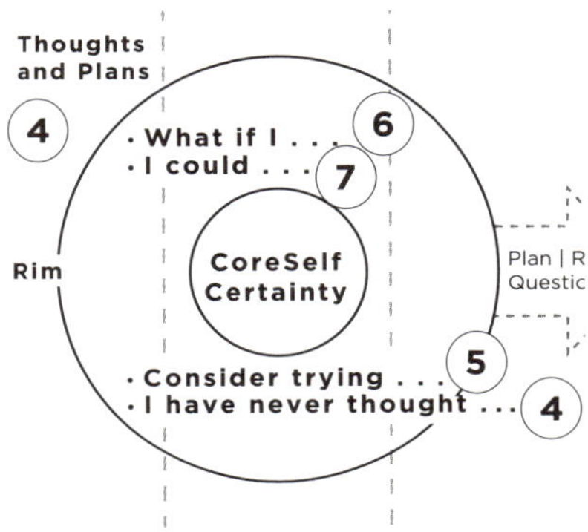


Figure 5.3 - **Thoughts and Plans Example**
Level of Certainty: Scaled Individually

Simply write down any thoughts or plans that may come to mind without censoring and second-guessing their potential to get you where you want to be. Treat this part of the CoreSelf Mapping as a brainstorming or to-do list exercise. Fill this circle with possible next steps. Listen to your Internal Observer's feedback.

One individual blurted out enthusiastically during this exercise,

*"This is like grading my own paper."*

It is exciting to hear one's inner self communicating possibilities in a new way. What is even more exciting is that you are only halfway through this CoreSelf journey.

## Outside-In, Then Inside-Out

During the first four steps of the CoreSelf Mapping, one's Internal Observer is activated and providing valuable feedback while one is *observing* the situation. As we move to Step 5 of the CSM, Situation, an important shift occurs; one's Internal Navigator is activated and begins offering insights about how to maneuver to improve the situation.

CoreSelf Mapping provides multiple powerful lenses that show us the fascinating, sometimes uncomfortable, inevitably alluring intersection of psychology and neuroscience—*where we are* and *where we want to be*—merging to provide guidance to a desired destination.

By selecting one of the many daily challenges we face and doing the work in each CoreSelf circle, we are able to align our feelings, values, and thoughts to identify a sustainable best next step. This process is especially helpful in times of crisis that might involve heightened emotions when surges of adrenalin put your body on high alert.

The CoreSelf process provides an opportunity to channel and counterbalance heightened emotions with values and practices exercises that center and surprise us with not just a better response, but the best response.

> **"What makes sense of a passion so intense is that, essentially, it** *[the Internal Observer]* **answers a question you didn't know you were asking. It is a solution to something you've struggled with all along. It is something that proves a point you didn't know you had to make. It is self-evident to you. It is some kind of liberation or transcendence. Something about it gives you a high, which means that it's familiar, and it's serving as an antidote."**[44]

Movement from the *rim*, a place of discomfort and uncertainty, towards the *core*, a place of comfort and certainty, in any one circle can help us become more centered in all three circles! (Notice the dashed line connecting each of the CSM cores on left side of worksheet.)

**Q: How can moving closer to our CoreSelf in one circle, move us closer in the other CoreSelf circles?**

**A: The CoreSelf Map is a behavioral guide to how the brain wants to work; it wants to predict, simulate, and compare to resolve a situation.**

The brain is able to accurately *predict* the strength of relationships within current and desired locations. It can *compare* what matters most with potential plans and *simulate* strategies and questions that can allow us to *resolve* a challenging situation.

Activating one's Internal Observer is an intrinsic superpower that each of us possesses. The Internal Observer is a part of our brain that is watching, listening, learning, and recording our actions—making note of when our choices are or are not in alignment with our values, asking Real Questions, and determining best next steps that are in alignment with our long-term values.

Inside each of us resides our proverbial best friend or mentor, who has our best interests in mind, for the long haul—who is *always available* to talk or listen.

It is a part of the monitoring function of our brain that we refer to as the "Internal Observer and Navigator," which is a conscious part of our brain that is non-judgmental, aware of all of our experiences (good and bad), and focused on our Big Picture.

*Don't let the distance between where you are and where you want to be prevent you from exploring Best Next Steps or Real Questions.*

It turns out that focusing on a single, specific Situation at a time can bring a moment of certainty versus the uncertainty and apprehension that thinking about everything going on in life at once can create.

**"It's not about how much you get right, it's about how much you get better."**

**Q: Why the focus on a Best Next Step instead of the final result or outcome?**

**A: One Best Next Step at a time creates momentum that leads to significantly better big picture final outcomes.**

We live in a fast-paced world where we are expected to deliver correct answers, productive results, and desired outcomes—in both our personal and professional roles. It can be difficult, possibly uncomfortable, to step away from urgent tasks to slow down to complete a CoreSelf Map. Taking the time to leverage our Internal Observer and Navigator can provide unexpected insights and strategies.

## Step-by-Step: Directions and Wins

Similar to the way our preferred GPS can provide us step-by-step directions to our final destination, our brain can also provide "mental maps" that can provide us with a sequence of best next steps to our final destination, Our brain's highly tuned monitoring function can provide us a specific best next step in alignment with our important values, resulting in increased CoreSelf: Trust, Respect, and Certainty.

"Our ability to pilot a car or airplane—or even to walk through city streets—has been completely transformed by the invention of the Global Positioning System (GPS). How did we navigate, though, before we had GPS? Recent work has shown that the mammalian brain uses an incredibly sophisticated GPS-like tracking system of its own to guide us from one location to the next."[45]

Similar to how step-by-step directions can get us to our desired destination, small wins built one upon another can lead to large wins over time.

Small wins build commitment and the will to proceed further. Long-term goals and positive change are based on having a big idea, then taking small steps toward it. Our research and work with individuals—personally and professionally—indicates that each of us can employ the CSM process to *discover how to get where we want to be, one best next step at a time.*

# **PLANS** and Thoughts

"Your mind has been endowed with the power to think, to aspire, to hope, to direct your life toward any goal."

- **NAPOLEON HILL**

*Andrew Carnegie (Scottish-American industrialist and philanthropist. 1835 - 1919) embraced the thought that with a little bit of endeavor ordinary individuals could easily unlock the key to the secret of personal success; he considered that achieving personal success was quite simple and required primarily loads of common sense. During his interview with Napoleon Hill, Carnegie was so impressed by his hard work and commitment that he gave him an assignment: Hill was asked to interview 500 of America's rich and famous people and find out what was it about their personality that made them successful.*

*Oliver Napoleon Hill (American self-help author. 1883 - 1970) is best known for his book Think and Grow Rich, which is among the 10 best-selling self-help books of all time. Hill's works insisted that fervid expectations are essential to improving one's life.*

*Carnegie armed Hill with his personal letters of introduction to these rich and famous people. What followed was 20 years of interviewing successful men and women including Henry Ford, Thomas A. Edison, John D. Rockefeller, William Wrigley, William Taft, F. W. Woolworth, John Burroughs, and Dr. Alexander Graham Bell, but it was these interviews and the analyses that changed the way Napoleon looked at life. Both he and Carnegie referred to the interviews' results as the "Philosophy of Achievement," and both men were of the opinion that every person who knew what personality characteristics brought success could develop and fine-tune their personality to enable them to reach their goals.*

*In 1928, the critical information from the "Philosophy of Achievement" was distilled into an epic masterpiece titled "The Law of Success," and was incredibly well-received.*

---

## *User Guide*

Moving from the left side of the CoreSelf Mapping worksheet to the right side shifts our monitoring function from *observing* to *navigating* the situation. Understanding what some psychology and neuroscience research has discovered about how our brain manages to position us physically and socially for success is quite fascinating.

## Brief Recap: Observing Left Side of CoreSelf Map

Your Internal Observer is alerted when you think of a specific situation and then draw a triangle on a blank piece of paper. It observes as you label it with two others involved in this Situation and indicate *who* is getting closer to or farther away from *whom*.

The *pilot light* of your Internal Observer is lit when you turn the CoreSelf Mapping worksheet over, and ask, "Where am I?" and "Where to I want to be?"

> A subtle but significant shift happens between the first two steps of CoreSelf Mapping: ***"Who"*** becomes ***"Where."***

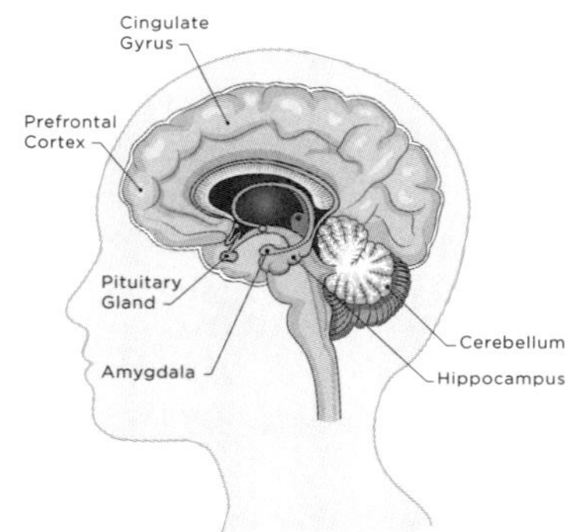


Figure 5.4 - **Structures of Limbic System**

A specific part of our brain, the hippocampus,[46] can precisely locate our current and desired location in both good and bad times, in calm and stormy weather. In simple situations, it can be as simple as waking in the middle of the night and needing to use the bathroom or get a glass of water. Our brain quickly determines "Where I am" and "Where I want to be." In complex, charged situations of high uncertainty or apprehension, this part of our brain can still execute regardless of our sensation of potential danger or our impulse to freeze, fight, or flee.

In *The Brain's Social Road Maps* (2020) Schafer and Schiller[47] explain:

> *"In this view, the brain operates like a telephone switchboard that maintains only reliable connections between incoming calls from our sense organs and outgoing messages to the muscles. But the behavioral switchboard was unable to explain the ability to correctly choose a shortcut right off the bat without having first experienced that specific path. Shortcuts and many other intriguing observations along these lines lent support to a rival school of thought promulgated by theorists who believe that in the course of learning, a map gets established in a*

*rat's brain. Tolman—a proponent of that school—coined the term: the cognitive map.*

*"Such model building or mapmaking extends to more than physical space. Mental maps may exist at the core of many of our most 'human' capacities, including memory, imagination, inferences, abstract reasoning and even the dynamics of social interactions.* ***Researchers have begun to explore whether mental maps document how close or distant one individual is to another and where that individual resides in a group's social hierarchy.*** *How does the brain, in fact, create the maps that allow us to make our way about the world?*

*"... the activity patterns of these 'grid cells' resembled highly regular, equilateral triangles. Like a spatial metric, these cells fired when an animal passed over the vertices of the triangles. The discovery of these cell types sparked excitement because of the emerging picture of how the brain controls navigation. Place cells and grid cells could* ***provide a means to locate oneself in space and determine distance and direction. These navigational tools are crucial for building mental maps.*** *(O'Keefe and the Mosers received the 2014 Nobel Prize in Medicine or Physiology for their work on place and grid cells.)"*

*"Maps let us simulate possibilities and make predictions, all within the safety of our own heads. The mental shortcuts we can so readily conjure up might have their basis in the same system that allows us to figure out a detour around a traffic jam. We have just begun to discover the varied properties and capacities of this system. Mental maps do more than help us find shortcuts through physical space—they enable us to navigate life itself."*

## Moving from Executive Functioning to Monitoring

Beginning with a blank piece of paper gives our brain's executive function nothing to try to figure out; we have put it in a temporary *wait state*. Next, we think about a single, specific situation that is top of mind. Once we have one, we draw a triangle, which might awaken our executive-functioning mind; however, instead of asking a resolution type of question (e.g., What, When, How), we ask an observing question, "Who else is involved?" Our brain's monitoring function awakens and our executive mind remains in a paused state. Our Internal Observer's alertness increases as we label the vertices of the triangle with others involved and consider the relationships between ourself and each of the others.

*__Who__ becomes __Where__, as our Internal Observer and Navigator engage to provide information, insights, and questions to answer: "__How__ to get there."*

Our fast-thinking, goal-oriented world focuses on answering questions correctly, and teaches us to quickly assess complex information and processes. Consequently, we hone our executive-function skills to deliver expected results. These skills benefit us personally and professionally in making daily decisions like driving in traffic, efficiently delegating to others, and prioritizing our daily roles and responsibilities.

Hard skills tend to be related to specific technical knowledge and training and are often easier to measure. Soft skills impact how we lead, communicate and manage our time. Both are equally important, however early education tends to focus on and grade hard skills at the expense of soft skills.

| Hard Skills | Soft Skills |
|---|---|
| Talking | **Listening** |
| Reacting | Reflecting |
| Answers | **Questions** |
| Rescuing | Limit-Setting |
| Decisions | **Thinking** |
| Delegate | Collaborate |
| Critique | **Understand** |

Figure 5.5 - **Hard & Soft Skills**
(Executive versus Monitoring-Centric)

## Four States of CoreSelf Certainty | Middle Circle

### State 1 - The "Rim"

In its simplest state, the Middle Circle represents an intersection between the Bottom and Top Circles. This circle creates a repository for *initial thoughts and plans* that have the potential to move you closer to where you want to be in your immediate Situation.

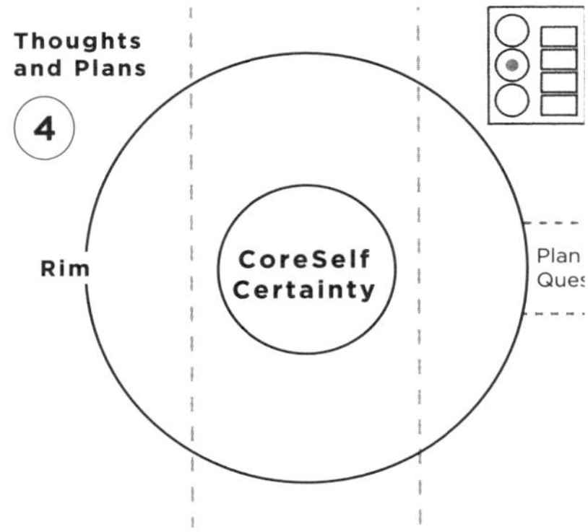


Figure 5.6 - **Middle Circle - State 1**
(aka Thoughts and Plans)

Begin by simply writing down inside the middle circle any thoughts or plans that "pop into your mind" that might contribute to moving closer to a more ideal position. A good prompt is: *"Don't over-think, just write anything that comes to mind."*

You can *brainstorm* a list of possibilities—without the storm—regarding this Situation by jotting them down inside the circle.

Before leaving this step, jot down a number that reflects your current level of certainty that these ideas or plans could collectively resolve the Situation (on a scale of 1-10, with 10 = highly certain). Some prefer to rate each idea or plan individually (see Figures 5.2 and 5.3).

### Reacting versus Best Next Step

The *Rim* in this state represents a place of randomness or impulsivity, as it relates to plans and choices made to resolve the situation. The CoreSelf Framework encourages us to *slow down*, allowing time to calibrate *where* we are and *what* values are most important to help us discover *how* to get where we want to be.

Each Best Next Step moves us closer to our desired destination.

## State 2 - The "Core"

In this detailed version of the middle circle (Figure 5.7), we have illustrated the elements of basic *impulse.* You will notice additional rim-based reactions each with a corresponding and counterbalancing action that can help us to move closer to our core.

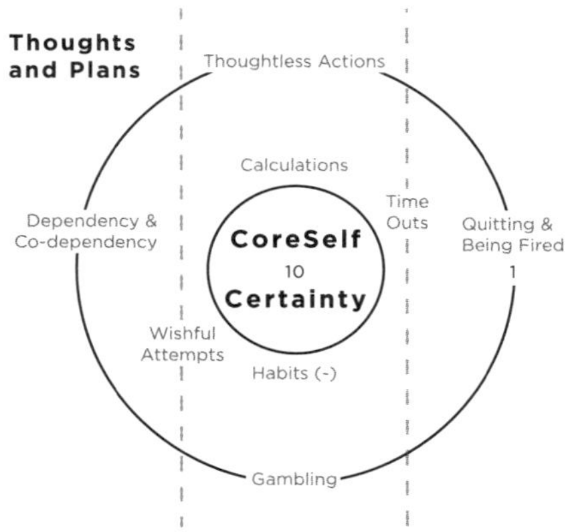


Figure 5.7 - **Middle Circle - State 2**
(Rim and Counterbalancing Core)

The expanded view (right) has poles added for additional clarity; each *Rim* emotion has a corresponding action that can move one closer to their *Core*. For example, taking a *Time Out* before saying something in a heated moment, can prevent oneself or others from *Quitting* or worse, *Being Fired,* for insubordination.

An alternate visual example of each of the four *Rim* categories has corresponding and counterbalancing Core categories that look like this:

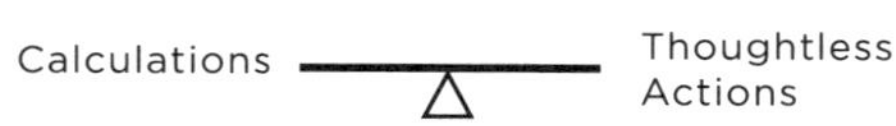


Think of the fulcrum (triangle) as moving back and forth to represent the 1-10 scale from rim to core. The challenge is to move farther from the Rim of *Thoughtless Actions* and nearer to one's Core near *Calculations*. For example: "Where Am I?" is answered with a "2" close to *Thoughtless Actions;* "Where do I want to be?" is answered with a "6" towards *Calculations*, so I am less likely to take action without being aware of potential missteps.

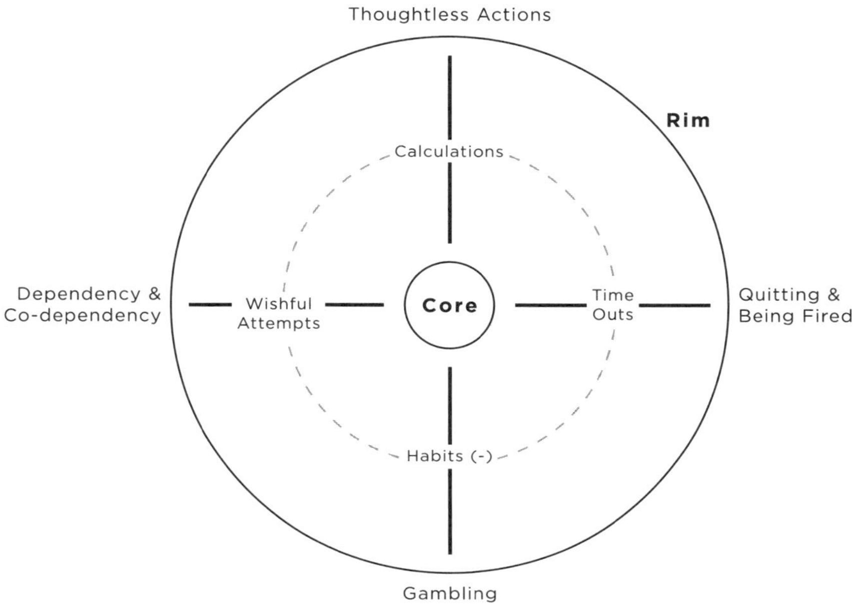


Figure 5.8 - **Middle Circle**
(Core Counterbalancing Rim)

| Executive Function | Monitoring Function |
|---|---|
| Believing | *Valuing* |
| Reacting | *Responding* |
| Feeling | *Energizing* |

Figure 5.9 - **Mental Process**
(Thinking Fast versus Slowing Down)

## State 3 - The "Flow"

In this state, we move from the energy of words to the energy of forces and the pressure those forces can exert— *this is where energy potentially changes its form*—or combines with other forces.

Randomly responding to life's outside pressures—Random Behaviors (RB)—with impulsive responses or decisions can invite unwanted future stress impacting one's emotional energy, potentially triggering critical judgments of one's choices. Conversely, slowing down to take inventory—the Who, Where and What of a situation—can offer a powerful How in the form of a Best Next Step (BNS).

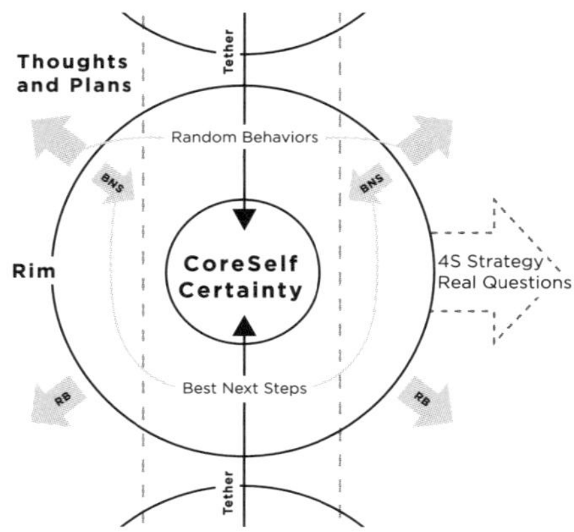


Figure 5.10 - **Middle Circle - State 3**
(External and Internal Forces/Pressure)

In both Step 2: Emotional Energy (bottom circle) and Step 3: Values (top circle) we encouraged the reader to take note of the *tether* that connecting both of those circles to another; here in Step 4: Thoughts and Plans we can see both circles tethered the middle circle.

## Counterbalancing and Tethering

The CoreSelf-Certainty circle acts as a bridge between one's current CoreSelf Trust circle (bottom), containing our emotional energy and sensations, and one's long-term CoreSelf-Respect circle (top), encompassing one's values and practices.

This single-lane bridge is suspended and tethered to both of these important areas of our self. One's Internal Observer assists us in our journey—switching the traffic light at each end between green, yellow, and red—helping us navigate to the best off-ramp on this bridge that can help us arrive safely to a better place.

## State 4 - The "Practice"

Effectively moving one's energy from the Rim—a place of impulsivity and reacting—to one's core—a place of reflection and certainty—on a consistent basis requires practice.

Practicing daily journaling can strengthen one's ability to consistently identify *Best Next Steps* that are aligned with one's values.

With practice one will be able to observe patterns and experience increased certainty in making choices that can combine CoreSelf-Trust and CoreSelf-Respect.

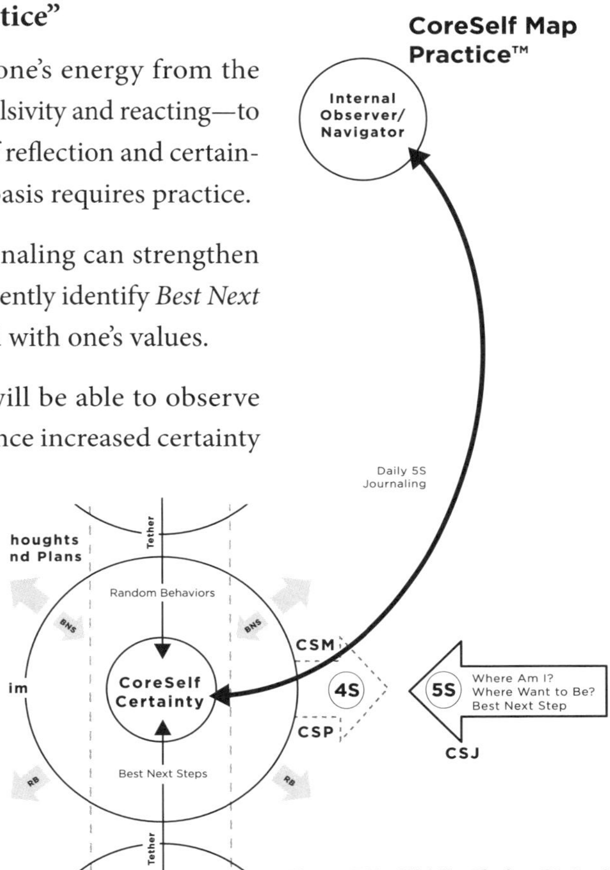


Figure 5.11 - **Middle Circle - State 4**
(Practicing Flow and Strengthening Self)

This last state provides a vantage point to observe the dynamic flow within the middle circle, which channels feedback from one's Internal Observer. Practicing the 5**S** CoreSelf Journaling (CSJ) strengthens one's ability to observe, locate, and understand their thoughts and plans; mastering this component of CoreSelf Agility can help us identify Best Next Steps that are in alignment with our most important values, for which we are most likely to hold ourselves accountable.

The graphic above highlights a significant inflection point that occurs between the two arrows (labeled 4**S** and 5**S**), albeit differently, in all the three areas of this book:

1. CoreSelf Mapping—transitioning from one's Internal Observer to Internal Navigator
2. CoreSelf Positioning—two people *Getting on the Same Page* at work or home
3. CoreSelf Journaling—expanding *4***S** to *5***S** framework for challenging Situations

## <u>My Thoughts, Notes, and Questions:</u>

*(if on Fast Track, please proceed)*

# **SITUATION** and Emerging Details

" We are not victims of our situation. We are the architects of it."

— SIMON SINEK

*In Simon Sinek's Leaders Eat Last: Why Some Teams Pull Together and Others Don't, he writes: "Leaders are the ones willing to look out for those to the left of them and those to the right of them. Leaders are the ones who are willing to give up something of their own for us. Their time, their energy, their money, maybe even the food off their plate. When it matters, leaders choose to eat last." In the book, Captain Marquet explains, "Leaders are to provide direction and intent and allow others to figure out what to do and how to get there."*

*Getting on the Same Page™ with oneself—well before we may be called on to lead others—provides an opportunity to effectively assess challenging situations and determine sustainable best next steps. At the intersection of vulnerability and courage resides our greatest questions leading to our most effective strategies.*

---

## *Overview*

As you have completed the first four steps of CoreSelf Mapping and begin the remaining four steps, a significant shift is being initiated. During the first four steps, one's Internal Observer is activated and *observes* the situation; as the reader begins to write the top paragraph on the right side of the CSM, their Internal Navigator is activated and begins offering alternate possibilities for *moving through* the situation.

The power of the 4Ss—**Situation, Strengths, Struggles** and **Strategie**s—lies in their brevity. *Don't let the brevity of the next four steps/chapters reflect on or reduce their importance.* Your Internal Observer and Navigator, described in Steps 1-4, is activated and firing on all cylinders; this is where you are having an important one-on-one conversation with your monitoring core self to identify how to get where you want to be.

To recap the initial steps that brought us here:

1. *Think of a single, specific* **Situation** that is of interest, then draw a Triangle, and consider **Who**, besides yourself, is involved.
2. Then answer two questions using a 10-point scale regarding the Situation:

    1. **Where** am I?
    2. **Where** do I want to be?

High Energy — Low Energy

| 10 | 9 | 8 | 7 | 6 | 5 | 4 | 3 | 2 | 1 |
|---|---|---|---|---|---|---|---|---|---|

Low Tension — High Tension

3. Next, *temporarily* put the Situation aside and consider what is most important long-term—The Big Picture—by focusing on your Values and how you practice them to center yourself.
4. Finally, take inventory of your thoughts regarding this situation and consider potential plans that could move you closer to **Where** you want to be.

Now, in this fifth step, you will describe your "Situation" of interest in great detail, being sure to include any pertinent information—positive or negative—that would allow you to come back months later and recall this particular situation in its entirety.

(5) **Situation:**

______________________________
______________________________
______________________________
______________________________
______________________________
______________________________

**Don't think, just write.**

Without censoring or judging, put the pen on the paper and let it fly.

In observing this Situation, recall the Triangle of who else is involved.

+ + +

## Types of Situations

Our daily roles put us in Situations of many types and sizes. Challenging circumstances that are novel may spark curiosity, while others may create uncertainty and fear of the unknown. Add to this that each of us is wired differently in regard to our capacity, tolerance, and experience in finding solutions to a difficult or challenging Situation.

Consider your experience of learning to ride your first bicycle or obtaining your driver's license compared to others' experiences. Learning new skills impacts each of us differently. After attaining proficiency, each of us will adjust to our own level of comfort and respect for this new skill; it is the ongoing application of these skills that has the greatest impact on our future. Experienced pilots continue to rely on safety checklists for every flight. Unfortunately, many drivers permit avoidable interruptions to become distractions, for instance, talking on the phone while driving.

Difficult Situations can cause a considerable amount of apprehension for all parties. Psychological tension can result from one's lack of self-trust, self-respect or self-certainty, or a combination of them. External pressure can be caused by a high level of demands at work or school, by poor health, or by difficult relationships. Intense pressure over time can make these demands seem unmanageable. Sudden changes like loss of a job or illness in a close relationship can feel overwhelming.

Living a dynamic and meaningful life involves meeting many emotional and physical challenges. Emotional tension can negatively impact our feelings, behaviors, thoughts, and how our body reacts. However, consistent CoreSelf Mapping practice can help us learn to better navigate any situation. While some experiences weigh us down, others can lift us to new levels of understanding and progress. The benefits of a daily 4**S** practice will be expanded in Part Four: CoreSelf Journaling.

# **SITUATION** and Emerging Details

"Between stimulus and response there is a space.
In that space is our power to choose our response.
In our response lies our growth and our freedom."

— **VICTOR E. FRANKL**

*For Frankl (Austrian psychiatrist, author, and Holocaust survivor. 1905 - 1997), meaning came from three possible sources: purposeful work, love, and courage in the face of difficulty. In his indispensable memoir, Man's Search for Meaning, he wrote, "Everything can be taken from a man but one thing: the last of human freedoms—to choose one's attitude in any given set of circumstances, to choose one's own way."*

*Twenty-five years later, Susan David, in her Emotional Agility newsletter ("The Space between Stimulus and Response," April 26, 2022), would refer to Frankl's quote and add, "While our emotions can be valuable data, these scenarios show the danger in treating them as though they were directions we must follow."*

---

## *User Guide*

The *Overview*, above, contains a brief but comprehensive recap of the steps you have completed prior to this fifth step. Having completed a CoreSelf Map, you have already experienced the flow of this brief summary.

It bears repeating not to let the shortness of the next four chapters/steps reflect on or reduce their importance. The power of completing the exercise we call the 4**S**s— **S**ituation, **S**trengths, **S**truggles, **S**trategies—is undiminished by its brevity. Internal Observer and Navigator functions are activated and firing on all cylinders; this is where you are having an important one-on-one conversation with your core self to explore how to get where you want to be.

This step asks, "What does my situation look like right now?" This is *very* different from asking for more information about what you are working on.

The CoreSelf Framework highlights and demonstrates unique abilities that only we possess. Use your wide-angle lens and know that this is a very unique homo sapiens capability to self-observe. The capability to tell a detailed story about oneself is something that does not exist anywhere else in nature. No other species has the ability to tell a complex story. Yet we switch on our Internal Observer part and say to ourselves, "It is there. Just write it down." When you have put it down in writing, you can observe it objectively on the paper. You may see it on the page as it takes on its own objective reality as a narrative, and then you may want to cross it out or start over. Your Observer continues its work taking notes about the Situation until you decide to take your next action.

A narrative is different from the problem one is working on. The problem can feel like something to be defeated, something that you need to crash through or get over with; the Situation happens in "stop action," as when you have a camera and you hold the shutter down and take a rapid series of shots. The little changes in the series of images that go on from one moment to the next capture the Situation. Our minds actually capture those images, and then stores them in a memory bank (a.k.a. monitoring function) in our brains. In addition to all the small details, it is also aware of all of our Big Picture values.

Individuals writing 4**S** statements with their Internal Observer and Navigator (I/ON) engaged are actually observing themselves from beyond the perspectives of the Bottom, Top, and Middle circles; they are using the perspective of the 4th I/ON circle.

As you try to recall any significant situation, you may be flooded with fragments of experience. Psychologists describe a "gestalt" phenomenon in which some information "comes forward" and some fades in importance. As one describes a Situation in writing, what is important becomes more clear and as that process unfolds, navigation begins.

The 4**S**s: **S**ituation**,** **S**trengths**,** **S**truggle**s,** and **S**trategies—are important in two areas:

1. Approach & Perspective
2. Future CoreSelf Journaling

First, let us consider approach and perspective. When a Situation is challenging and intensely personal, consider pausing to write a response from your *Observer's perspective* (third person). A change in your vantage point can help reduce emotional intensity and provide new insights. It can also increase your ability to develop and sustain this perspective in conversation with others if you choose to share it. With practice, this approach will become second nature. You will be surprised how well your comments from this "new place" will be viewed.

*Changing one's approach to documenting a situation can provide new perspective that tends to increase one's ability to first consider and then sustain a centered response.*

Over time, and covered in Part Three: CoreSelf Positioning, writing in this way will allow you to share your 4**S**s with others to *Get on the Same Page, literally.*

Second, in Part Four: CoreSelf Journaling, we will share a short-hand methodology utilizing the 4**S**s to quickly and effectively journal on a daily basis. The practice of journaling will strengthen your proficiency in *Being on the Same Page* with yourself, which can improve relationships that matter most.

## My Thoughts, Notes, and Questions:

*(if on Fast Track, please proceed)*

# **STRENGTHS** and Resources Available

"Grant me the serenity to accept the things I cannot change, the courage to change the things I can, and the wisdom to know the difference."

— **REINHOLD NIEBUHR**

*The Serenity Prayer (1943) is attributed to Reinhold Niebuhr (American theologian, ethicist, and professor. 1892 - 1971). It has been adopted and popularized by Alcoholics Anonymous and other programs. It reminds us that change can be difficult and invites us to be courageous in our journey.*

---

## *Overview*

"Strong" is an adjective that traditionally describes an individual or an organization; as a noun, "Strength" is the quality or state of being strong, physically or mentally. Consequently, when asked about *strengths or resources that we can count on,* most of us wish to be self-reliant. We ask, "What can I do? Read, study, or contemplate?

How can I change or resolve this difficult challenge?"

There is much written on strength and resources available to us—sometimes referred to as the courage to ask for help. Consider Brené Brown's comment: "You can choose courage or you can choose comfort, but you cannot choose both!" or Isabel Allende, "We don't even know how strong we are until we are forced to bring that hidden strength forward."

(6) **Strengths:**
(resources available to you that you can count & call on)

____________________

____________________

____________________

____________________

____________________

In this step, we also ask you to consider *strengths in action.* Who besides yourself could you *call on*—as a resource —to assist with resolving this challenging situation? What external resources are available to ask for help? (Don't overthink this or eliminate possibilities by deciding if they would assist or not.)

Resources available are not limited to those immediately available. Some might represent past experiences, a course of studies, or acquaintances that could be useful to reframe challenging situations.

Treat this exercise as a brainstorming session with yourself and consider all the resources available to you that you can count on, *internal*, and call on, *external*, to get you to where you want to be. Actively engage your curiosity about this opportunities to positively resolve the situation. Do not be afraid to "think out of the box." Be creative.

Make a list of resources available to you that you can count on or call on to help you to resolve your situation. Resources that could help you to get to "where you want to be" in a positive, productive fashion.

Here are some prompts for readers who have a preference for a visual approach to learning:

**Strengths:** (Resources available to you that you can count on) *(internal)*

- Immediately available to make a change in the Situation.
- Skills or experiences that can come forward from your past.
- Abilities or ideas that you have not tried to call on before.

(Resources available to you that you can call on) *(external)*

- Friends or family who might have input or feedback on the Situation.
- Others who may help but you are not sure when.
- Professional resources, even if you have not identified them yet.

The CoreSelf Framework can be used to extract and access the value of *Getting on the Same Page* with one's CoreSelf. Each of us has a pool of *trapped value* within our being. Considering others as valuable resources available to be called on can have a multiplier effect and therefore change our vantage point. Their ability to share insightful experiences regarding similarly difficult situations can be incredibly helpful to us.

+ + +

**It Is Okay To Ask For Help**[48] https://vivekasrani.com/ | Jul 31, 2021 |

***We like to do things by ourselves. It not only gives us a sense of confidence, but in a way it validates our belief that we are capable of managing alone. But sometimes being good at what we do can stop us from asking for help. It is a subconscious belief that asking for help could be a sign of weakness or not being good enough.***

***Nothing can be further than the truth.***

***We don't necessarily know everything. Asking for help not only supplements our knowledge and information, but also gives us a perspective we may not have considered. Our decision-making gets better when we ask for help.***

***Acknowledging that there is someone who could bring out the best in us, not only keeps our ego in check but also takes our performance to a different level. The best sportspersons have the humility and sensibility to be guided by their coach.***

***The principle of synergy is a powerful one—"the whole is greater than the sum of its parts."' When we ask for help, we are seeking to collaborate effectively, achieving much more than we could individually. Alone we may go fast, but together we may go far.***

***When we ask for help, not only do we allow someone else in our life, we open the door for them to approach us when in need. Asking for help need not be an obligation, it could be the demonstration of our closeness to someone making us comfortable enough to reach out. Asking for help build bonds.***

***Sometimes a situation can emotionally drain us and things we could do easily become difficult. Asking for help gives us the much needed support at a low point in our life, to not only help us, but also protect and take care of those depending on us. Even the tallest tree needs temporary support when the wind is too fierce.***

***Over time, as we become proficient in what we do, we also start realizing the degree of our inter-dependence in the world. And we soon realize***

***that the joy of life is not about proving how good we are, but by working together to see how much good we can do for people around us.***

***But it is only when we drop our arrogance and conceit, and understand the connectedness of life, will we be comfortable asking for help. And if our ego stops us from reaching out and asking for help, let us remind ourselves of the simple truth—asking for help is not a sign of weakness, it is a display of strength.***

# **STRENGTHS** and Resources Available

"Sometimes a situation can emotionally drain us and things we could do easily become difficult. Asking for help gives us the much needed support at a low point in our life, to not only help us, but also protect and take care of those depending on us. Even the tallest tree needs temporary support when the wind is too fierce."

— **VIVEK ASRANI**

*This excerpt from Arsani's "It Is Okay To Ask For Help"*[49] *is included in its entirety (at the conclusion of the preceding chapter); his message is empowering and beautifully highlights the strength that asking for help displays.*

---

## *User Guide*

You who have already experienced CoreSelf Mapping know the importance of making a list of resources. Resources you can call on *internally* or *externally* to help resolve a challenging situation and help navigate to where you want to be.

Napoleon Bonaparte said, "Courage isn't having the strength to go on—it is going on when you don't have strength." This reminds us to summon all our resources and to muster the courage to ask for help in difficult times or situations.

Lisa Barrett, author of *The Secret Life of the Brain,* posits that our ability to predict and plan best next actions is one of our greatest internal resources. She suggests that we have a "built-in spotlight of attention"[50] based on our previous experiences.

Broadening that spotlight is as simple as expanding our experiences. There are limitless opportunities for those motivated to spend the time and resources to learn a new language—inexpensive and effective—or travel to foreign countries—more expensive and equally rewarding. She comments:

> *"If you change your current experiences today, you can change who you become tomorrow."*

If one has ever been allowed in the family kitchen during special events, there is a universe of food preparation and enjoyment to explore. Opportunities to nurture ourselves and others can open dimensions of relationship that are rewarding in several ways. Considering external resources available to us might allow us to exchange our spotlight of attention for a floodlight that can illuminate other additional important resources that are available. For instance, learning to cook expertly requires us to embrace curiosity and willingness to experiment, and to trust in our desire to learn and be more comfortable with asking others for feedback. As we practice new relationship skills, we will gradually become more curious about trying new *recipes* and sharing our new skills with others.

### The Lenses of Our Lives

The CoreSelf Framework invites us to view circumstances through a variety of lenses. Zooming in on intense emotional energy in a challenging situation, then zooming back to remember values that matters most to us, then considering both of these views through a wide-angle lens can reveal Best Next Steps and Real Questions.

When deliberating a difficult decision, consider creating a list of resources you can call on and count on. You will find it is the same as having a well-equipped camera with many viewing lenses available. With practice, you can quickly focus on the subject of interest, fade out unimportant details, and simplify the composition of the entire scene. The degree of improvement in one's ability to see the *big picture* is priceless.

### Thinking Outside the Box

A story about how CSM helped someone get out of a box at work.

> **Suddenly I'm not boxed in anymore when I am given a view that provides a view from another elevation. Our strengths come forward when we look at them from another perspective.**

I was practicing the CSM with him and his *situation* was that his new boss, the Vice President of Sales, had said, "I'm going to be meeting with you and I want you to present to me strategies that you are going to use going forward that your team hasn't been using so far."

Suddenly, I could see the light bulb going on and he said,

*"I've been doing this practice with myself that really helps me with my imagination and with creativity and I've never shared that with my team. I'm really good at it and I'm kind of an expert at it, but for some reason I've never told them about it."*

This was an exciting idea that came to him only because I asked, "What is a strength you have not necessarily called upon?" Suddenly he was certain he had the answer. That's what he ended up sharing with his boss, and ultimately his team. Slowing down to complete a CoreSelf Map provided alternate perspectives and Best Next Steps that a standard SWOT analysis would not have generated—to the plaudits of all involved.

I will always remember this CoreSelf Map because it illustrates so clearly the power of asking a Real Question. This can evoke an immediate, very constructive response from one's Internal Observer.

The mind can filter and sort very creatively if we give it the room and the encouragement to recall experiences that have not been obvious or visible to us prior to switching on our Observer.

# **STRUGGLES** and Receiving Credit for Past Efforts

"Strength and growth come only through continuous effort and struggle."

— **NAPOLEON HILL**

*There is no doubt that Napoleon Hill believed one's struggles could make them stronger. Is it possible that he also was aware that giving ourselves credit for our efforts would make us stronger? Did he know that our continuous effort in taking small steps forward could position us for even greater growth?*

---

## *Overview*

Struggles are defined as good faith efforts that have not yet paid off. Imagine a sort of bank account, in which you have made deposits of effort and you are waiting, curious, about what the final balance with interest might be over time.

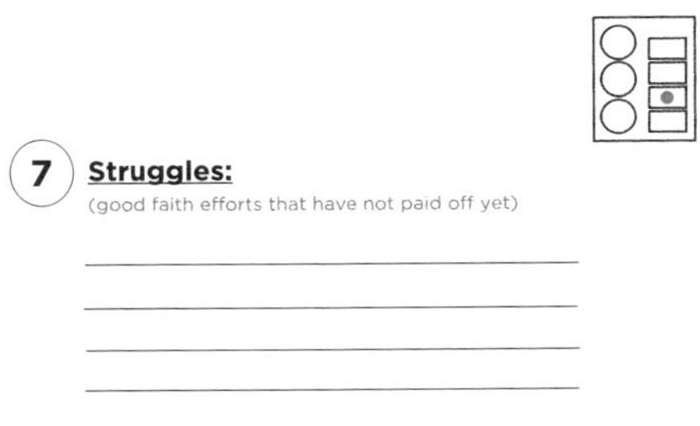


In this step we are acknowledging our past efforts and giving ourself credit. You know in your mind that this was an important way to invest your energy, although the outcome is still unknown. Writing down the details of your investment of time, energy, and creativity is an important part of this 4**S** exercise. Give yourself time to account for how hard you have worked to try to change the situation that you described. **It matters!**

"Struggles" are not another opportunity to document how difficult your problem was. They are recognition for effort expended and something in which you can take real pride, regardless of what it says on the scoreboard at that moment. Unfortunately, in life, *when we are in the game, we should pause to give ourselves a high five.*

Make a list of any good-faith efforts you have made pertaining to this situation. What proactive personal or professional efforts have you initiated, even though you do not know the outcome of your effort yet? Brainstorm on any preparation that you took the time to carefully consider or action that you took before knowing the final result. The goal we are describing is about investing in the process and not being totally results-oriented. The goal is to have this type of exchange with oneself in the midst of any tough competition:

> *"I worked really hard to return that shot. I scraped my knee when I got really low to return that ball, hoping it would go inside the line. But you know what?* ***It hasn't landed yet and I don't yet know if the effort was successful, but it was definitely worth it."***

This is acknowledging that every effort counts. They all matter.

+ + +

# **STRUGGLES** and Receiving Credit for Past Efforts

"It is worth remembering that the time of greatest gain in terms of wisdom and inner strength is often that of greatest difficulty."

— **DALAI LAMA**

*It is important, especially during difficult times, to find ways to give oneself credit for proactive investments of time and effort that we have expended—not to compare our effort to those of others to keep time or to keep score. Looking at a complex situation from a different vantage point allows one's mind and heart to remain open to possible new strategies to resolve a difficult situation; to formulate a question that, if answered, could reframe the entire situation. When feeling in danger of failing, deciding not to exchange self-confidence for internal criticism can make all the difference. Thomas Edison famously extolled, "I haven't failed. I've just found 10,000 ways that won't work." He also said, "The best thinking has been done in solitude. The worst has been done in turmoil."*

*For some, it will be a* ***struggle*** *to give themselves credit for past efforts.* ***Do it anyway.***

---

## *User Guide*

A sound mental foundation consists of many individual building blocks: taking inventory of where we are (self-awareness), envisioning where we want to be (values and goals), building and refining positive practices which can become habits (self-discipline and regulation), proactively taking a breath or pausing to reflect (self-care and reflection), determining sustainable best next steps (self-direction and learning), and practicing gratitude (affirmation and appreciation). Combined, these practices create a reliable compass of character, resilience, and contribution that can help us successfully navigate the vicissitudes of our life's journey.

*This step is about rewarding yourself for efforts that really matter.*

Positive self psychology suggests giving oneself a break when things are not going too well, then reengaging with new effort and better focus. Struggles are not another narrative about *The Problem.*

*Too often we are hard on ourselves and need to be redirected toward what we have done instead of what we have not. Take time to focus on what might work instead of what did not work. Build yourself up instead of tearing yourself down.*

Dr. Martin E.P. Seligman, the director of the University of Pennsylvania's Positive Psychology Center, says:

> **"Humans are built to attend to the things that go badly in their lives. A lot of the exercises in positive psychology are ways of teaching people to savor and pay attention to what goes well."**

Approaching difficult situations with a growth mindset instead of a fixed mindset can have life-changing benefits. Carol Dweck's groundbreaking research and book, *Mindset*, reminds us that:

> **"In the fixed mindset, everything is about the outcome. If you fail — or if you're not the best — it's all been wasted. The growth mindset allows people to value what they're doing regardless of the outcome. They're tackling problems, charting new courses, working on important issues. Maybe they haven't found the cure for cancer, but the search was deeply meaningful."**

It's not about the score on the scoreboard at the moment. How do we make additional effort when it looks like we are about to lose? How do we reframe our outlook on a loss, so that we can show up and play the next game with our best effort?

### Effort Creates Momentum

The effort that we put in creates momentum that quite often we do not give ourselves credit for. *Take a moment to appreciate it*. Feel it.

Jonathan shared;

> **"When I tell people learning CoreSelf Mapping that the key part of the 4S exercise on the right side of the CSM is to give themselves credit, I see them relax a bit. They already know on some level that they are due recognition for how hard they've already worked to try to change a very difficult situation. Feeling that credit matters. And then they relax a bit more and say, "Yes, in fact I am the kind of person that pushes hard to make something work out. It's good to hear that I am already due credit for my efforts even without yet knowing whether those efforts are going to move me to where I wish they would." That internal shift in their thinking gives them a boost in terms of their momentum; practicing CSM helps people break out of situations in which they are stuck, where they've been stuck, or where they potentially could get stuck, by giving them a sense of their positive trajectory, their purposeful movement with focus toward an important goal."**

It is quite possible that giving ourself credit may be related to practicing gratitude. There is no doubt that it is a simple step that offers accountability and builds self-esteem. It is also quite possible that self-credit provides an important release of dopamine to the brain that boosts happiness.

### Self-Validation

Psychologists use the term "validation" to describe the need that most people have to be recognized for their positive contributions. When that is missing from a situation, individuals may not know how to provide themselves enough credit. They may wait for other people to validate them, putting them at risk of being disappointed. They may feel unappreciated without knowing why.

Positive self psychology teaches us that we have the capacity to learn to encourage ourselves, give ourselves a break when we are stuck, step back to reframe and refocus our attention freshly. All this can happen because a part of them, the Observer, uses a *wide-angle lens* to see that they have worthwhile opportunities, even if there are some obstacles in the way. That Observer function can say, ***"Don't quit. Don't give in. Don't stop. Reorganize your efforts and know that you have what it takes."***

Sometimes in tough situations we wish we had a knowledgeable source of wisdom and encouragement to talk us through the next few steps. External messages of encouragement and validation are so powerful when they say: "I get it that you are doing the best you can with this, even though it is still not looking like you want it to look."

External messages of validation can be a tremendous help. CoreSelf Mapping is a simple way that *we can give ourselves that kind of message in our own time, with the same benefits.*

### Intersection of Efforts and Values

How did I make that good play when it looked like the game was lost? How do I keep putting out my supreme effort when it feels like I am not being appreciated by the people that I depend on for support at that moment?

It is really about being aligned with my own values, with my own efforts, with my best self doing what I am able to do. If I can say,

> *"Yes, I do really deserve credit for that, and I can even give that to myself. I can write it down as a struggle that is worth recording and looking at as part of the picture of this situation."*

## My Thoughts, Notes, and Questions:

*(if on Fast Track, please proceed)*

# **STRATEGIES** and Real Questions

"When you have exhausted all possibilities, remember this: you haven't."

— THOMAS A. EDISON

"To ask the right questions is already half the solution to the problem."

— CARL JUNG

*We have all heard the story about Edison's discovery of the lightbulb and his powerful ability to reframe what many would view as failure: "I have not failed. I've just found 10,000 ways that won't work." Add to this Einstein's "If I had an hour to solve a problem, I'd spend 55 minutes thinking about the problem and five minutes thinking about solutions." All of these quotes remind us of the importance of making time to survey our challenging situations from different vantage points. It is equally important to consider not just our best next step, but also pertinent questions that, if answered, would change the situation.*

---

## *Overview*

In this last step of the CoreSelf Framework, you will consider Strategies and Real Questions to move the Situation forward. They might originate in flashes of insight from the past that were not written down or included in a successful action plan.

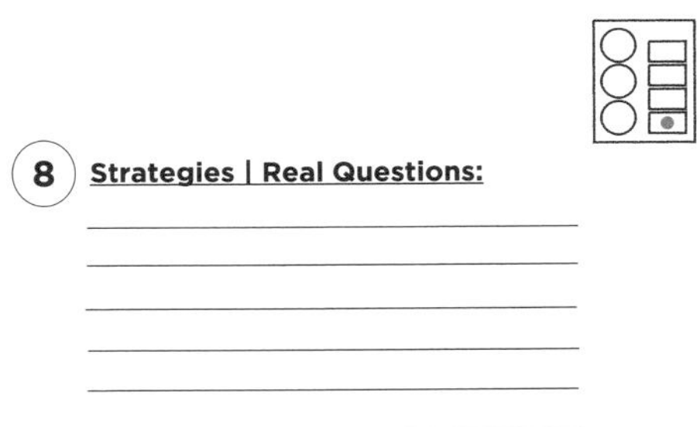


Take the time now to make a list of any thoughts, ideas, or plans that occur to you that might resolve the situation, or at least move you closer to where you want to be.

*You have the target in your sight and are willing to let the arrow fly.*

As we mentioned in Step 4: Thoughts and Plans, when one's Internal Observer is activated, possible solutions for the situation are likely to occur; moreover, one's Internal Navigator has joined the conversation at this point to provide Strategies that are in the form of turn-by-turn directions. After you have jotted down one or more strategies that could move you closer to where you want to be, pause to consider which option represents the Best Next Step for you.

It turns out that there is usually one Best Next Step each time you do this exercise. It may not show up immediately and it may require more than one step to ultimately reach your goal. What is fascinating about getting feedback from one's Internal Observer/Navigator is that their suggestions reinforce your personal Values (that matter most) and are achievable in a reasonable amount of time.

## Internal Observer & Navigator-Driven Real Questions

Occasionally when completing this last step, one may write a question instead of a strategy—we refer to these as Real Questions which meet these four criteria:

1. I don't know the answer.
2. I want to know the answer.
3. I am willing to ask it.
4. I am willing to consider further steps toward arriving at an answer.

Real Questions (RQ) are opportunities to course-correct or get new information. Think of it as if you were driving: You leave with a set GPS destination and drive for a while. Upon re-checking your GPS, it offers new possible routes which may save you time or avoid trouble in reaching your final destination.

**Asking oneself a Real Question is an opportunity to discover the answer to this overall puzzle:**

## *What are Questions regarding this Situation, that, if I had the answers to them, would change the Situation?*

Trusting this process may seem to you like a difficult challenge, but it *will* lead to new levels of insight and ways forward when previously you were convinced there were none. It will also demonstrate how creative messages from your Internal Observer/ Navigator can provide new routes and course corrections to your destination.

### A Final Question

Once you have completed this step, there is one final question related to Step 2 when you asked yourself two important questions: 1) "Where am I? and 2)"Where do I want to be?"

Reconsidering these two questions and your original answers (On a scale of 1-10 how far are you from the very center of the Bottom Circle?), have you now moved any closer to where you wanted to be as a result of completing the remaining six steps? If so, make a numerical note of where you are now on that bottom circle and put a *box* around that number.

+ + +

## Thank You and an Invitation

In recognition of your having completed Part One of this book and the investment you have made in becoming better acquainted with your CoreSelf, we would like to extend to you an invitation to have a Certified CoreSelf Advisor walk you through a CoreSelf Mapping experience; during the 45-60 minute session they can answer any additional questions you may have.

Speaking with an advisor has real value—but is not a requirement—and we are offering it as our thank you. It is simply an opportunity to heighten your experience of combining eight chapters into a single, cohesive CoreSelf Mapping experience.

If this invitation is of interest, scan the QR code or visit:
www.SimpleNotEasy.org

After selecting a preferred date and time, then completing your information, select "Redeem Coupon" and use this code for 50% off the $95 fee: **CSM4FF**

---

## Overview and origins of the 4Ss: Situation, Strengths, Struggles, Strategies

Because this component of the CoreSelf Framework is significant and foundational to Part Four: CoreSelf Journaling, it makes sense to share—between the *Overview* and *User Guide*—another interview (circa June 2021) with *Simple. Not Easy* co-founder Jonathan Thomas, MSW, which we believe provides enriching detail and background information:

We've gone through the triangle and the three left circles and today will run through the 4Ss. Could you share an overview of the 4Ss, which we have described as the thirty-thousand-foot view?

> **Of course. The title "4Ss" was a gift to me from someone that helped discover the process. The 4Ss: "Situation, Strengths, Struggles, Strategies," represent four terms summarizing something new that we were originally doing with clients in family therapy. The wide-angle view or the thirty-thousand foot perspective is when we describe a situation while the Internal Observer is activated by work on the CSM, a process that helps us to construct a story about the most important things going on in our lives. The Observer function operates better when we're writing. We can use either longhand or typing, maybe even dictating. It's about "turning on the Observer function," and what happens falls under the overall term of "journaling." People have written journals or**

**diaries for thousands of years to tell the story of their life, details of their day, or where they were going on a trip. The CoreSelf mapping process takes some of the data from the left-hand side of the map, the four circles, and integrates them into a detailed portrait of that particular historical moment using the narrative writing process. It's been a fascinating experience for me to have watched so many people so vividly capture their important vantage points doing the CoreSelf Mapping process.**

**The observation has to be objectively black and white somewhere on the paper, or on the screen. It's got to be something that's outside your mind. I worked with many people who had been diagnosed "depressed" or "anxious." After further inquiry some decided that they might have just been "confused." However, the whole process changed when they wrote it down. If they just kept going over and over their story in their mind, they didn't get anywhere. A lot of psychotherapy happens while that reviewing continues. After learning the CSM process, many of these same individuals found it to be an efficient and useful adjunct to psychotherapy or a valuable historical document on its own.**

*"I had to graduate from that business of just sitting there watching people spin around, and eventually got to the point of saying: 'Here's your clipboard, here's your map. Here's the space called "Situation." Write down what comes to mind. They did, and then we were in a whole different ballgame."*

I was curious if you could share the origin and significant history of the 4Ss.

**Sure, that was a really wonderful and amazing time in my career when I was a supervisor in a psychotherapy clinic. We had one group of 18 clinicians who worked with complicated family cases, people who had very challenging problems. This was a resource group for the therapists to learn new strategies. I taught the group members enough of CoreSelf Mapping technique that they could do an abbreviated map with new clients which they would then bring to our meeting to share with the group. The therapist would write a letter to the parents summarizing the 4Ss that the family had discussed in session. When the parents offered edits, they would be added to the document. We did this for about ten years. There was also an outside consultant who observed and helped us refine the mapping process.**

**Obviously one strength of this approach is that there were multiple levels of observation and collaboration in drafting the letter. Ultimately, after using letters drafted by therapists for several years, we encouraged parents to write a 4S letter to their children about ways that the family could improve their situation. It was a great dialogue tool and people came back to us sometimes months or years later, the document in hand, and said, "This really worked!"**

**Later, we presented the process to a hospital accreditation board. We shared our work with them, and they said, "We're talking to people all over the country. You've got something here. This really works: it's current, it's concise, and it's constructive."**

**It's wonderful when creativity is a shared process between all the levels of an organization. Everyone contributed to the success of the 4S Letter Project, from the clients to the staff, the administration and a national board. The final product was something that they all could endorse.**

**But you asked about who originated the 4S document. Dan Sontag is his name. He said, "It's the situation; it's the strength that you bring to the situation; the struggle is what you've tried to do already. And the next thing you're going to do is the strategy."**

**As simple as it is, it's always worked.**

# STRATEGIES and Real Questions

"Your mind has been endowed with the power to think, to aspire, to hope, to direct your life toward any goal."

— NAPOLEON HILL

"Learn from yesterday, live for today, hope for tomorrow. The important thing is not to stop questioning."

— ALBERT EINSTEIN

*All of the great thinkers and creators in history have understood the power of the mind and often seemed able to tap into a hidden superpower.*

---

## *User Guide*

As your proficiency with CoreSelf Mapping increases, it is not uncommon for *Best Next Steps* (BNS) to surface before arriving at the last step of *Strategies*. Your Internal Observer and Navigator (I/ON) has been ignited—ongoing CSM practice increases the intensity of the I/ON burner. BNS often surface in Step 7: Struggles.

### Strategies and Best Next Steps

It is important to note that Real Questions (RQ) are embedded in the CSM process. Answering "Where am I?" the first RQ is primed and visualized with "Where do I want to be?" The RQ just beneath the surface is "How do I get there?" It breaks that surface as one completes their CSM and arrives at Strategies and Real Questions.

### Real Questions

In Simon Sinek's introduction to *Start with Why*, he comments:

*"… if we're starting with the wrong questions, if we don't understand the cause, then even the right answers will always steer us wrong … eventually."*

Some senior English scholars think the current dependence on technology means we are "spoiled" because we take for granted how easily we can search for information. It is often distracting, especially at dinner, how quickly someone will grab their mobile phone to search for an immediate answer to a question that arises.

When researching topics online, the specific words one uses in the search can lead to dramatically different results!

In Step 6: Strengths, I was looking for an appropriate quote … Contrast these two searches and their results:

> "best quotes on using our resources efficiently"
>
> "best quotes on leveraging our strengths and asking for help"

Each search delivered valid responses. However the former focused on resources that are free, like our time which costs us nothing, and quickly morphed into resources of the economy and its sustainability, whereas the latter was most appropriate to our context and offered encouraging quotes found throughout this book.

The importance of crafting the right search question for the context is paramount for identifying our Best Next Step and answering our Real Questions.

## Importance of Crafting the Right Situation

As one progresses in their proficiency with CSM, the ability to craft a unique Situation with specific parameters can have a positive correlation to success in identifying potentially successful Strategies and uncovering Real Questions.

## Outside-In, Inside-Out CoreSelf Map Correlation

The left-side of the CSM (Internal Observer) correlates with the right-side (Internal Navigator), creating a multiplier effect that can provide a rich supply of insights and Real Questions.

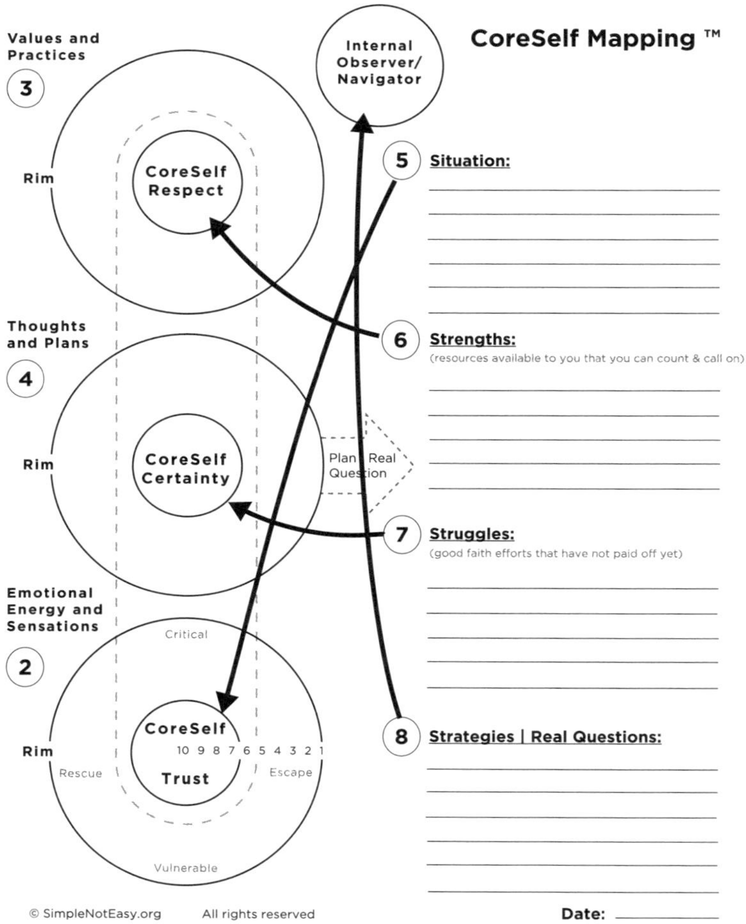


Figure 9.1 - CoreSelf **Map Correlations** (Internal Observer + Navigator Combine)

The left side of the CSM is more objective and observation-based, drawing upon the situation's facts and data, whereas the right side is based more on impressions and takes the form of language creating a narrative.

## Reviewing the Mapping Process After Completing a CSM

First, questioning their Observer, a Mapper observes their current location in the Bottom Circle (closer to the Rim or to the center of the Core on a scale of 1-10) and is able to ask:

**Q:** **"Where am I?"** then

**Q:** **"Where do I want to be?"** related to the Situation.

They are sensing the answer, mostly by deciding what feels safer or more comfortable. Next we go from the bottom circle to the top circle for a reason, because the top circle is about values and practices. The values and practices that they write down in the middle of that circle directly correspond to their S*trengths,* which is the second block on the right-hand side. Then we ask them about good-faith efforts in S*truggles*. These relate to movement that they have made toward practical plans, even if they have not paid off yet. Any practical solutions that occur end up in the center of the middle circle, which is C*ertainty*. Good-faith efforts get us closer to the core of the middle circle. Finally we arrive at the bottom of the right-hand side where we are going to actually write out possible S*trategies*. This is where *Best Next Steps* and *Real Questions* surface. There is only one place left to go: the top-right Internal Observer/ Navigator circle. They have done the map twice by doing both sides—the left-side observing and the right-side navigating. Both sides of the map have collaborated to provide an emotional energy and value-based practical perspective. All these efforts have been supervised and endorsed by one's Internal Observer/Navigator.

The final question is about movement and giving ourself credit for the work we have done:

**Q:** **"Am I any closer to where I want to be?"**

**A:** **Indicate if there has been movement towards the Core (scale of 1-10). It is possible to complete another CSM or read on.**

# PART TWO

## *CoreSelf Guidelines*

## **Three Guidelines** That Reveal *Real Questions and a Best Next Step*

"For values or guiding principles to be truly effective they have to be verbs.
It's not "integrity," it's "always do the right thing."
It's not "innovation," it's "look at the problem from a different angle."
Articulating our values as verbs gives us a clear idea—
we have a clear idea of how to act in any situation."

— SIMON SINEK

*Simon Sinek's quote reminds us that words can name a specific thing (a noun) or name an action (a verb). Notice that each of the following CoreSelf Guidelines are verbs that promote action. This reinforces your Internal Observer/Navigator's process of providing powerful insights and profound questions. In life, great guides lead to great experiences.*

---

### Real Questions Are The Foundation

The *Getting on the Same Page* and *Real Questions* material was developed as a scaleable tool which provides a broad range of applications and benefits for individuals and organizations of any size. It makes its greatest contribution when implemented on multiple levels of relationship networks. Real Questions create foundational relationships built with trust, respect, and certainty that result in long-lasting professional and personal same-page partnerships.

This book demonstrates how the CoreSelf Framework can be extremely useful to professionals in many disciplines. The need to get on the same page with associates, vendors, and clients touches every profession, especially when two or more professionals are working together to make positive change, resolve an impasse, encourage better choices, or make difficult structural changes. In the clinical arena, this material helps individuals and families understand and navigate many types of challenging situations. Real Questions are the keys to getting on the same page in all important relationships, CoreSelf tools promote positive personal and organizational change.

## The Paradox of Long-Term Partnership

New partners, personal and professional, who are well-matched and in low-stress situations, usually communicate thoughtfully and with minimal confusion. They are often able to create plans that work out to their mutual satisfaction.

However, some longer-term partners tend to speak or write to each other less often than when they first met. Small differences that before had been easily settled sometimes escalate into arguments. When conflicts go unresolved for weeks, the partners may drift into an uneasy silence until the next painful encounter. In moments of honest reflection, they may admit, "We just don't know how to communicate any longer."

Long-term partnerships can maintain healthy conversations by asking and answering "Real Questions." This is defined by taking the following position:

> **I don't know the answer.**
> **I want to know the answer.**
> **I am willing to ask it.**
> **I will respectfully consider your answers.**

Partners employing this communication style look forward to time together to catch up on what has been happening since they were last in touch. They tend to look forward to regular partnership sessions to discuss short- or long-term goals.

CoreSelf Mapping (CSM) was described in detail in Part One. It provides a concise step-by-step method to get on the same page with oneself.

CoreSelf Positioning (CSP) builds on previously acquired CSM skills. CSP recalibrates old and strengthens new relationships by using this formula:

***Real Questions + Real Conversations = Real Positive Change***

The CoreSelf tools have been thoroughly tested in a myriad of professional and personal situations. Teams, couples, and individuals have applied the CSP method over days or weeks to find that they are finally together in a magical moment: "signing off" on a co-constructed document. What makes that possible is asking Real Questions that activate the internal observers of all the parties involved. Practicing this process over time leads to the conviction that this result was always possible if it had been known and consistently practiced.

The experience of asking and answering Real Questions takes the mystery out of the same-page transaction and makes it readily available for everyday positive communications.

## Two Game-Changing Real Questions

There are two questions that our internal monitoring system, including the hippocampus,[51] is capable of answering at any moment. In addition to tracking our current physical location, the Internal Observer monitors our levels of safety and comfort within a given situation. In order to gain access to that important information we ask the Observer:

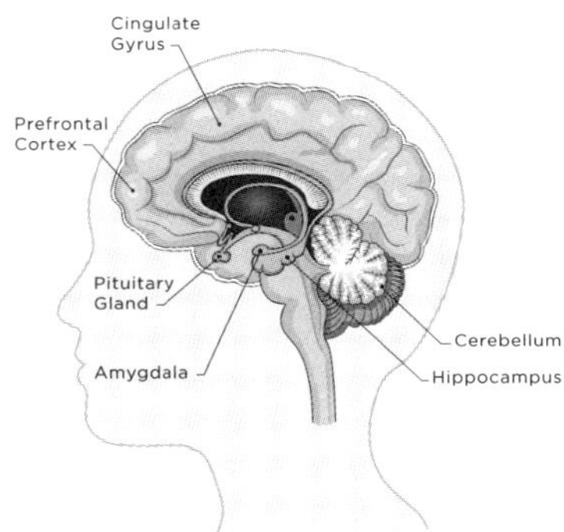


1. **Where am I?**
2. **Where is it better for me to be?**

These two questions create space to consider a plan to get us to a safer and more desirable place; when useful or truly necessary, these questions can also launch a longer equally effective process, CoreSelf Journaling.

In summary, learning and practicing *Getting on the Same Page* with oneself and others can result in a myriad of better long-term partnerships heading in the same direction.

# **SLOW DOWN** to Get There Faster

The test of learning psychology is whether your understanding of situations you encounter has changed, not whether you have learned a new fact.

It is wise to take admissions of uncertainty seriously, but declarations of high confidence mainly tell you that an individual has constructed a coherent story in his mind, not necessarily that the story is true.[52]

— DANIEL KAHNEMAN

*In "Thinking, Fast and Slow," an international bestseller, Kahneman (Israeli-American psychologist and economist, 1934-2024) espouses the benefits of slowing down and cautions against reacting: "A child, a flower, a car … The moment you encounter something, your brain has already prepared its reaction before you realize it. As soon as you feel like giving that reaction, you can stop and think for a second, and now you are in control."*

---

Life fills our days with plenty of things that need to be done with rarely enough time to complete all of them. We rush to and fro in our roles, our days filled with appointments, assignments, and deadlines. Rarely do we take the time to intentionally slow down. Too often, life forces us to slow down with an unexpected or unplanned event.

Proactively making the time to take care of ourselves can be a challenge. Fortunately, improving health is becoming increasingly important for many executives who want their people to be in optimal physical and mental health. The importance of supporting all employees' mental health has been recognized in post-COVID work-from-home initiatives. Research documents that mindfulness and meditation practices slow down and center the organization's most valuable asset—its people.

*The CoreSelf process represents a way for individuals and teams to accomplish that. Let's look at how that can happen.*

Organizations that are investing in the health benefits of mindfulness and meditation are searching for a tool that connects these desirable soft skills to accomplishing specific company goals, like improving certain measures of productivity.

Psychologists have demonstrated that the human brain has two primary functions:

1. **Executive functioning** refers to a set of skills that underlie the capacity to plan ahead and meet goals, focus attention, follow multiple-step instructions, and juggle multiple tasks despite interruptions or distractions. Summary: *Getting a lot of stuff done, lists completed, quickly and accurately.*
2. **Monitoring functioning** is a form of data-gathering which systematically observes and records specific events that include emotions, sensations, and behaviors. Summary: *Monitoring can be instrumental in determining if desired actions are being implemented as planned and are having intended results.*

CoreSelf Mapping (CSM) flips the switch from executive functioning to monitoring functioning, providing valuable feedback on what is most important to us personally and professionally. Being grounded in our core values also helps to clarify our priorities pertaining to a particular project or situation.

Maintaining focus on a single, specific situation leads to Best Next Steps and Real Questions for both teams and individuals. CoreSelf tools support the important skill of "zooming in and out" of key situations as needed, minimizing the need to multitask.

CoreSelf Positioning (CSP) slows teams down to proactively get on the same page, literally. A team CoreSelf meeting encourages everyone to contribute to a same-page plan: naming resources available; acknowledging all efforts invested year to date; collaborating to identify Best Next Steps and uncover Real Questions. All participants leave with a clear understanding of their role and its impact. All members of the team are accountable to fulfill their agreed upon role in the same-page planning document.

## Example: Executive Functioning

You have decided to change course and pursue a new profession or career. Your stage in life when you make this important decision will have certain implications and raise certain questions. Your *executive* function may simulate scenarios that raise challenging questions about your decision to change careers.

*Unfortunately, some of the executive feedback might include uncertainty and even doubt.*

## Example: Monitoring Functioning

Slowing down to engage your *monitoring* function can offer helpful new perspective.

| Stage | **Young Adult** | **Mid-Life** | **Early Retirement** |
|---|---|---|---|
| *Current* | *I think this . . .* | *I need to . . .* | *I have always . . .* |
| **Executive** | | | |
| **Emotions** | What if I am wrong? | What choice do I have? | What if I am too late? |
| **Beliefs** | I am invincible! | Do I have what it takes? | Should I just relax? |
| **Reactions** | What is cost/time? | I have responsibilities! | Is this worth time/cost? |
| **Monitoring** | | | |
| **Energy** | Will this get me closer to where I want to be? | | |
| **Values** | What values matter most to me? Will I be accountable? | | |
| **Plan** | Is this decision in alignment with my values? | | |
| *Destination* | *Where do I want to be?* | | |

Figure 10.1 - **Career Change at Different Life Stages**
Executive- versus Montoring-Function Perspectives

Getting on the Same Page with our self (CSM) might begin with this situation:

**Q: "I am considering a significant career change. Why would this be a good decision now?"**

**A: Ask the two Real Questions (RQ) via CSM (Bottom Circle):**

1. **Where am I?**
2. **Where do I want to be?**

Answering these RQs activates our monitoring (hippocampus) function called the Internal Observer which can use multiple lenses to provide vital information.

**Q: Why are both of these questions important?**

**A: They pause the executive function and fire up the monitoring function.**

## Paradox of Slowing Down

Slowing down can help us get to where we want to be faster *efficiently*. Faster is an interesting choice of words. Many would be satisfied to simply *arrive* where they want to be as quickly as possible.

Our executive function is efficient at quickly completing tasks. It can also rapidly access information that helps us make fast decisions. It is from slowing down that we can get valuable feedback from our monitoring function; feedback that can validate that our quick decisions are in alignment with our most important values. Slowing down helps ensure that we will not regret those quick decisions in the future.

The CoreSelf approach allows us to systematically understand all aspects of situations, especially what types of emotional energy the situation contains now and what outcomes will matter most to us over the long term. Combining these two perspectives can reveal unique strategies and insightful Real Questions.

New Year's Resolutions offer a great example of the benefit of slowing down to achieve our goals faster. Resolutions and goals are different and similar; the first focuses on an ambition and the latter on an action. The reasons that both can fail are similar.[53] Here is how to approach them:

1. Initiate Goals at a Time of Change
2. Expect Obstacles
3. Set Goals into Challenging, Measurable, but Smaller Chunks
4. Stress Accountability

"Researchers suggest that only 9% of Americans that make New Year's resolutions complete them. In fact, research goes on to show that 23% of people quit their resolution by the end of the first week, and 43% quit by the end of January."

Slowing down to engage your Internal Observer with CoreSelf Mapping provides:

1. Desired Position in Situation/Destination (goal)
2. Anticipate Resources Available to Create Momentum (obstacles)
3. Establish Best Next Step towards Goal (small wins)
4. Builds Self-Trust, Self-Respect, and Self-Certainty (accountability)

*Slowing down can provide greater clarity, an opportunity to harness your emotional energy and ultimately make better decisions.*

# **TRUST THE MAP** As You Engage

"All you need is the plan, the road map,
and the courage to press on to your destination."

—EARL NIGHTINGALE

*Nightingale (American radio speaker and author. 1921 - 1989) dealt mostly with the subjects of human character development, motivation, and meaningful existence. He also said, "Your problem is to bridge the gap which exists between where you are and the goal you intend to reach."*

*Bridging the gap between where we are and where we want to be is the problem. The CoreSelf Map can provide the roadmap.*

---

Most of us use Global Positioning Systems (GPS) to get us from points A to B, especially when searching for the route to a new destination. We now rely on technology to get us to our destination in the shortest possible time and keep us out of trouble by rerouting us around traffic.

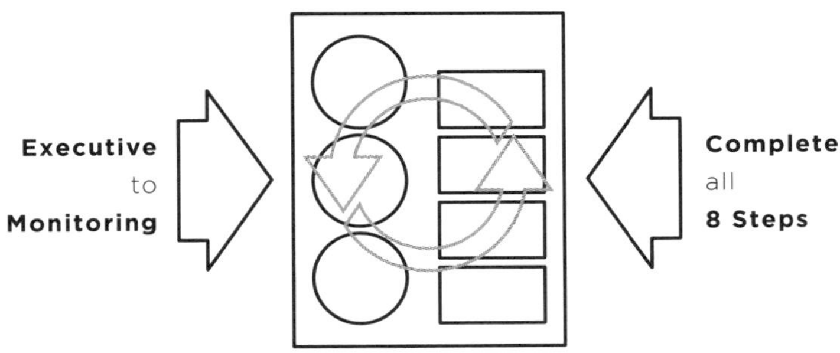


**Slow Down** shifts our mindset from Executive to Monitoring functioning. **Trust the Map** refers to completing all eight steps of the CSM worksheet.

Switching from executive to monitoring brain function is simple, but not easy in a world that operates at the speed of light. Daily life is filled with decisions and conscious choices regarding our personal (CSM) and professional

(CSP) roles. Some decisions require more time for thoughtful analysis.

**Q: How does the brain multitask, making decisions in rapid-fire fashion on multiple projects?**

**A: The executive function of our brain allows us to call on our experiences, emotions, beliefs, and thoughts to make decisions with maximum efficiency.**

Our executive mind has been trained to quickly access situations, compare and simulate with our experiences, then arrive at a reasonable resolution. This task-centric mode can make us feel productive and in charge most of the time. Unfortunately, this approach does not always serve us well (e.g., in difficult or high-stress times in life).

The CoreSelf Mapping process slows down executive function and increases monitoring function. The monitoring function can view a challenging situation from many different vantage points. This observing-centric mode can help us center ourselves and see components of the situation that may have been hidden. Moving from the left side of the map to the right engages resources available to navigate our best next steps.

Both sides of the map work together with the Internal Observer/Navigator to:

- **Observe** - our positions, emotional energy, values, and plans
- **Navigate** - adding language our observations, consider resources available, credit ourselves for past efforts, and identify step-by-step plans to arrive safely and in a timely manner at our preferred destinations

As we trust the map, we are trusting the process. The human brain has an internal navigator that is more sophisticated and more capable than most GPS tools.

## Getting a Roadmap to Where We Want to Be

Trusting the Map allows your Internal Observer and Navigator (I/ON) to chart a course to where you want to be. Your I/ON knows all of your experiences and values. It knows the best route for you to take. Specifically, it knows the best way for *you* to get there. Without a long explanation or any justification, *there is a part of you that knows what you will—and will not—sign up for*. **Read that again.**

CoreSelf Mapping (CSM) provides lenses for you to zoom in and out of any challenging situations. These lenses can balance heightened emotional energy with your value-based centering practices. They also help to capture insightful feedback from your Internal Observer and Navigator.

The structure of the CSM supports the way your brain wants to work. Allowing your brain to both observe and navigate can provide clarity and insight. This internal collaboration can provide a useful roadmap to arrive at your desired destination in the best possible way for you to travel.

There are many ways to get to the same destination. Each of us gets to choose the path that we will take.

The *founders* of the CoreSelf system have demonstrated with a wide spectrum of individuals in a wide variety of situations that the eight CoreSelf steps function as an algorithm, a step-by-step instruction guide that produces viable Best Next Steps.

## Trust the Map = Playing by the Rules

Similar to the three circles in the CoreSelf Map, Trust the Map tethers to Slow Down and Question Respectfully. Each guideline builds on and flows to the next.

Whether we are playing the "game of business" or the "game of life," these guidelines build "teamwork" and "relationships." They provide an environment where everyone feels safe to participate; where all communication is respectful; where everyone can learn; where everyone is committed to their particular team's success.

When an individual is completing a CoreSelf Map (CSM), it is important to:

1. Slow Down (ask Who and Where questions)
2. Trust the Map (complete all eight steps)

3. Question Respectfully (self and others)

Consequently, as two or more people are using CoreSelf Positioning (CSP) to get on the same page, these guidelines become even more significant.

1. Slow Down (not keeping time or score)
2. **Trust the Map** (have CSM available and follow the 4**S**s)

    - Listen with Curiosity (to others' input)
    - Communicate Collaboratively (look for a better way)

3. Question Respectfully (without critiquing, judging, or censoring)

In sports, rules are established for safety and to keep the game fair; the only consequence may be a time penalty or ejection from the game. We keep time to keep the game moving and we keep score to determine who wins.

In the "CoreSelf game," playing by the rules keeps everyone safe and the game fair; consequences of not playing by the rules can be costly. Getting on the Same Page with others never requires keeping time or score.

**My Thoughts, Notes, and Questions:**

*(if on Fast Track, please proceed)*

# QUESTION RESPECTFULLY
## and Actively Listen

"As with most things in life, the process of determining what we want is improved with targeted questions and deeper awareness. The more we ask and the more we listen - with both our heads and our hearts - the better the answers we receive. And every step we take is an opportunity to get feedback and make refinements."

— **JOSEPH DEITCH**

*In "Elevate: An Essential Guide to Life," Deitch (American business executive, philanthropist and author) offers powerful reasons to ask thoughtful questions and listen deeply to the answers we receive. The authors of this book call these Real Questions™ and highlight their importance to Getting on the Same Page™ with oneself and others.*

---

The guidelines work together, but this last guideline is the most important.

Trust and respect are the fundamental building blocks of all important relationships.

Questioning Respectfully with Real Questions is the most important key to building trust and respect. This process requires listening, learning, and curiosity.

Definition of a Real Question (RQ):

1. **I do not know the answer.**
2. **I want to know the answer.**
3. **I am willing to courageously ask a Real Question.**
4. **I am willing to listen to the reply and reflect before answering.**

The skills learned in Part One: CoreSelf Mapping and the values of building our CoreSelf-Trust, CoreSelf-Respect, and CoreSelf-Certainty become more important as we move to Part Three: CoreSelf-Positioning—Getting on the Same Page with others.

When we let another person know that this relationship is important to us, we are asserting balance between ourselves and others. Being assertive is a positive quality that communicates self-respect and more importantly, respect for the other person.

Communication is key to healthy professional and personal relationships. The CoreSelf Positioning process shared in the next chapter operates differently than other communication tools.

*Respectfully ask the other party to commit to try this communication process. Share with them the importance you place on this relationship and on creating a dialogue that works for both of you.*

Getting on the Same Page with others expands on CoreSelf Mapping skills. The collaborative insights and Real Questions in CoreSelf-Positioning will extend these skills.

**Bookmark these three guidelines to build and accelerate Getting—and Staying—on the Same Page in your most important relationships.**

---

## Bookmarks in our Minds that Can Change Us

Ironically, I had the fortuitous opportunity to meet Jonathan in October 2009, as the result of a troubled relationship—and this book is about improving relationships with self and others. At the time, he bookmarked three words in my mind:

> ***Everything I am going to teach you is simple, not easy.***

It took thirteen years before I would ask him what he meant by those words, which led to this book and the formation of Simple.Not Easy., LLC in 2017. His response:

> **What I said then and what that sentence means to me now are**

**essentially the same. Completing a CoreSelf Map is simple when you know the difference between Executive functioning and Monitoring functioning, when you can allow your Inside Voice/ Observer to use the pen or keyboard to do the writing in a relaxed way. As we know, for most of us who are conditioned to respond with some urgency to a writing prompt and want to be the first one done with all the right answers, not being worried about getting it wrong when filling out a questionnaire is a challenge in itself. We are also conditioned to expect the best response to come from an outside rather than an inside source. "Planning to be surprised," is a confusing/ contradictory activity for most human beings that takes some practice to fully appreciate.**

**We learned in the beginning stages of this project that there is a consistent and valuable reward for slowing down, trusting the map, and questioning respectfully. As we reflect on our current position on the CoreSelf Map by jotting down brief statements about our Situation, Strengths and Struggles, we also gain a unique perspective on possible Best Next Steps. We have been gratified to learn how much CoreSelf Mapping/CoreSelf Positioning practices benefit everyone who has made those skills key parts of their professional and personal identity.**

- JONATHAN THOMAS' RESPONSE (CIRCA OCT 2022)

I recently asked Jonathan what his top three life lessons year-to-date were, if a grandson or young adult were to ask. Without pause he replied: "Over all these years, it has not changed:

***Slow Down, Trust the Map, and Question Respectfully."***

# PART THREE

# *CoreSelf Positioning*

# **CoreSelf Positioning:**
## Getting on the Same Page *with others*

"Human life is interdependent! We can combine our talents and abilities and create something greater together. Interdependent people combine their own efforts with efforts of others to achieve their greatest success."

— STEPHEN COVEY

*In Covey's The 7 Habits of Highly Effective People, he espouses self-mastery to become independent in the first three habits, then growing towards interdependence with others in the next three habits. Similarly, CoreSelf Mapping begins with a focus on independent mastery of self, followed by interdependent relationships—getting on the same page with others.*

---

Most of us have heard from leaders, managers, parents, or significant others—or thought to ourselves—***"we need to get on the same page."***

**Q: How is it that such a simple sounding arrangement can be so elusive and difficult to achieve?**

**A: When most people use the phrase, "on the same page," they are only speaking metaphorically.**

The phrase has come to mean that "somehow by some unknown means, we will come to understand and accept our differences. We can then create a common platform for moving forward and our previous disagreements or misunderstandings will not block our future progress." *The page to gather on* represents a wish and sometimes a desperate need for an effective plan on which all parties can sign off and execute together. Some may picture this as getting out of their own bubble. *On the same page* with ourself encourages us to consider where we want to be prior to considering others' perspectives.

This sounds like a simple and obvious plan. In reality, it is never easy for two parties to get or stay "on the same page" when that means close collaboration on a complex plan to address important issues. The parties sometimes find themselves on completely *different pages* trying to figure out how they got so far apart. Often elements of time and life's storms have interfered with the parties' best intentions. Navigating back to a "safe harbor" for working and living together can be a daunting challenge.

*More often than not, "getting on the same page" is camouflaged under the tarp of a desire for consensus. Often, we settle for asking rhetorical questions to see if others can arrive at the "correct answers," which in fact are veiled attempts to persuade others to our own way of thinking.*

We intuitively know it is critically important to be clear, honest, and direct in the personal and professional relationships that matter most. We also know that rising to that challenge may require determined effort.

In the spirit of Covey's "Begin with the End in Mind,"[54] we will begin with a step-by-step guide to *Getting on the Same Page* and follow with supporting data and explanation.

## A Step-by-Step Illustration

Building on the foundation of *Getting on the Same Page* with *oneself* (Part One: CoreSelf Map), let us add the framework for *Getting on the Same Page* with *others.*

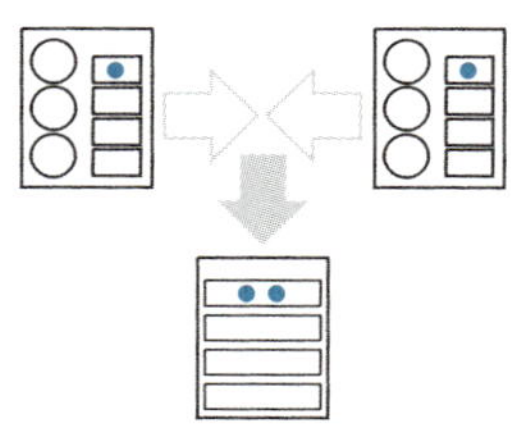

Figure 11.1 - **Getting on Same Page with *one* other** (Individual CSM's to Co-create a joint 4**S** document)

In its simplest form, it can be described by the equation:

I do a Map + You do a Map = We do a Map together.

The blue dots highlight the importance of *co-creating a specific* Situation that each party will utilize in their personal CSM, prior to a joint 4**S**.

## CoreSelf Positioning in Relationships | Partnerships

In CoreSelf Mapping (CSM) we discussed the importance of selecting *a single, specific situation* that is important, interesting and that creates intense curiosity, for more information, to resolve predicaments that are very uncertain or causing apprehension.

In CoreSelf Positioning—Getting on the Same Page with others—we add the significant layer of selecting a single, specific and common situation. It is important that both parties are thinking about the *exact* same situation, before each spends time to complete a personal CSM, which is called Getting On The Same Page with *oneself.*

### Co-Creating on the Situation

Before you each make time to complete your personal CSM, take time to discuss and agree on a single, specific situation you would both like to discuss and address. Invite one of you to describe the situation as they see it without interruption, then add anything that you feel is missing or could make the description more specific. As you co-observe the situation, do not attempt to resolve or influence the description of the situation into something that has an obvious solution. Maintain a spirit of observation and curiosity as you collaborate on describing the situation. Look forward to working together to identify a Best Next Step that realistically both of you can endorse.

*Describe the Situation that you would like to discuss as an observer of a crime scene, without the crime. Consider yourself a reporter and describe the scene as though you have just arrived.*

Go to your separate spaces and complete your individual CoreSelf Map using the agreed upon situation. Do not share your individual maps with each other yet. You will experience informative insights and Real Questions as you each take inventory of your unique positions regarding this situation.

## Collaborating on a Joint Map

You will recall that the right side of the CoreSelf Map (CSM) contains four paragraphs that we refer to as the **4S**s: **S**ituation, **S**trengths, **S**truggles, **S**trategies. Consequently, we sometimes refer to Getting on the Same Page as creating a joint **4S** document. As you reconvene, it may be helpful to review your prior personal CSM to remind yourself of where you were and wanted to be in this Situation: "Step 2: Emotional Energy and Sensations" and insights from "Step 8: Strategies or Real Questions."

To draft the joint Situation, one of you will start by writing down your draft Situation and reading it aloud slowly, sentence by sentence. After the writer is finished, the other will suggest any changes they think are warranted, or will state their own version of the description of the situation. This is an incredibly important component of the 4S process; respectfully take all the time needed to complete the full first paragraph.

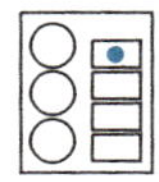

(5) **Situation:**

______________________________
______________________________
______________________________
______________________________
______________________________
______________________________

During this joint brainstorming opportunity, consider three of Stephen Covey's *The 7 Habits of Highly Effects People*[55] when completing the **4S** exercise [added by authors]:

4. **Think Win/Win**
5. **Seek First To Understand, Then To Be Understood**
6. **Synergize**

Keep the three CoreSelf guidelines, in Part Two, front of mind as you continue:

*Slow Down, Trust the Map,*
*and Question Respectfully.*

Completed CSMs in hand, we *co-create a* **4S** *document* including observations of our specific **S**ituation; **S**trengths—resources available to count on and call on; **S**truggles— giving each other credit for effort invested; **S**trategies—common actions, or Real Questions, that can move us closer to where we both want to be.

CoreSelf Positioning (CSP) expands the benefit of CSM and *Getting on the Same Page* with *others*. **Summary**: two or more individuals identify where they are in a **S**ituation and jointly collaborate on the best way to get to where they all want to be. CSP leverages each participant's unique I/ON to culminate in a specific one-page agreement. As you work through the remaining three S's: **S**trengths, **S**truggles, and **S**trategies, pass the baton back-and-forth allowing both parties to contribute to the document. Record all initial thoughts without censoring or judging either party's suggestions. Each of your Internal Observers and Navigators (I/ON) will be firing and providing feedback. After recording all thoughts, read them aloud, discuss, and draft an agreement.

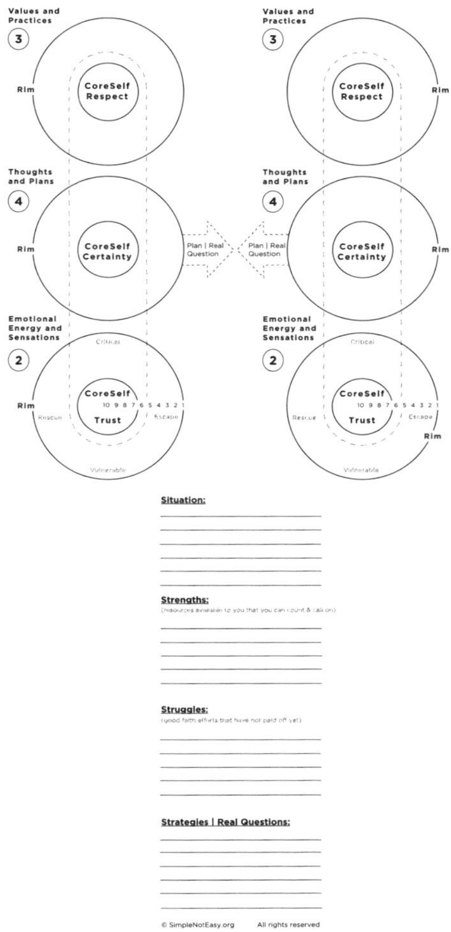


Figure 11.2 - **Getting on Same Page with another** (Combining Individual CSM's to a Joint 4**S**'s)

Note: If a refresher on the 4**S**s descriptions is needed, refer to CSM Steps 6-8. Refer also to your personal CoreSelf Map regarding this situation as you add to this joint 4**S** document, as your collaboration may spur additional strengths, struggles, strategies, and Real Questions that had not occurred to either of you before.

Finally, considering all the written options, is there any one Strategy-or any Real Questions–that jump out as a Best Next Step that you both can endorse?

## Highlight it!

When you conclude Step 8 and have documented all potential strategies and plans that could help move each of you to "Where we want to be," consider this question:

**Q: Are there any questions, that if we had the answers to them, would change this Situation?"**

Give each other a moment to pause and jot down any new questions that might have surfaced.

Below are a few 4**S** samples; in essence, they represent a jointly created right side of the complete CoreSelf Positioning. Both participants can consider, at the end of this effort, if they have moved any closer to where they wanted to be in their individual CSMs. As both parties become proficient with the joint 4**S** exercise, they will be able to move more smoothly and efficiently to consider and record: "Where are we now? Where would we like to be? What is our Best Next Step?"

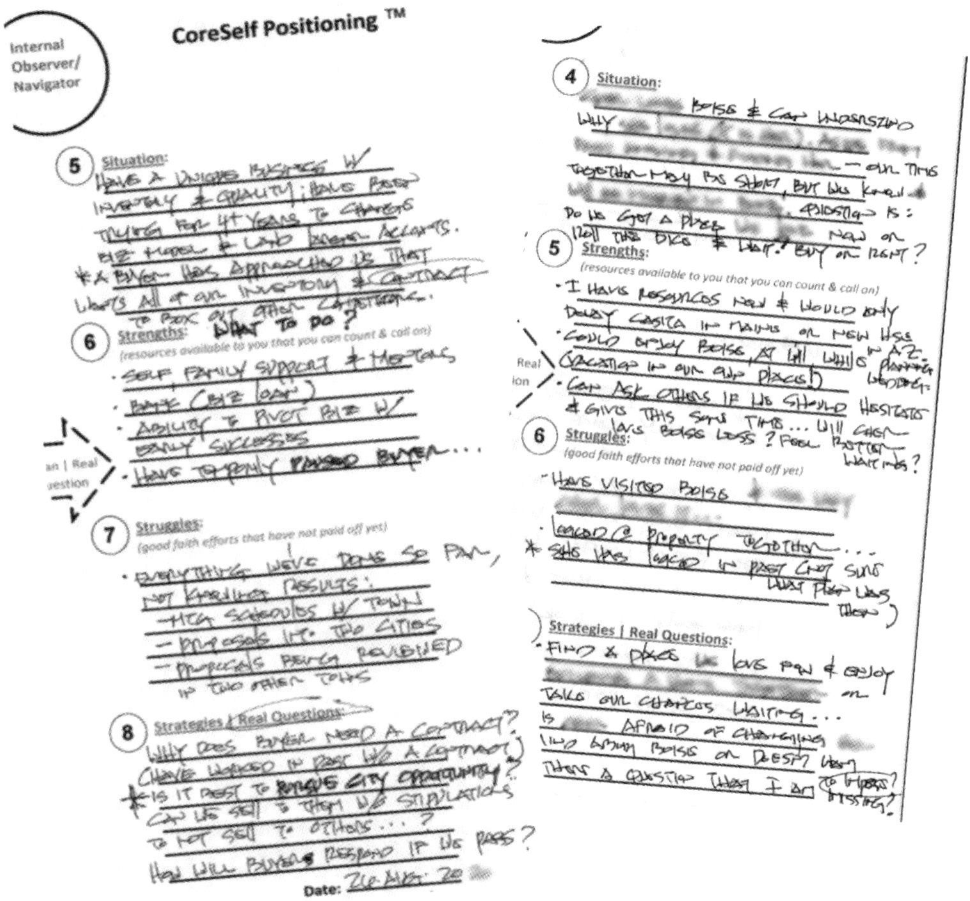


Figure 11.3 - **Joint 4S Sample** (Professional and Personal: Real Questions vs Strategies)

## CoreSelf Positioning in Organizations

We will discuss expanded applications of introducing CoreSelf Positioning into organizations to help teams: *Getting on the Same Page* using a different part of their brains that can extract trapped value to effectively create and collaborate with others.

Trapped value exists when opportunity is visible, but the individuals are each *stuck in their own bubble*.[56] Releasing trapped value is a key to success professionally and personally. *Bubble thinkers* have become stuck by their reliance on traditional methods and models. Consider the value that could be available when opportunities become more clearly visible and everyone at the table has a voice.

Leaders are tasked with creating long-term strategies that maintain sustainability and grow shareholder value. Managers are responsible to deliver short-term results that progress to long-term goals. Traditional workshops deliver short-term skills, ideas, and momentum, but often lack long-term impact. The CoreSelf Framework provides both desired short-term benefits and long-term impact at both the professional and personal levels. CSM and CSP uniquely teach both soft and hard skills along with the practice of recognizing and implementing Real Questions.

To set the stage, let us highlight the order of how our CoreSelf Framework is initiated and delivered:

1. **Identify Situation:** specific, shared, inclusive (co-craft or co-create)
2. **Share Situation:** all attendees complete their own CSM prior to collaboration
3. **Collaborate on Situation:** review resources available, investments made, potential strategies, Real Questions that would change the situation
4. **Select and Deploy a Best Next Step or Unpack Real Questions**
5. **Celebrate Learning a New CoreSelf Language**

*Encourage everyone on the organizational train to change their seat from passive passenger to active participant.*

Note: *Simple. Not Easy.* conducts numerous CSP Workshops. We advocate that organizations certify a key member of the team as an internal certified CoreSelf resource, providing self-sufficiency within of the organization (e.g., training, HR, reviews).

## Co-Crafting the Situation

The basic equation of *Getting on the Same Page* with others is simple; deploying it in an organization for the first time adds a few extra variables to the equation. When a certified CoreSelf Advisor is facilitating the initial workshop, the critical role they play with the management sponsor is to offer guidance on "crafting the best Situation." Taking the time to create an open-ended, inclusive situation in which all attendees may actively participate fosters development of unique insights and Real Questions.

The importance of management taking the **time** to step back to appreciate the contributions of **all active participants** in the workshop can unlock key insights to develop and describe a **compelling** situation that is **inclusive** and **accessible**.

Once the situation is crafted with the sponsor, the CoreSelf Positioning (CSP) pre-workshop work begins and each attendee is guided through their personal CoreSelf Map (CSM) as it pertains to the crafted situation. This gives them an opportunity to observe and navigate their position, values, and thoughts prior to the workshop.

Once each participant has experienced and completed their CSM prior to attending the workshop, each participant's Internal Observer and Navigator has been activated. They have taken the time to articulate and inventory the unique value they bring to the organization. Each participant is primed and ready to make significant collaborative contributions to the workshop. The crafted Situation is reviewed and clarified as needed, prior to jointly completing the CSP exercise.

## Co-Creating a Description of the Situation

Co-creating a description of the Situation facing them is an essential task for a newly formed organizational team. This initial task provides the best foundation for their ongoing work by supporting innovative collaboration, curiosity, confidence, and change. This written document leverages what Amy Edmondson called "team psychological safety (PS)," defined as "a shared belief held by members of a team that the team is safe for interpersonal risk taking." The team is continuously strengthened by practicing *Getting*—and staying—*on the Same Page.*

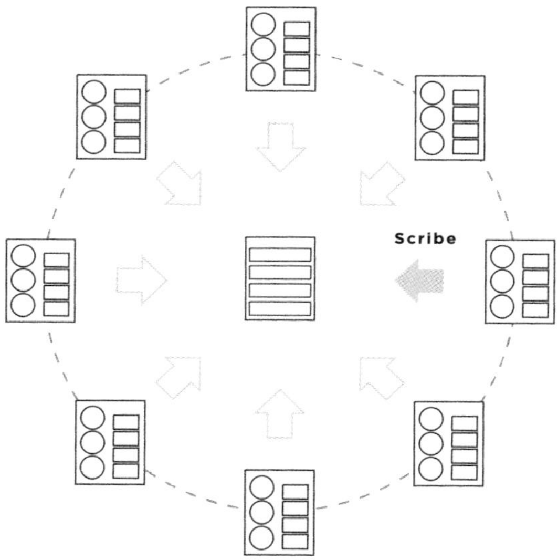


Figure 11.4 - **Getting on Same Page with *many* others** (Personal & Professional Relationships: Participating)

The following illustrations speak to the complexity of "Getting on the Same Page" with *many* others. The basic methodology remains the same; we each do a CoreSelf Map regarding a predetermined Situation (if sponsored) or a jointly collaborative Situation (if Team-driven). Next, each participant spends time completing their individual CSM, which then provides input into the collective, collaborative **4S** document (the highlighted arrow represents the designated scribe, as opposed to leader of the dialogue). Take note of the traditional *outside-in* direction of contribution in this illustration.

A reciprocal transformation—multiplier effect (X to 1/X) — occurs as organizations and teams practice the Getting on the Same Page with others framework. While the scribe remains the same, the feedback loops intensify and their input multiplies; each participant's unique Internal Observer and Navigator is firing with powerful insights and Real Questions. Note how the direction of contributions transitions to add key *inside-out* feedback.

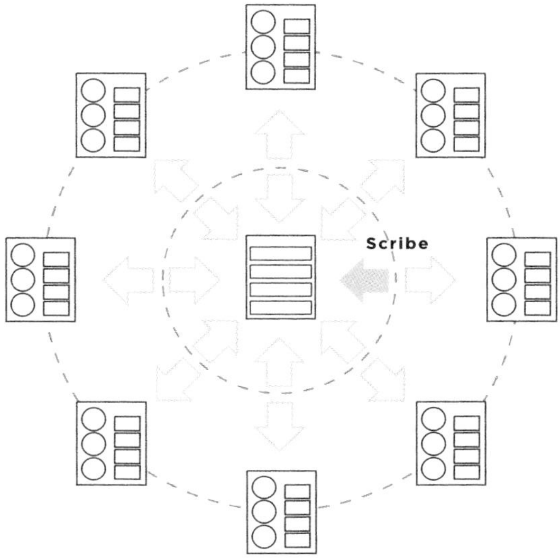


Figure 11.5 - **Getting on Same Page with *many* others**
(Same Page Partnership: Dynamically Collaborating)

## Share the Situation

Once the specific situation has been recorded and every effort has been made to include all participants' comments in the Situation draft, each team member completes their personal CoreSelf Map (CSM) based on the agreed upon "Situation" draft.

This CSM exercise provides value in many areas, including exploring:

**How do I *Observe* the Situation?** The opportunity to review in detail their current and desired position, energy and unique values, thoughts and potential solutions, and possible answers that could impact the Situation ahead of time. (*Getting on Same Page* with *oneself.*)

**How do others *Observe* the Situation?** Arriving with one's collected thoughts on an important situation can encourage curiosity about others' thoughts prior to working together to identify the best strategy with which to move forward.

**How do we *Navigate* the Situation?** Collaborating to Get on the Same Page with others garners clarity and meaning for each team member, which directly impacts each participant's accountability and dependability in playing their respective role in executing on the agreed upon Best Next Step.

Note: Encourage attendees to bring a copy of the right side of their CSM, the 4**S**s for reference, and a note of their beginning position in the Bottom Circle that described: "Where am I?" And "Where do I want to be?" (for example, in shorthand, 4 > 8).

## Collaborate on the Situation

As participants reconvene to embark on Getting on the Same Page with each other, remember Covey's three habits of interdependence listed above (page 166) and the three CoreSelf guidelines are worth repeating:

*Slow Down. Trust the Map. Question Respectfully.*

As the team works through the remaining three S's: **Strengths, Struggles**, and **Strategies**, allow all participants to pass the "talking stick" back and forth, allowing everyone to contribute to the draft. Record all initial thoughts without anyone censoring or judging anyone else's input. Everyone's Internal Observer and Navigator will be firing and providing feedback. After all thoughts have been recorded, read them out loud, discuss, and verify that all input has been recorded accurately.

As you conclude the Strategies section, have all attendees review and actively discuss all strategies that were collected to determine a Best Next Step for *this* team.

During this exercise, Real Questions (RQ) may arise and the scribe will record them. Before discussing any RQ that percolated, participants should ask themselves this question:

*Are there any questions that—if we knew the answer to them— might change the Situation?*

Give the group a moment to reflect on this question and record any and all questions without censoring or judging. Enjoy and embrace this brainstorming opportunity.

Occasionally, a Real Question is raised that warrants further collaboration that could lead to an unexpected and insightful Best Next Step. When such a Real Question presents itself, take time with the team to make this RQ the new Situation and collaborate utilizing the 4**S** methodology that all have just completed.

A valuable option at the end of *Getting on the Same Page* with others is for the facilitator to take a poll of the participants to ultimately answer: *Where are we now?*

**Q: Based on the collaborative work we did today, have we moved closer to where we want to be? Can we measure it?**

---

Participants can be invited to share their thoughts about the collaboration or movement they have experienced from their prior individual CSM work. For example, a manager might want to share where they were on a scale of 1-10 and the movement they experienced during the CSP workshop. Others will reciprocate and the magic starts.

In addition to the Team's Best Next Step, each participant may find it useful to identify an additional Best Next Step that they can individually pursue. Why? Because we want to keep participants active, instead of delegating a team Next Step that one usually owns . . .

Below is an illustration of how each participant's unique Internal Observer and Navigator is concurrently communicating with all aspects of their CoreSelf.

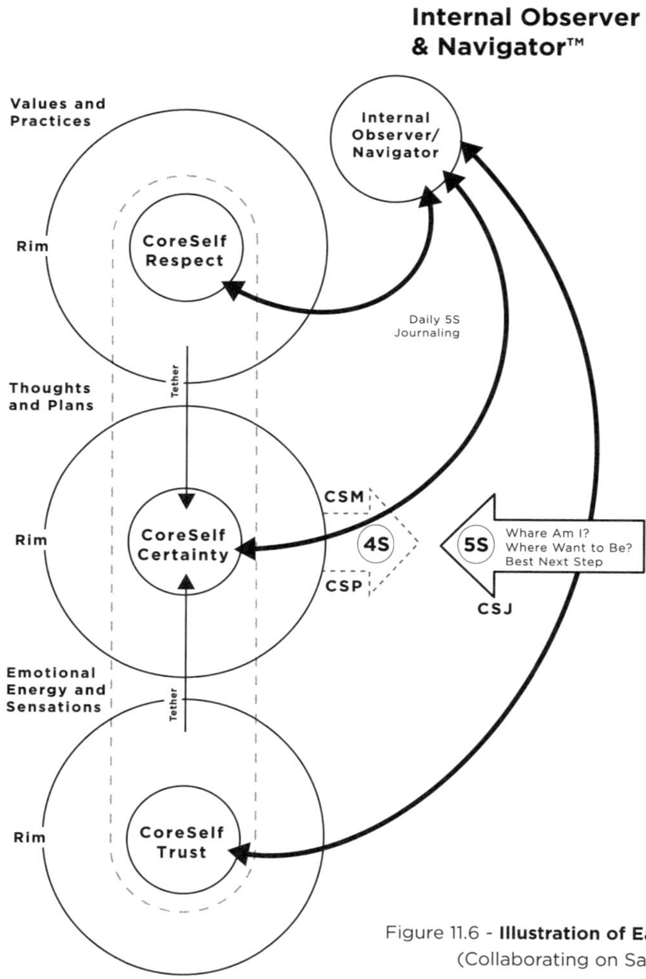


Figure 11.6 - **Illustration of Each Participants Flow**
(Collaborating on Same Page Partnership)

Following is a copy of a jointly created 4**S** document. While the scribe can record all participants' feedback in whatever format is most efficient at the time—it will ultimately be digitally transcribed for distribution to all participants for their review.

**4S Recap: Real Questions, and Best Next Steps - Strategic Products (SP) Team**

During the workshop each attendee was completing their CoreSelf Positioning worksheet; below are the collective notes for the team, shared to promote all attendees in Getting on the Same Page, *literally*.

**Situation:**

- How can I/We best optimize my product specialist skills, balance my time [being on the same page] with the entire sales team and maintain the responsibilities of my business transformation sales role?

  Being on the Same Page = closing with strong sales reps.; teaching weaker sales reps.; strategizing, planning, executing, and providing status reports; getting on and staying on the same page with team.

**Strengths:** *(resources available to us that we can count on and call on)*

- This Team: bouncing ideas off each other, collaborating, brainstorming, networking, et al
- Regular contact with
- organization-wide willingness to invest in employees growth
- Team's 'Reach' (e.g., LinkedIn) and Subject Matter Expertise
- Number of Training Classes being taught
- 'Ride Alongs' and number of client installs
- PodMeetings@ (team was invited by IT)
- The Power and Effectiveness of Real Questions and Answers

**Struggles:** *(good faith efforts that haven't paid of yet—giving ourselves credit)*

- Marketing efforts ( YTD efforts were highlighted) ...
- Everyone on this team has invested in becoming a Subject Matter Expert (SME) ...
- Many that are new to SP Team have asked how to access resources ...
- Network Effect: current, happy customers that move to other companies and call us ...

**Strategies | Real Questions:**

- How do we access organized resources (e.g., Sandler)?
- Like and Share each other's LinkedIn articles & blogs — leverage this team's expertise
- Leverage 'Network Effect' — classes being taught, happy clients, A/E's, sales teams
- Actively engage in 'ride alongs' and attend installs
- Consider offering 'Lunch & Learn' sessions with Strategic Products to those interested (no 'no shows')
- Identify 'Insights' — "What's the word on the street," What's trending in the industry? With our Clients?
- See Something. Say Something. (referrals from A/E's, tech. support, accounts receivable, sales reps.) What am I looking for? What does it sound like?
- Be respectful of Sales Team's time by creating helpful SP descriptions & resources that resonate. (Ideas included & evolved: baseball cards > battle cards > strategy cards)
- Best Next Step for Team collectively and individually by each workshop attendee (see below)

**Best Next Steps**

**Team:**

- Battle Cards for each Strategic Product -> ICP (Ideal Client Profile) with 4-5 questions

Figure 11.7 - **Organization's 4S Sample** (Sample Co-Created 4**S** Document)

The authors' intent from the start has been to offer actionable ideas and tools up front. For those interested in additional information, perspectives, or examples, supporting information follows.

## Narratives and Equations in Life

We all instinctively know Getting on the Same Page with our *self* and *others* is important, but why is it so elusive and difficult to accomplish?

Remember the following three narratives from CSM Step 1: Triangles (page 22), when we were focused on *Getting on the Same Page* with yourself. In CoreSelf Positioning we expand this skill to *Getting on the Same Page* with others.

***A young adult*** *who is a serious student, develops strong friendships, and volunteers in the community, goes on to college and then secures a good job in an area of interest. Their future seems quite promising and their persistent efforts are being rewarded appropriately. However, a close family member then experiences an unexpected tragedy. This young adult* ***feels an overwhelming obligation to interrupt their own plans completely to come to the rescue of that family member,*** *even though it is unclear if any of their efforts will have a positive outcome.*

***A working couple with children*** *are both doing the best they can to "make ends meet," balance individual work responsibilities and the needs of growing children that never seem to tire, leaving little to no time to attend to each other's needs. Time passes with each playing their respective part as years pass and the children become more independent. Eventually, each partner* ***finds that they are feeling increasingly distant from the other.*** *Communication is not effective and planning becomes exclusively based on individual needs.*

***A small company*** *spends its early entrepreneurial years just trying to survive. Through years of persistence and shear grit they succeed in becoming a sustainable, midsize company, balancing profits with expanding costs and staff. More time passes and the company starts to grow by acquiring other small companies; this organic growth continues and the shareholders are pleased. One day management* ***notices that all these disparate acquired companies came with their own cultures and ways of doing things,*** *and no one seems to be concerned about a common plan.*

What should happen next? What usually happens?

### What are the Real Questions?

Below is another way to view these three narratives. This illustration is similar to **Mapping Our Narratives** (Figure 2.3) in CSM. In CoreSelf Positioning we are sharing our narrative positions with others involved in the situation. The "I" becomes "We."

| Stage | **Individual** | **Partners** | **Professionals** |
|---|---|---|---|
| *Current* | | *Where are We?* | |
| **Executive** | | | |
| **Emotions** | Overwhelmed & Uncertain | Vulnerable & Unfair | Surprised & Critical |
| **Beliefs** | Responsible & Obligated | Partnership & Children | Profits & Growth |
| **Reactions** | Why me? | What happened? | How do we . . . ? |
| **Monitoring** | | | |
| **Energy** | | Will this get us closer to where we want to be? | |
| **Values** | | What values matter most to us? What will we sign up to do? | |
| **Plan** | | Is this decision in alignment with our values? | |
| *Destination* | | *Where do We want to be?* | |

Figure 11.8 - **Sharing Our Narrative Positions** Getting on the Same Page with others (CSP)

The situational benefits of Getting on the Same Page with *oneself* prior to getting on the same page with others include:

- Self-awareness: Who else is involved (closeness and distance)
- Self-trust: Where am I and where do I want to be (core position)
- Self-respect: Know my values are and how I practice them (center self )
- Self-certainty: What are my thoughts and plans (aligned with my values)

Coming prepared to the CoreSelf Positioning communication table allows us to slow down, trust the map, and question respectfully. All parties can collaborate on resources available to them. All can honor the efforts that they have invested towards a solution. Each participant has taken time with themselves and can make space for others to be heard.

What could happen next? What will happen next? **Ready for a different equation?** Initially, we described Getting on the Same Page with *others* with a simple equation:

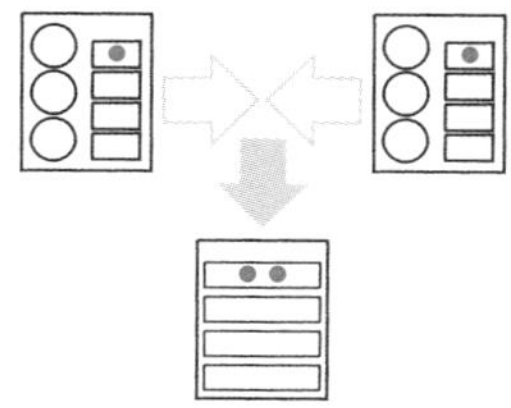

"I do a Map + You do a Map = We all do a Map (4**S**) together."

Why is it so elusive? Because, all too often:

**1 + 1 = 1.5**

In business, when one company acquires another it can be attributed to: economies of scale (reducing costs by eliminating duplicate departments like accounting and administration), loss of momentum (misunderstood or misaligned cultures, goals, roles, and expectations), market reaction (both clients and vendors), and timing.

---

I remember calling the VP of Sales of our primary vendor, excited about an offer to acquire our company and prepared to share with him all the reasons this acquisition would be good for both our organizations.

> *Ken, this is Tim and I am excited to let you know that another company has made an offer to buy ours. I would like to share all the benefits of this acquisition and ask you to endorse it.*
>
> ***[silence]***
>
> *Ken ... are you there?*
>
> ***Tim—my apologies for not sharing in your excitement; it is just that every time this happens it is good for all your companies—however, it is rarely good for our company, as 1 + 1 rarely equals 2 and often equals 1.5.***

I was stunned with his response; fortunately, the acquisition did go through and we vowed to ardently insure that our sum equaled more than two. His response has lingered with me *for years.*

Before we suggest a new formula for *Getting on the Same Page* with others—in both our professional and personal lives—consider this perplexing equation:

**I + I = \ /**

The equation above represents an unexpected—and all too common—outcome of joining two people, teams, or organizations together that are not yet in alignment. Not only do they *not create* a "greater sum of their parts," but they find themselves on different paths with no apparent convergence. Finding ourselves in this situation as a partner in a relationship or as the leader of an organization often prompts the following: "We should get on the same page." The Real Questions—at times, a request and at other times, intense pleas—are close by:

**Q: How did we get on such different pages?**

**Q: How can we get back on the same page?**

Which brings us back full circle to the exercise with which we started:

***"I do a Map + You do a Map = We do a Map (4S) together."***

Let's consider the multi-faceted benefits of a better equation:

**I + I = I I**

This equation illustrates the synergy of two people, teams, or organizations, standing beside each other looking in the same direction. Neither party is in front of or behind the other. Each provides enough space for the other to grow yet remains close enough to offer stability in challenging times. Each encourages the other to bring 100% of their value to the equation to create a combined sum greater than its parts.

*A partnership is any relationship in which two people are equally committed to the success of their work together and intentionally strive to demonstrate trust and respect toward one another. Partnerships occur in every area of human interaction and across levels of social and financial status.*

Another component of this equation contains a subtle reminder. If we visualize the sum of these two entities as a graphic symbol, **I I**, it is the "**PAUSE**" button used countless times when listening to a book or watching a video.

It can be a powerful reminder—in relationships that matter most—to pause and take the time to Slow Down: breath in and out, count to ten, create space to observe, reflect, calm our emotions, center our thoughts, hear one's "inside voice," consider our response, and ask questions respectfully. **This collaborative CoreSelf equation is a game-changer.**

*Getting on the Same Page represents an* ***opportunity*** *for each participant to allow energy to* ***flow*** *from one place to another* ***internally*** *and from one person to another* ***externally*** *for extraordinary* ***results!***

Once all parties have agreed that *Getting on the Same Page* is a mutually beneficial goal, then all can embark on the journey of creating and sustaining a productive, collaborative conversation.

*Start by giving each other the gift of a "****pause.****"*

This can provide a valuable "reset" moment when parties find themselves headed in different directions for an extended period of time. It will be important to share with others that "we are experimenting with and learning a new approach." It may seem unfamiliar or inconsistent compared to past behaviors or actions. For example, any of the following actions could be misinterpreted: asking for input, listening without censoring or judging, asking Real Questions respectfully, recording another's answers, being curious as opposed to condescending. Acknowledging that past attempts to communicate may have gotten us off the same page indicates respect for others. Statements of respect for others build trust.

The power of a pause can create space to *Get on the Same Page* with important others. That space can provide an opportunity to positively change our equations.

Rebuilding trust and respect takes time yet pays significant dividends for all parties.

For those no longer in alignment, experimenting with new techniques can bring a wave of fun and excitement. *Getting on the Same Page* can feel invigorating and refreshing.

Ray Dalio, in *Principles: Life and Work*,[57] states it wonderfully:

> *"The most meaningful relationships are achieved when you and others can speak openly to each other about everything that's important, learn together, and understand the need to hold each other accountable to be as excellent as you can be. When you have such relationships with those you work with, you pull each other through challenging times; at the same time, sharing challenging work draws you closer and strengthens your relationships. This self-reinforcing cycle creates the success that allows you to pursue more and more ambitious goals."*

Ray Dalio goes on to quote in his book *Principles*: ***"Meaningful relationships and meaningful work are mutually reinforcing, especially when supported by radical trust and radical transparency."***

## Getting Each Participant's Input by Slowing Down

The benefit of *slowing down* in each component of Getting on the Same Page can't be overemphasized. Let us take a moment to expand on each of these areas:

### 4Ss: Situation | Strengths | Struggles | Strategies

Above we described different ways to arrive at an open, accessible Situation that all participants can explore separately and together. Let us consider another subtle aspect of describing situations that can have significant implications for the "Where are we?" and "Where do we want to be?" conversations. When describing situations, be careful not to assume that all participants are using the same definitions of the words used in describing a situation; take a moment to re-examine key terms framing an important Situation. For example:

| <u>Situation description:</u> | <u>Potentional Meaning:</u> |
|---|---|
| *overcome* | * difficult times in our relationship or business |
| *experienced* | * change in environment or loss of ... |
| *healed* | * invested time with a coach (or therapist) |
| *arrived at* | * a good place as a result of effort to ... |

When collecting key words, thoughts, and input from each participant, it may be helpful to visualize three columns on a piece of paper with a participant on the on the left column and another participant on the right column—both feeding the joint middle column.

This method can be effective for collecting Strengths and Struggles that represent a unified view of all participants' feedback.

<u>Slowing down is key, whether one is mapping a complex organizational challenge or a puzzling personal predicament.</u>

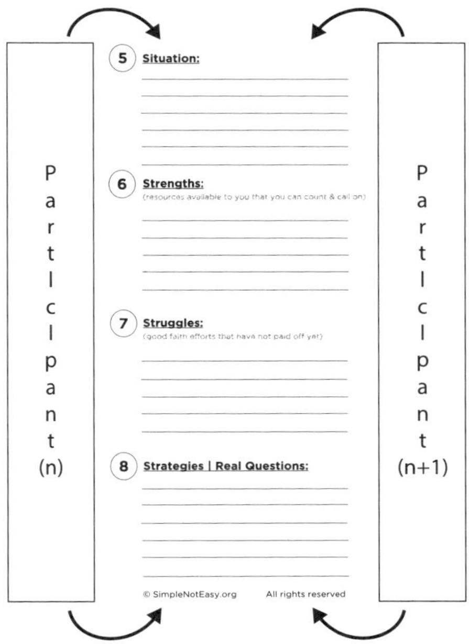


Figure 11.9 - **Getting Everyone's Input Illustration** (Slowing Down to record all participants' input)

## Complementary Curiosity: Perspectives, Strategies, and Real Questions

There is plenty of writing by others that reinforces and complements our CoreSelf Framework. Here are some of our favorites.

It is important to note that many of the perspectives and references we share refer to *leaders* and *leadership*; however, do not dismiss their advice if you are not currently a recognized leader whose job description includes responsibility for others. **We must all take responsibility for our own behavior and achievement.** Lead yourself to become the best version of yourself, and it is highly probable that one day you will positively influence others to meet their own highest standards—as a friend, partner, parent, manager, or business owner.

---

Stew Friedman (American professor, speaker, and author) created the concept of *Total Leadership* in education and authored the book of the same title with the caption—*Be a Better Leader, Have a Richer Life.*[58]

When exploring "Work/Life Balance" he implores us to "drop the slash and look for integrated, synergistic wins." He then reminds us that the word "balance" implies equal give and take on each side of the slash. He adds, "Consider a jazz quartet metaphor in which we play richly textured music with the sounds of life's various instruments; it is not about muting the trumpets so the saxophone can be heard."

Getting on the same page encourages all participants of the organization, team, or quartet to play their unique role while collaborating with all the other team members.

His answer to:

**Q: What do Leaders do that is so important?**

**A: "Inspire commitment to produce results that matter to the collective, through the path/goal model or experimental model."**

In *Part III: Be Innovative - Acting with Creativity* he reminds us that, "Small wins build commitment and the will to proceed further." He also encourages us to persevere:

> *"Obstacles are everywhere if you're trying something meaningful and they can be particularly daunting in the work domain, where careers are on the line. This amplifies the need for you to be skillful in adapting. You're going to confront unknowns when you cut new paths. Persisting in the face of resistance, having the courage to lead change derives from having a sense of purpose, taking intelligent risks, and knowing how to adjust quickly. It comes from knowing that you're contributing to the success of others, building stronger connections among others, and increasing everyone's sense of belonging to something bigger."*

He adds: "Leadership is a performing art and you're the instrument."

---

Peter F. Drucker (Austrian-American management consultant, educator, and author. 1909-2005) considered one of the most widely-known and influential thinkers on management—some say, the father of management thinking—offered many valuable reasons to get on the same page with *self* and *others*, in his wonderful article *Managing Oneself*.[59] The article challenges readers to take responsibility for managing their futures, both *in* and *out of the office*.

While discussing two people working together, he highlighted "manners," which many might consider soft skills and states: "**It is a law of nature that**

**two moving bodies in contact with each other create friction. This is as true for human beings as it is for inanimate objects."**

He eloquently writes:

> *"Success in the knowledge economy comes to those who know themselves—their strengths, their values, and how they best perform."*

Expounding on the "knowledge worker" leveraging strengths versus areas of low competence, he writes: "Energy, resources, and time should go instead to making a competent person into a star performer."

Lastly, his excerpt in the same article under the subheading "*Responsibility for Relationships*" is a profound reminder that the majority of us need to work with others to accomplish significant results. Finding a common language of trust and respect leverages the unique skills of each participant on our team. Occasionally there are those few that appear to be exceptions and do not need anyone else to accomplish some great feat; that said, maybe some of them should credit much of their accomplishment or insight to those that came before them.

> **"Very few people work by themselves and achieve results by themselves—a few great artists, a few great scientists, a few great athletes. Most people work with others and are effective with other people. That is true whether they are members of an organization or independently employed. Managing yourself requires taking responsibility for relationships. This has two parts."**
>
> **The first is to accept the fact that other people are as much individuals as you yourself are. They perversely insist on behaving like human beings. This means that they too have their strengths; they too have their ways of getting things done; they too have their values. To be effective, therefore, you have to know the strengths, the performance modes, and the values of your co-workers."**

**“The second part of relationship responsibility is taking responsibility for communication.”**

**“The first secret of effectiveness is to understand the people you work with so that you can make use of their strengths.”**

---

In the early 1990s, Andy Grove (Hungarian-American engineer, professor, and author. 1936-2016.), then the CEO of Intel, coined the term ‘Strategic Inflection Point’ (SIP) to underline the importance of business leaders taking action during such times. He described an SIP as, “An event that changes the way we think and act.” These SIPs, if noticed, can prompt a change in strategy, organization, or operations, individually or all at once.

Why do we think SIPs are relevant today? Because each of us experiences these types of important life events, professionally and personally, that can change our course. These life-changing events can be a result of chance, an unexpected disruption or the consequence of a choice. They may feel overwhelming at the moment, even catastrophic, yet their significance and impact can almost never be ignored.

Grove is also credited with the motto, “Only the paranoid survive.” In 1999, he wrote a book[60] by the same title which included nine key ideas that expanded on and explained this phrase. It’s an excellent read both professionally and personally, as illustrated by:

*“Change in the business environment can come from anywhere—even from within. Therefore, it’s important to stay on the watch and get information from as many sources as possible.”*

Grove's insights complement What It Takes To Accelerate Through A Strategic Inflection Point[61] by George Brat, which references five BRAVE questions[62] that encompass environment (Where), values (What matters), attitudes (How), relationships (How), and behaviors (What).

Our last reference before wrapping up this section comes from Joseph Deitch's wonderful book *ELEVATE: An Essential Guide to Life,*[63] filled with insights related to awareness and skills to promote action. His insights reinforce the importance of *Getting on the Same Page* with oneself and others.

We have highlighted *The Paradox of Self* throughout the book, starting with CoreSelf Mapping: "Part of me is feeling this way and part of me is feeling that way." Deitch adds his own "amazing paradox:"

*"A key to dramatic growth is to recognize an amazing paradox: by accepting and actually embracing our limitations, we allow ourselves to open up to the knowledge, experience, and insights of others."*

> "Deluded by myriad bits and bytes of data, we make choices at every moment of our lives. If our perceptions are clouded or constrained, then our decisions will be suboptimal. They may not even be conscious; instead, our decisions may amount to nothing more than automatic responses to stimuli based on our current desires and past conditioning. But when we begin to remove those obstacles, we find we have heightened sensitivity, greater cognitive clarity, and more astute discernment—all of which lead to more creative analysis, wider choices, and far more satisfying outcomes. It also begins with awareness—and a decision to open those doors and windows."

Later in the book, he offers this "1% Solution:"

> "In the best-selling book Raving Fans,[64] authors Ken Blanchard and Sheldon Bowles reduce success to three primary points: (1) **know what you want**, (2) **know what your customer wants**, and (3)

**implement "the 1% solution," in which everyone keeps improving things bit by bit.**"

"... when we implemented this process at work, we enlisted the support of every employee and explained that every improvement adds up and we all have something to contribute."

"What happened next was remarkable. The self-images of individuals and teams started to change as we kept making incremental gains. They quickly realized that if we could easily find ways to improve by 1%, there was no reason we couldn't do it again and improve by 2% or 3% or more. Before long, the sky was the limit, and the results followed the trajectory of our expectations and beliefs."

Take a moment to consider the long-term benefit if you could make *Getting on the Same Page with yourself and others* just 1% better on a daily or weekly basis. Who are the most important relationships—energy holders—in your life?

---

*Getting on the Same Page prompts:*
***real questions** that impact **real conversations***
*that result in **real change**.*

## The Basic Triangle - Who Else is Involved?

Let us revisit and expand on the basic concept of Step 1: TRIANGLES and Others Involved, introduced in Part One: CoreSelf Mapping.

In addition to identifying "Who else is involved," the triangle allows us to graphically ascertain two important Situational facts:

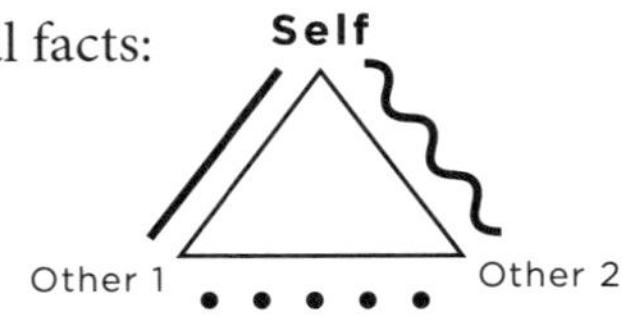


1. Closeness & Distance
2. Over & Under-Functioning

Though simple, there is quite a bit of valuable information in this triangle. Granted, the relationships between self and others represent a snapshot in time, however they also provide Real Question-level feedback: "Am I closer or farther away from the most important person in this relationship? What did I do to create this current relationship status? **Is there anything that I can do differently?"**

Getting on the Same Page with self creates an opportunity to understand our *personal* relationships and a tool to better understand *situational* relationships.

Aside from slowing down one's executive-function, a significant benefit of the triangle is that: **Who becomes Where** (when we move to Step 2: ENERGY).

Note: *Be aware that all illustrations with triangles can be inverted and maintain the same meaning. For those that actively practice "Servant Leadership," refer to CSM (page 28).*

## Interlocking Triangles - A Dynamic Conversation Changer

Getting on the Same Page with *others*, creates an opportunity to understand our *professional* relationships and a tool to better understand *situational* relationships, on a much larger scale.

Let's begin by building on what you've already learned utilizing CoreSelf Mapping (Part One) and consider what a few professional triangles might look like:

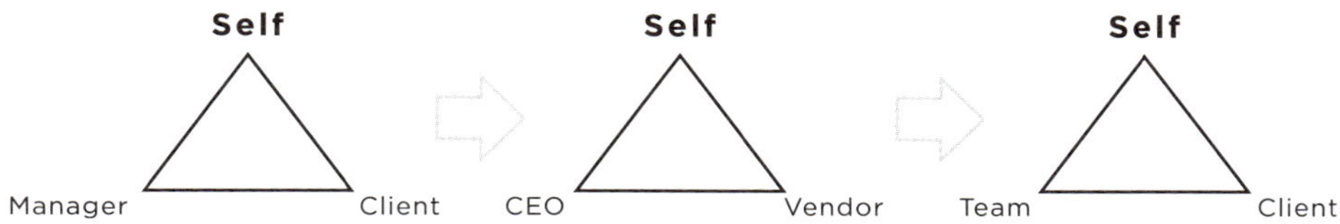


The illustration above shows progression of **Self** from employee to manager to owner. Take a moment to picture yourself in each of these roles, currently or in the future.

**Q: What might the relationship of each leg of the triangle look like?**

*Can you feel the excitement and the **energy** of those relationships, the potential **tension** that distance can create, and the growing **curiosity** to know more?!*

Consider a simplified business organizational chart:

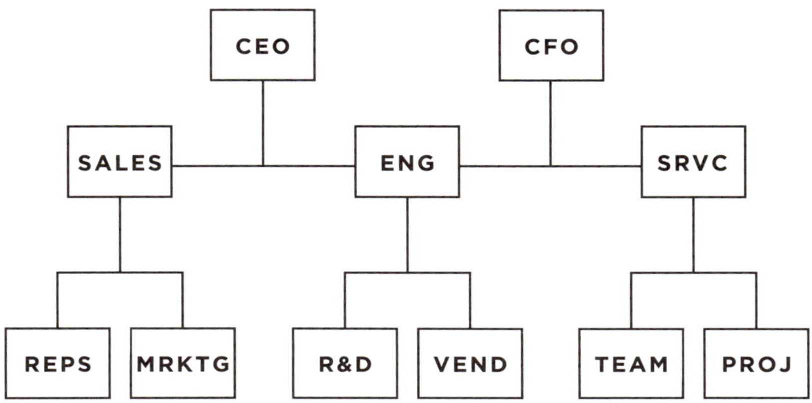

Now let's have some fun by overlaying triangles over this chart to understand relationships and answer questions. Power triangle? Influence triangle? How things get done? Decisions?

Organizational charts basically provide a view of the internal structure of an organization, including roles, reporting relationships, and who to contact if a problem occurs; in addition they can be utilized to anticipate gaps in staffing, as well as areas that could be strengthened with additional resources (e.g., training, more staff ).

**Q: So what do triangles and organizational charts have in common?**

Whether you are inside an organization—which is much more interesting—or studying organizational dynamics, consider the following questions for this org chart:

**Q: Where is the "power triangle?"**

**A: The key triangle of who makes final decisions; the triangle that contains the one person who can say, "No" when everyone else is saying, "Yes."**

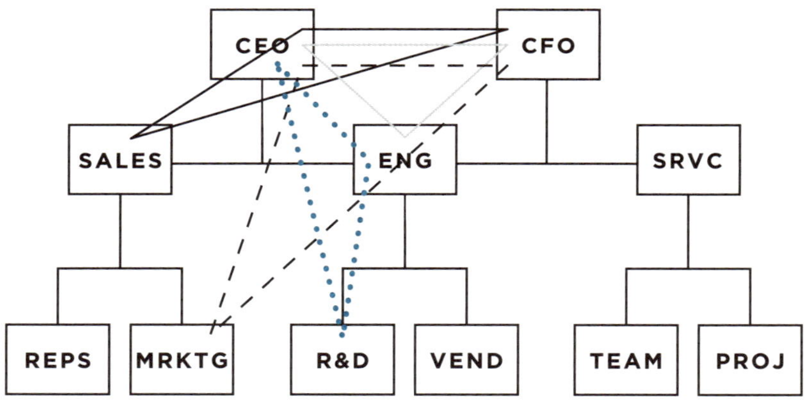


Each of the three triangles above might represent a "power triangle" based on a variety of valid variables—and each triangle contains interesting information about closeness and distance with potential for over-and under-functioning. Before dismissing this last comment and assuming that both C-levels are closer, consider the origins of a CEO that came from ENG compared to one that came from SALES; it's possible, some would say probable, that this CEO might favor—be closer—to their comfort zone of origin.

There is more. Remember the phrase, "Things are not always as they appear."

**Q: Where is the "influence triangle?"** ....

Granted, most organizations have a power triangle; however, as an organization gets larger, primary influencers arise and many in power rely on them for expert advice. See the dotted triangle, as an example.

For anyone who has ever participated in any sort of lifecycle management or attempted to document process in an organization, this question will resonate:

**Q: Where are the "how things get done" triangles?**

And where are the "how things *really* get done triangles?"
*(that aren't documented)*

Note: Before exploring additional ways that triangles can provide organizational insight and dynamic conversation, we wanted to once again give credit to Murray Bowen, MD, for his use of the triangle to understand complex relationships. He was instrumental in using triangles to view family units using his Family Systems Theory. While we are focusing on organizational structures, many of our examples mirror his work with families. As we highlighted in Step 1: *TRIANGLES and Others Involved*—if one inverts an organizational (org) chart, it resembles a family tree (Fig. 11.10). For those wishing to explore Bowen's Family System Theory[65], much is written.

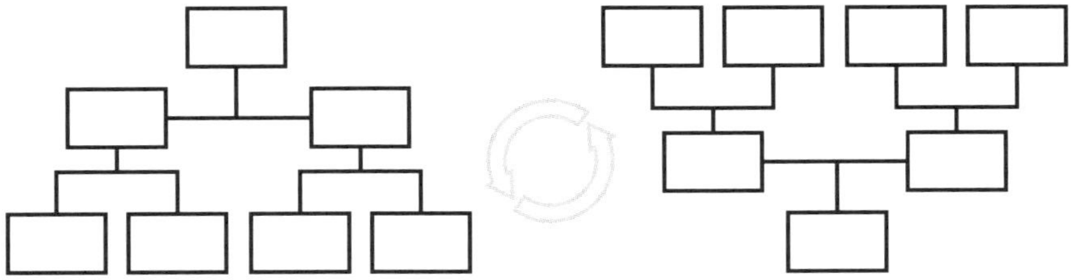

Figure 11.10 - **Organizational Charts & Family Trees**
(An inverted family tree can resemble an organizational chart)

## IT'S NOT ALWAYS JUST ABOUT US

Take note that in all three of the triangles below, there is an outside, *other* involved:

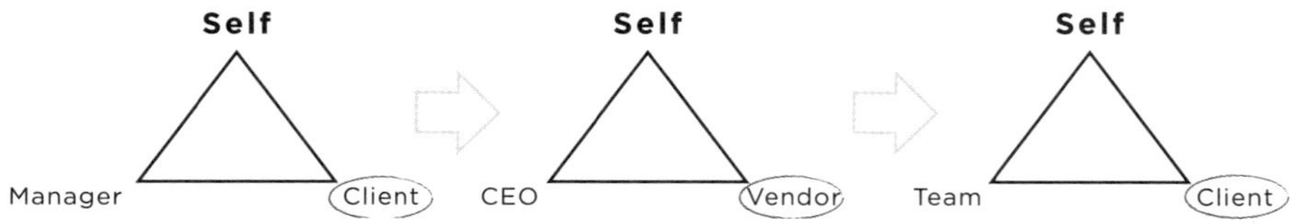


The *others* involved make for an interesting and exciting expansion of interlocking triangles both inside and outside the organization. It can be a game-changer when it comes to dynamic conversations and insights.

For this illustration, let us use two simplified org charts to represent a reseller (DISTributor) and vendor (OrigEquipMfg). Each represents a different company with unique goals, structures and, expectations of the other.

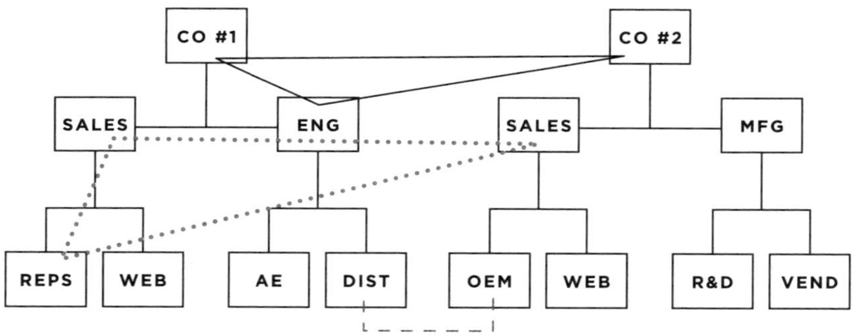


The *only* invisible bridge that connects how these two companies earn income occurs layers deep, even in this org chart; the Reseller (**DIST**, on left) earns revenue by distributing the OEM's offerings and the Vendor (**OEM**, on right) earns revenue from the Reseller's efforts. **The level of trust and respect that will translate into alignment and success for each organization lies in the relationships that are created. If the relationships are strong, then the bridge will move to the top layers of the organization. However, if the alignment is weak, then success and strong relationships for either entity will be limited.**

Consider the same "power" and "influence" triangles we did before; however, now it gets more interesting:

**Q: Does the OEM earn revenue one way and expect the DISTributor to earn revenue a different way?**

Think about 2D/3D printers: The OEM's annuity (primary revenue) is the *ink*, yet most DISTributors are expected to earn revenue with *printer* sales.

Does the OEM reserve "house accounts" or are they totally vested in the success of their DISTributor?

**Q: Who drives the solution to the prospect?**

Does all communication to DISTributor's sales REPS flow through from Reseller or does Vendor occasionally attempt to boost sales with promotions?

> *Alignment between disparate organizations is built on a relationship of high trust and respect. Consequently, the achievement of collaborative success can be measured by their alignment. In business, all too often, this litmus test is:* ***Do we achieve revenue goals exactly the same way?***

## IN THE FINAL ANALYSIS IT IS A FIELD OF RELATIONSHIPS

At the end of the day, the collective *we*—self and others—crave meaning and understanding of how it is all working. Observing situational and organizational dynamics with triangles can create understanding that can have significant advantages in our "Inner Work Life."[66]

## INTERLOCKING TRIANGLES DYNAMICS

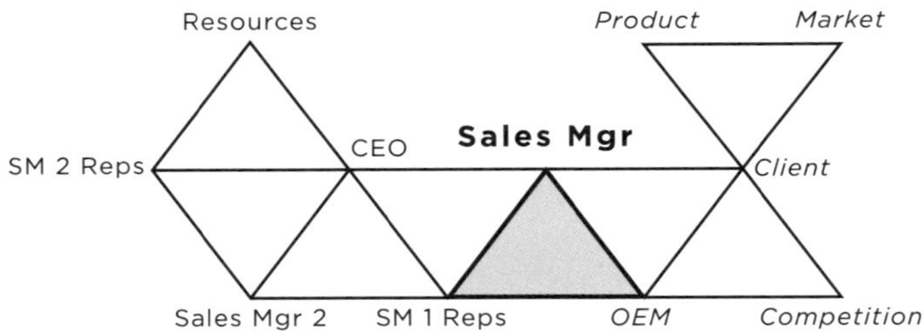


Figure 11.11 - **Interlocking Triangles** (Visually Mapping Relationship Dynamics)

Consider how one*self's* triangle (**bolded**) and the dynamic interlocking triangles (**shaded**) with *others*, each have their own dynamics. The illustration above is a simple representation of a few interlocking triangles; others (*italicized*) outside of the organization come with their own expectations that influence other triangles.

> Interlocking triangle maps contain dynamic game-changing conversation opportunities inside—and outside—the organization.

I recall sharing a CoreSelf Map with a **Sales Mgr**. After we finished our conversation, he returned to his initial triangle (Step 1) and we spoke for another hour. He said, ***"I just got off the phone with our OEM about their instructions for one of my Sales Reps., of which I was unaware. I used a triangle to explain the conflicting instructions that we were each giving the salesperson."***

The ability to connect the dots to create understanding can have significant advantages in our "Inner Work Life."[67] Being aware of how stressors within interlocking relationships can disrupt our sense of balance can help us successfully counterbalance back to our **sweet spot of self.**

Expectations of Self or Others can push or pull on our emotional energy—adding momentum or unwanted tension (reminiscent of CSM: Step 3).

Both our professional and personal roles with their responsibilities can add momentum or tension into our important relationships.

Learning to navigate the daily vicissitudes of life can be trying, even on our best day.

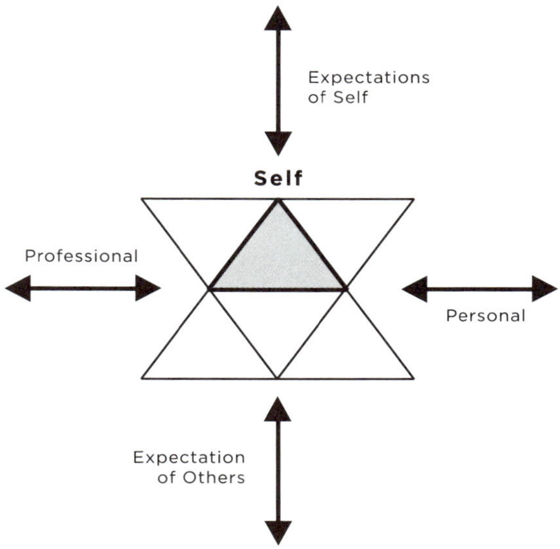


Figure 11.12 - **Interlocking Triangles Influencers** (Providing Stressors or Momentum Builders)

*CoreSelf Mapping and Positioning provide a camera with lenses allowing us to move our focus in, out, and around the scene to effectively observe difficult situations in order to navigate to places of understanding and greater certainty.*

Getting everyone on the same page with others who are moving in the same direction, solving for the same outcome—is priceless! CoreSelf Positioning starts and ends on the same page, giving all participants the ability to sign off on the project together, then measure their outcomes separately.

## Real Questions Bursts

While CoreSelf Positioning is a powerful tool to Get on the Same Page with others to identify strategies, it can also be effectively used to surface Real Questions.

We instruct participants that, while strategies and best next steps may emerge—and we will write them down—our focus will be on identifying Real Questions that are related to the situation on which we are collaborating. Specifically:

***What are the questions that, if we had the answers to them, would change the situation?***

This may seem like traditional brainstorming from the outside-in; however, the inside-out CoreSelf approach delivers an interesting component. Each participant's unique Internal Observer and Navigator provide fascinating feedback from everyone, not just those arriving with strong inclinations towards a direction that all should pursue.

In our research, you can practically hear participants' silent response after the instruction, which sounds like: "Okay. I will only focus on and think about questions that might reframe this situation."

In Hal Gregersen's insightful book, *Questions Are The Answer: A Breakthrough Approach to Your Most Vexing Problems at Work and in Life,*[68] he states:

> **"Great questions have a catalytic quality — that is, they dissolve barriers to creative thinking and channel the pursuit of solutions into new, accelerated pathways. When problem-solving, the emphasis far too often falls on finding a single correct answer. However, the power of a great question has the potential to ignite a type of innovative thinking that is essential to our globalized, digitized, and disruptive world."**

Moreover, Gregerson encourages us to "Listen for the Unexpected" and reminds us of "the Power of the Pause" and to "Listen to Understand versus Defend." All of these complement Covey's fifth habit, "Seek First to Understand, then to Be Understood." All of these provide excellent opportunities to benefit from our collaborative curiosity.

---

### An Invitation to Organizations—Large and Small—Wanting More

For those organizations wanting to unleash the power of CoreSelf Positioning (CSP) internally or externally, Simple. Not Easy has created a number of experiences:

- **CSP Workshops** - single and multi-day events focused on your real challenges. Each participant will become proficient in completing their CoreSelf Maps prior to event.

- **CoreSelf Certification Program** - designate internal resources within your organization to deploy your own CSP Workshops. Self-directed utilization.

- **Same Page Partnership Program** - this eight week program lies at the intersection of short-term individual benefits and long-term win-win partnerships. The first three week focus on team members unique CoreSelf-Trust, CoreSelf-Respect, and CoreSelf-Certainty; the next three weeks explore these fundamentals within your organization, your vendors, and ultimately with your clients.

For more information visit:

https://www.simplenoteasy.org/coreself-positioning/

# PART FOUR

# *CoreSelf Journaling*

# CoreSelf Journaling:
## *Practicing Daily to Maintain Focus on What Matters Most*

"I don't know what I think until I write it down."

— JOAN DIDION

*On October 4, 2004, Didion began writing, "The Year of Magical Thinking," a narrative of her response to the death of her husband and the severe illness of their daughter. She finished the manuscript 88 days later on New Year's Eve. Written at the age of 70, this was her first nonfiction book that was not a collection of magazine assignments.*

*She refers to the quote above in a wonderful NPR interview (September 2005) responding, "Well, that was part of why I wrote it. And, well, as a writer, the first thing you think of doing when you don't know what to think about something or what you're going to say, and so you work it up. I mean, that's the phrase. You get the information." She added: "I had no control over anything at all. I could not control anything. So what I interpreted as craziness was probably a reaction to a perceived loss of control."*

*One doesn't have to be a writer to journal and benefit both personally and professionally.*

---

Journaling is the practice of writing a story, perhaps in several episodes, about an event or an idea that is important to the writer. It's a record of that experience and its ongoing impact. The motivation for continuing to write in a journal begins out of curiosity about the meaning of a series of events that evolves toward greater clarity about important feelings, thoughts, and beliefs.

A journal can be used as a memory box into which one tosses things, then later re-examines them as a collection. Observations of events with adjacent commentary is the journal's important contribution. One entry might be significant on its own; however, laying them all out next to each other creates unique connections and new levels of meaning. Journaling provides a place to explore different aspects of, perspectives on, and outcomes of important moments. We can also review alternate choices that might have changed the ending or altered our experience.

While journal and diary share similar definitions as nouns: "a daily record, of the writer's own experiences, observations, feelings, and attitudes," we have chosen to highlight journaling's definition as a verb: "to write self-examining or reflective journal entries." Daily journaling supports and facilitates personal and professional growth in that it provides the opportunity to better understand and come to terms with dimensions of self and relationships with others. The privacy of the journal offers unique opportunities to explore the challenges of current situations and to consider possible strategies that promote beneficial outcomes.

How the brain sorts and stores the details of our complicated lives and interprets their meaning are primary topics in both psychology and neuroscience. Virtually all significant experiences are recorded by the human brain, although only a tiny percentage is consciously available. Our conscious access to these memories is in part determined by our brain's "body budgeting"[69] function, a role that manages available emotions and energy, experiences and solutions, actions and reactions.

The Internal Observer has knowledge of and access to any of these memories at the conscious level. The more remote memories can sometimes be accessed by certain medications or hypnotic techniques.

CoreSelf Mapping is a tool to explore personal history with timelines, then use 4**S** journaling to explore particularly puzzling physical or emotional connections. Real Questions that emerge will merit additional research. Some users of CoreSelf Journaling have asked the following:

**Q: Why isn't the Internal Observer/Navigator information always available?**

**A: Having some experiences stored out of awareness is a necessary part of our brain's self-protection system.**

Keeping those memories out of awareness (but not forgetting them!) means that the individual has most of their energy and focus available to deal with immediate events.

Frightening experiences may be recorded and saved in a mental compartment behind what Dr. Ernest Hilgard called an "amnesia barrier," so that they don't have to be focused on immediately.

We have previously shared the overall organization of the CoreSelf Mapping worksheet (reference Fig. 12.1). Its most basic feature is a combination of three large circles on the observing, left side of the map which include emotional energy, values, and plans; the navigating, right side of the map adds language to expand on prior observations. The left and right sides of the map collaborate to provide direction and best next steps toward safety and positive accomplishment.

CoreSelf Journaling builds on skills learned in CoreSelf Mapping and leverages access to our Internal Observer/Navigator in a simple, yet effective format.

**Q: How does CoreSelf 4S Journaling leverage the entire CoreSelf Map (CSM)?**

**A: CoreSelf Journaling can reference prior CSMs and update them to our current position by re-asking two Real Questions:**

**1) Where am I?** and **2) Where do I want to be?**

Once the Internal Observer has been activated by CoreSelf Mapping, it remains on duty. The 4**S** CoreSelf Journaling format provides continuous access to the CSM's Bottom Circle whenever prompted by asking the two "observing" Real Questions again.

## The Ultimate Benefit of Daily Journaling

There are many journaling tools available in both paper and digital formats; the most important task is to find one that will work for you on a daily basis.

**Q: What do I gain from journaling daily?**

**A: You will develop and maintain the essential skill of articulating and then answering Real Questions; CoreSelf skills will be strengthened and be readily available when needed.**

The ultimate benefit of journaling is identifying significant Real Questions in your life. Daily journaling provides valuable time for reviewing the past and considering future plans. Real Questions can provide new perspective and spark curiosity. Their answers can be insightful and life-changing.

Refer to Chris' Real Question earlier in the book, ***"Why have I spent my whole life taking care of others instead of myself?"*** Another example: The mother whose daughter had just returned home after a long in-patient battle with addiction, asking, ***"How do I raise the child I have instead of the child I wanted?"***

Articulating these Real Questions is a major step towards generating greater self-trust, respect, and certainty about life decisions. Every answer can become a roadmap that can be explored with the possibility of alleviating or altogether avoiding future crises.

***"Asking Real Questions in a structured format (CSM) helps identify Best Next Steps in all Situations."***

CoreSelf Journaling represents a simple and repeatable tool in a world filled with complex systems and tools. The structure can easily be accommodated into one's current system and provides a methodology that can effectively be used on a daily basis.

### External Benefits of Daily Journaling

Psychology has developed tools and procedures that complement the CoreSelf Framework to safely explore difficult emotions and experiences and help an individual heal or reframe traumatic events from the past. CoreSelf Journaling is a viable tool for mental health clinicians to use in short-or longer-term work with selected clients to empower them to explore complex psychological and relational issues in a productive way.

CoreSelf Mapping, CoreSelf Positioning, and CoreSelf Journaling can also be used to drive team development to positively impact organizations' strategic goals and effectiveness.

## A Simplified Journaling Technique

While Jonathan has been journaling for decades, when I met him, journaling was a new skill for me. It occurred to me that journaling with the 4**S**s could be a powerful tool to reinforce and strengthen my CoreSelf Mapping skills. I started experimenting in July 2020 and have continued this practice daily. The benefits began presenting themselves in just four weeks; within two weeks I supplemented with a personal 1505, (a shorthand technique that will be elaborated on that answers four key questions and takes no more than fifteen minutes to write and five minutes to read).

Fundamentally, the 4**S**s: **S**ituation, **S**trengths, **S**truggles, **S**trategies on the right side of the CoreSelf Map (CSM) represent the foundation of CoreSelf Journaling (CSJ), with one addition when warranted.

Since you've already completed a CoreSelf Map, there are a number of components that you can leverage and revisit as needed. Daily Core Self Journaling will reinforce and amplify your skillset in a variety of ways.

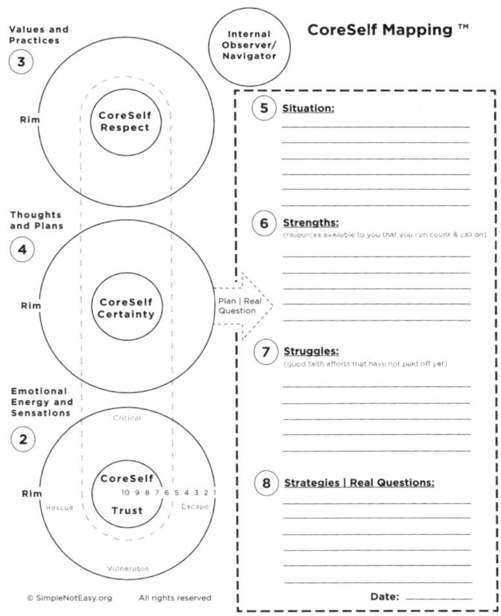


Figure 12.1 - **CoreSelf Journaling subset of CSM** (Individual Daily 4**S**s)

First and foremost, the initial CoreSelf Map you completed lit the "pilot light" of your Internal Observer/Navigator, and now waits for your future questions. It remains ready to reveal new Strategies and Real Questions aligned with your Values (Step 3) that can counterbalance difficult emotional situations.

Next, the **4S**s can be easily accommodated to one's existing journaling medium and format; if you do not have a journaling practice, we'll share ours. The key to daily journaling is finding a format that fits your schedule. It needs to be easy to access and easy to complete in a few minutes each day to become a habit.

Finally, be aware that during stressful or challenging Situations, when a full CoreSelf Map (CSM) is not feasible for whatever reason, an additional "5th **S**: **S**tation Point" should be added to capture the answer to the two important questions from Step 2:

**"Where am I?"** and **"Where do I want to be?"** Record the answers on the 1-10 scale.

High Energy | Low Energy

| 10 | 9 | 8 | 7 | 6 | 5 | 4 | 3 | 2 | 1 |
|---|---|---|---|---|---|---|---|---|---|

Low Tension | High Tension

Recording these answers (e.g., 3 > 7) in a journal entry will send a message to your Internal Observer/Navigator, "I need to talk. I'm in need of some feedback and a bit of relief from this highly charged situation to maneuver closer to where I prefer to be."

*It is comforting to learn that you have an internal advisor that you can call on at any time, that has your best interests in mind, is non-judgmental, and knows everything about you before you share anything with them.*

Daily journaling will better prepare you for productive conversations with employers, clients, colleagues, friends, family, and coaches—in short, all important relationships.

Daily journaling is an effective portal to self-discovery and growth. The authors' intent from the start has been to offer actionable ideas and tools up front and add supporting information after, especially for those who desire additional information, perspectives, or examples of Real Questions.

## A CoreSelf Journaling Journey (TP)

Early in my journaling practice, I reviewed over two years of my daily entries. It was interesting to observe past experiences of growth and setbacks, satisfaction and frustration, joy and sadness. Those years encompassed spending a significant amount of time with a good friend and his wife as he was battling ALS, a COVID pandemic, purchasing a new home in AZ, evolving our business while writing this book, and of course, a few challenging personal relationships. Reading this material was like watching an action-packed movie—the movie of my life—filled with colorful joy, profound sadness, and insightful learning.

Here are excerpts of my approach to **4S** journaling that illustrate my initial progress, including experiments and initial insights; I hope it is of benefit to others as they develop their own daily journaling practice.

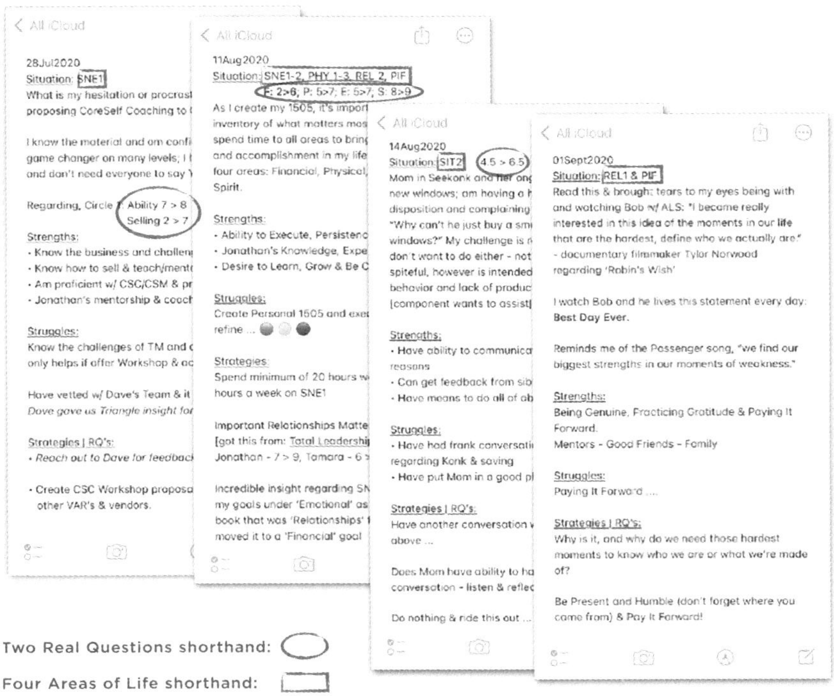


Figure 12.2 - **CoreSelf Journaling Excerpts** (TP)

Earlier, we emphasized the importance of asking two of the most important Real Questions (page xli) and recording those values in your journal entry to "fire up" your Internal Observer and Navigator; I've shared my shorthand above. Choose your own.

I found it useful to create a shorthand for both my journaling (Fig. 12.2) and for my personal 1505 (Fig. 12.3). Each intentionally correlates to the other:

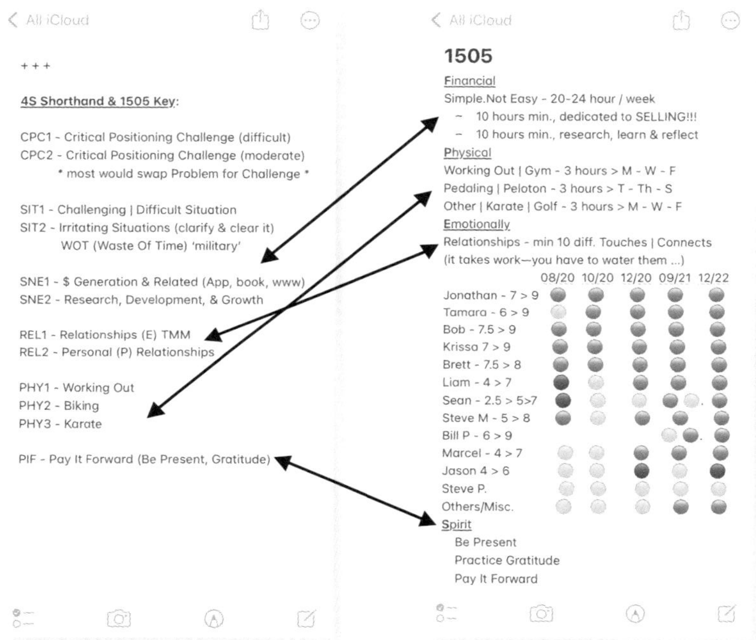


Figure 12.3 - **CoreSelf 4S Journaling & 1505 Keys** (TP shorthand to correlate both documents)

The 1505 (right) lets me monitor goals set in four important areas of my life. As time progressed, I found myself updating some of the components in these categories (e.g., REL1 - Relationships That Matter Most). My shorthand provided two benefits:

1. Knowing (and prompting me) when to ask the two Real Questions; and to
2. Experiment looking for patterns in my life.

The benefits of practicing gratitude have been studied and documented by many, so I decided to include it in my weekly journaling. Initially I selected Friday as my day to practice gratitude (and give myself a break from daily journaling). Unexpectedly, gratitude began leaking into my daily journal entries—it works! As journaling became a habit, I found that I didn't need a day of rest—a break— from daily journal entries.

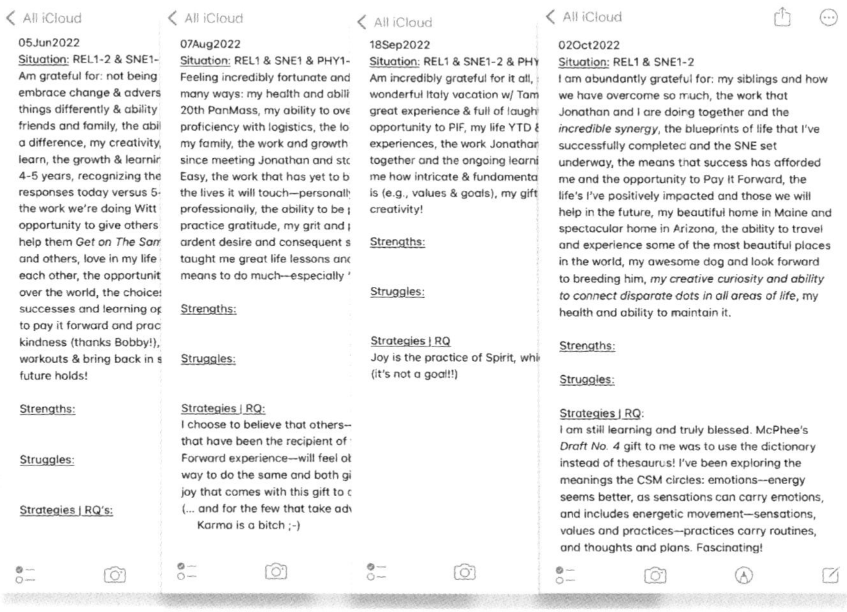


Figure 12.4 - **CoreSelf Journaling Excerpts** (TP Sundays of Gratitude)

**What's a 1505?** A business practice introduced to me by Phil Mydlach, in which:

- **Key metrics** are defined and agreed on (inserted into rows of a spreadsheet)
- Takes **no longer than 15 minutes to write** (employee creates for manager weekly)
- Takes **no longer than 05 minutes to read** (manager reads, both discuss weekly)

- Visual **green light** (GO) if on track or **red light** (STOP) if off track, then answer four questions:

    1. What happened?
    2. Why did it happen?
    3. How long will it take to fix?
    4. When will it be fixed by?

Below is a progression of my personal 1505s that span the same week over three years (Take note of the shorthand, notes to self, and growth of weekly relationship touches.)

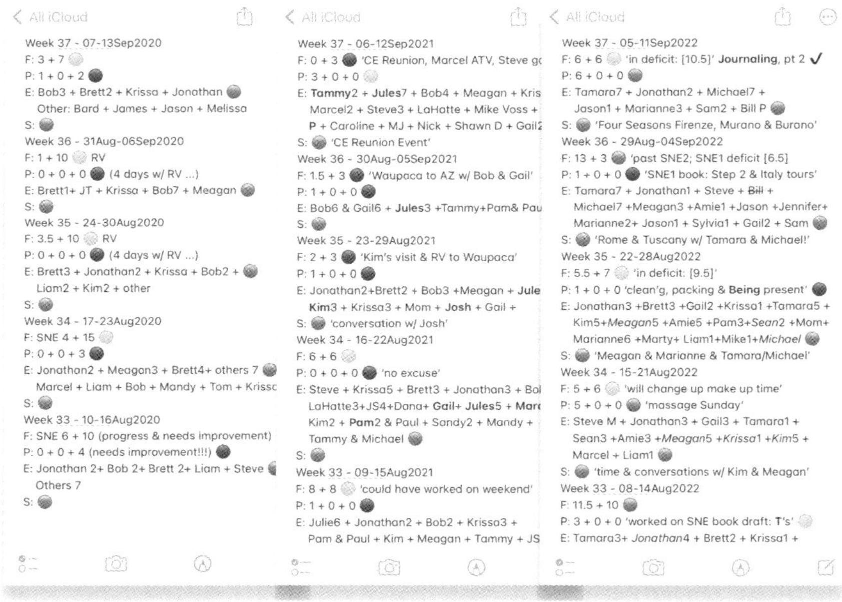


Figure 12.5 - **Three Years of Personal 1505** (TP shorthand provides quick, visual feedback)

In professional 1505s, colors are only green—on track—or red—off track; however, I strongly feel that with a personal 1505 it is important to add yellow—*intentionally* off track. Why, you may ask? In short, to give myself permission to shift where I spend my time knowingly, and not beat myself up later for being off track. For example, intentionally spending time with people (E) or projects (F)—in that order—That Matter Most (TTM) will negatively impact my physical (P) goals. Lastly, Spirit (S) is an important value to me, and this keeps it front of mind and I give myself weekly credit.

*Time Monitoring with 1505*
*may be as powerful as Time Blocking.*

Finally, I would like to share some promising experiments that I have done with my digital journaling; I mentioned earlier that one of the reasons for my shorthand (a.k.a. code lists) was to look for patterns in my life.

A few Real Questions were: **"Are there ways that one's journal could visually present itself to show patterns over time? Is there any benefit to comparing one timeframe of a journal to another?"** The answer is an exciting, **"Yes."**

Figure 12.6 - **Three Months of Journaling** (TP cut-and-pasted into free WordClouds.com)

The WordClouds experiment above represents three months ( Jul-Sep2020) that I cut-and-pasted into a free wordclouds.com visual representation without any edits; both are different views of the same data and I did not edit out the 4**S** **S**ituations, **S**trengths, **S**truggles, **S**trategies | RQ, so these were counted over 90 times, which makes them more prominent than if they had been filtered out. When you visually filter out the 4**S**s, you notice **keywords** that visually jump out (note that WordClouds makes all words lower case):

- **bob** - my good friend with ALS
- **jonathan** - my partner in SNE and co-author of this book
- **time** - a keyword in all of our daily lives
- **csm** - CoreSelf Map shorthand

Notice some words are prominent but smaller than above, as they appeared fewer times over three months, but enough times to percolate up from smaller words:

- **pam** - my sister, **gail** - bob's wife, **sne** - Simple. Not Easy, and **challenge** - situation

### What Checklists and Journals Have in Common

In *The Checklist Manifesto,*[70] Atul Gawande, a Harvard surgeon, showed that even experienced surgeons can improve the performance of their teams dramatically by using a simple checklist. He cautions:

> **"After using the checklist for a few days, you will probably decide that you can run through it mentally. You'll reason that it's so simple, you already have it memorized. Resist that impulse. Without looking at the physical checklist as part of your daily routine and recording your thoughts, you'll be likely to stop doing it altogether. Next thing you know, daily progress, catalysts, and nourishers will have slipped off your mental agenda."**

Swapping "checklist" with "journaling" in the above paragraph offers a compelling reason to maintain the habit of daily journal entries in our preferred format.

Journaling keeps us focused on important daily progress, including small wins, that add up over the week to let us know that we're on track with our long-term plans—big picture—and with the people who matter most.

Daily life offers us warning signs of wrong turns or exceeding speed limits, provided we are aware of our surroundings and paying attention to the dashboard of our life. Daily journaling can keep these warning signs front-of-mind to arrive safely.

Recording day-to-day entries gives us the ability to periodically step back and observe patterns—or holes in the pattern—that can provide both insight and powerful learning experiences. Over time these conversations with our

CoreSelf can lead to new courses of positive action that can strengthen our self-trust, respect, and certainty.

Conversely, journaling only when feeling overwhelmed or experiencing high anxiety might provide short-term relief and temporary safety; but rarely does it maintain the desired steady state—that centered place that we hope to maintain long-term. Daily journaling allows us to course-correct with small directional changes prior to encountering strong headwinds that could push us off course.

---

**Jonathan's answer to a frequently asked question: "I have a therapist. Why do I have to journal?"**

In therapeutic relationships, the counselor is often following "maps" and "protocols" of which the client is not aware. Many therapists feel confident that clients do not need exposure to the level of training which they have experienced themselves. There are a few branches of psychotherapy that teach the theory on which they are based and strongly recommend that clients study that theory on their own. Occasionally clients are encouraged to spend a significant amount of time outside formal therapy sessions practicing skills and methods for change. In recent years, many clients have been encouraged to study and practice disciplines like yoga and mindfulness meditation. These activities generally complement clients' work in session.

However, in most cases, the benefit of psychotherapy depends on direct contact, either in person or remotely, with the "provider." Often progress is measured by insight gained within the therapy hour and specifically validated by the therapist. A statement classically used by providers at the close of a session, "**We can explore that next time**," indicates that the clinician's wisdom is the key ingredient to progress. When intensely positive or negative moments occur between meetings, clients are usually expected to contain their feelings and wait until the next therapy appointment to explore them in greater depth with expert guidance.

My long experience on both sides of the psychotherapy encounter leaves me grateful but unsatisfied. I have come to question the hierarchical nature of the therapy relationship. The professional's knowledge and expertise make some progress possible; however, when psychotherapy pauses or stops for any reason, the client must carry on alone, although often welcome to return if they "feel stuck" at some point. **I believe that the traditional psychotherapy system used by itself lacks an opportunity for true collaboration, for a process of knowledge-sharing that both parties can develop further with or without immediate contact with the other.**

Tim Preston and I have been developing CoreSelf Mapping, Positioning, and Journaling since 2017 to address some of these concerns. Diagrams describing the relationships of multiple mind functions in a daily one-page journaling exercise are important means by which information about current situations and progress towards specific goals are shared. The method is primarily educational, with the intention to provide participants the tools, skills, and practice they need to move forward in their CoreSelf *Agility* skill level. The central focus in our work is increasing the participants' ability to explore their own constellations of resources and challenges by recording their observations and "course changes" with respect to key relationships. They can then become more confident planning sustainable short-and long-term strategies for themselves and the partnerships most important to them.

This "note to self" was written early in the process of including CoreSelf Mapping in my everyday practice as a licensed psychotherapist:

> **"I have been sensitive to the differences between psychotherapy and education for many years now. In many schools of psychotherapy, the relationship between the practitioner and the client is the medium through which therapeutic interventions are delivered. Demonstrating particular strategies and techniques in session is "education as a part of therapy."**
>
> **Education on its own involves a different contract. A client who is dependent on therapy "needs" to see the therapist and waits impatiently for the next meeting, whereas a student feels empowered to grasp the new tools they are learning to use and to practice**

**them independently in productive ways before the next "check-in." The knowledge gap between psychotherapist and client is very great; the gap between teacher and student is mostly years of practice.**

**I have concluded that while psychotherapy "successes" can be important and satisfying, teaching/learning "successes" are exciting in very different ways. Witnessing moments in which the student reports on work being done independently brings a deep and abiding satisfaction to the teacher. The student is connecting with inner resources that the therapist did not create and cannot sustain. Validating the success of such a CoreSelf connection is always an important contribution to the student's life going forward."**

Tim and I wholeheartedly agree with the folk wisdom that "a picture is worth a thousand words." Therefore, we have taken care to illustrate in detail the steps of CoreSelf Mapping, Positioning, and Journaling. The goal of providing the suggestions and mapping diagrams we have included is most definitely not to diminish or replace the vital role of the psychotherapist/client relationship. Our goal is to provide an alternate and parallel practice in which CoreSelf Journaling becomes a readily available resource that can both supplement and complement the therapist/client relationship. In such an arrangement, both participants may experience higher parallel levels of empowerment and satisfaction in ongoing CoreSelf Journaling work than they might have from the psychotherapy relationship alone.

We encourage clients and colleagues to take the time and make the effort to monitor and appreciate their movement, intentional and/or situational, with relationship to the core and the rim of all three of the major circles on the CoreSelf Map on a day-to-day basis. For all those who establish consistency in their Journaling practice, our experience as advisors of the process is that those efforts will enable them to be able to count on steady, measurable progress toward their specific professional and personal goals.

---

## A CoreSelf Journaling Conversation with Jonathan

Because a daily journaling practice is so instrumental to becoming the best version of our self, we'd like to share a conversation between the authors: Jonathan Thomas, MSW and myself, which was filled with informative and thought-proving comments. Some of this dialogue was expanded in other parts of this book. (circa April 2023): Enjoy!

Welcome back. Let's kickoff the morning with a quote from my journal notes: "The benefits of journaling are well documented; however, the key is to find an efficient 'shorthand' that will assist you in making it a daily habit."

That's a key bullet point but it also occurs to me from reviewing my notes that different people journal in different ways. Some create a shorthand that's easy and, I want to say, "fun." Granted, I don't know if I initially considered journaling fun, but it was intriguing, and soon did become a habit. Habits are things that we do without thinking about them. While journaling about difficult topics or challenges may not be fun when we're in the moment, we feel better when we're certain about a best next step or know that we're moving towards a safer place.

**What is the "secret sauce" that you make when you do a map? What changes in terms of your communication with yourself and your important personal and professional contacts through consistent CoreSelf Mapping?**

Journaling about a particular situation with a CoreSelf Map opens my mind. I've done many maps, but after the first one, there was a "pilot light" that ignited that we refer to as the Internal Observer & Navigator. When that light goes on, it becomes a conversation about where I am and how much emotional energy I have regarding whatever I'm going through and the stress of it, the tension, the pull. The next important question is, "Where do I want to be?"—meaning the destination, the goal, the different place I'm striving for. And that question provides space to think, instead of being stymied by the stress of a particular situation or challenge.

Being able to zoom in and out of the situation when mapping or journaling allows me to observe the situation through different lenses. We've talked about the metaphor of arriving at the scene of an accident. Sometimes the ability to step back and observe the situation for a moment, even if it is uncomfortable, helps one to see the situation from a different perspective and be clear about where one would be safer and better able to get needed help—knowledge that can make all the difference in an urgent situation.

**Yes, could not agree more.**

"Observing the situation" was a skill set that I learned over time. Even though I had never journaled before, it took only a few weeks. Learning to journal as an observer of my own situation changed me and my relationships with others for the better.

Writing as an observer has highlighted three important dynamics:

- Journaling doesn't reduce the importance of resolving the situation; it helps me filter some of my own intense feelings, allowing me to consider my beliefs and thoughts more carefully.
- It also allows my thoughts about a situation to be more easily shared with the other parties involved.
- Observing can help filter any impulse I might have to blame someone else for my painful feelings, which would only intensify already heightened emotions; journaling helps me to take responsibility for my own emotions by naming and keeping them in context.

Observing the situation or challenge, naming resources that are available to improve the situation, then acknowledging previous good-faith efforts to do so, provides clarity and new perspectives on possible best next actions. Writing in this way offers an unexpected benefit of journaling: it helps to approach getting on the same page with others—especially in some important personal relationships.

What I've found fascinating is that sharing my observation of a situation, casually and unexpectedly, has invited others to do the same. My best intention is to reduce tension and stress through sharing my journal entry. Unfortunately, despite all my best efforts, it is sometimes necessary to part ways and my 4**S**s provide me some closure.

**Yes, I agree. Reviewing what happens when I journal about the map and how it helps me get on the same page with others is why I'm such a huge fan of our structure. To make the rewards of the CoreSelf Mapping process evident by sharing one or more daily journal entries can be a great benefit to all involved.**

As you were talking about "safety deposit boxes" the other day, I was thinking about the term "compartmentalizing," which reminds me of another important benefit of journaling that might help others. Recording a journal entry creates some needed distance from a highly stressful situation. In a remarkably different way than compartmentalizing, journaling allows me to address and acknowledge an issue, even if I don't have all the answers yet. I know that my mind will keep working to resolve it, and I will find a better solution than if I reacted impulsively. I know how important this is because, as a young person, I became great at compartmentalizing intensely stressful situations because they often triggered painful migraines, which took a lot of time and effort to resolve.

Let's reset and return to the basics of journaling; I'm a huge fan of the 4**S**s: **S**ituation, **S**trengths, **S**truggles, and **S**trategies. The one thing I'd encourage people to do when they find themselves in a stressful situation that has built up a lot of energy or heat is to review their current CSM and then ask themselves these two Real Questions: "Where am I?" and "Where do I want to be? This is important because our Internal Observer and Navigator have already been turned on by CoreSelf Mapping, and these questions were the igniters.

**The other day you added another metaphor when you said your Internal Observer and Navigator are like coaches on your**

**team who want to help you become the best version of yourself. Knowing I've got these coaches on my team and that I can ask them the two questions is powerful. To be able to engage with them at will: "Hey, coach, I've got some questions for you and I'm looking for some feedback. Now, please!" I don't have to pick up the phone and approach them with: "Hey, do you have availability on Friday at two?" I don't have to wait until our next coaching session. I don't have to wait till the next time that we're in the gym together or on the field. Any time of day, I can just ask, "Hey, can we talk?"**

That accessibility is pretty huge. Can you share how you journal, what works for you, and why it's worked? Techniques that you figured out over the years? I've seen some of your writing and know we have different styles.

**Yes, but first I want to add something that occurred to me while you were sharing, and then I'll come back. Since the map was very young, there's always been an "observing" left side of the map that's using images and a "navigating" right side of the map that uses language; they work together to create a pathway leading to a more satisfactory destination. [This is] our brain's ability to function like a GPS that can provide "turn-by-turn" directions that bring us closer to our goal.**

**Let's look at how those two different functions happen in the mind. One of the ways the CoreSelf Map works is to improve focus on specific important facts about the current Situation. For instance, are we participating in an active Triangle right now and: who is closer or more distant from whom? Another way is to track the flow of emotional responses/reactions, both positive and negative, between the individuals involved.**

**My questions evoke my Observer's responses, which I have learned to trust and record. Therefore, when I ask at the conclusion of the map, "Where am I now?" relative to the rim and the**

**core of my major circles, it's extremely fortunate that my Internal Observer/Navigator has been tracking my position through this conversation and can precisely plot my current position. By consulting my CSM, I have plenty of data from which to choose my next move.**

**Okay, so here's another metaphor for you. People have solo-circumnavigated the globe on a private boat; they have a way to secure the tiller while they are sleeping but still moving, and when they wake up, it's a new day and time to ask: "Where am I now, compared to when I checked in last?"**

That's a great comment.

**If I had to say in fifty words or less, that's what I think journaling is. It's focusing on important new locations. However we do it, with a nautical tool, a sextant, or GPS, or whatever—it's putting a pinpoint on the map about where we are now. And then time goes by and events happen. Maybe we're out of awareness for a while and then we get to check back in. Always, stuff has happened, but we're able to track the segments of the journey. And not just to find out where we are, but also to find out where we've been and what the total experience of being on that boat has been.**

*As we process questions and get new information, internally and externally, we actually move closer to where we want to be in a measurable way.*

**In moving toward a resolution of my situation, I can easily pick a location "where I was, closer to the rim," and "where I want to be, closer to the center." When I journal, I pay very close attention to where I am on that line. My observer will quickly calibrate where I am quickly and precisely. For example, if I started**

**at a "5" and wanted to be at "7," looking at the map and having followed all the steps of the map, I can pick the point that tells me my current location.**

The key point is to journal daily in whatever format works best for you and visualize where you are on the map. There's a sort of magic that occurs when observing a CoreSelf Map in the context of a single, specific situation or challenge; the elements of the map have a way of interacting with each other and making things clearer.

**Right, which is why when I was doing psychotherapy, this whole thing started with me drawing while I was listening to my clients in session. "Where are they?" is one of the things that I had to ask myself. Are they in the bottom circle, or are they in the top circle, or are they in both? Have they moved anywhere closer to the middle circle? I was tracking all that in part because I was trying to be responsible in my job. But I was also just fascinated by the process of transferring what was going on in the room into another medium; I translate what a person is saying into their movement in the circles on the page.**

In essence, you were creating the "visual language" of CoreSelf Mapping.

**I was, because I am a visual learner. But I did it originally as a service to others because I could give them clearer feedback if I indicated "where I thought they were" on the CoreSelf Map at that moment. And then I would turn the clipboard over and say, "This is what I understood from what you just told me about where you were. Is this what it looked like to you?"**

**And they'd say "yes," or "no," or it would lead into another conversation. So the "where" question became a very key part of that process of trying to understand where they were and how they got there and where they wanted to go, and then I didn't have to tell them where to go next. They figured it out themselves, which was incredibly comforting to me because I didn't want to be "driving their boat."**

Your last comment was really interesting—"I didn't have to tell them where to go next. They figured it out themselves." How can journaling soften critical thoughts, provide safety, or provide direction? What are your thoughts?

**I think there's an "on" switch that moves the journaling process into "ongoing mode." So once I've even entertained the idea of doing a map, I think that's already got some current going through that switch. Then I've got more access to my Observer than I have when I'm just being my executive self and getting things done. Of course, most of the time I am focused on completing tasks in functioning mode, but when I choose to "hit the switch" by doing a CoreSelf Map or Journaling, I get clarifying feedback on the situation from my Observer. I think the important question for me is: "How often do I take steps to tune into my monitoring function/Observer, and for how long, before refocusing on the project of the moment?"**

**For me, pottery is a good metaphor because actually that's what I had been doing when I started studying the process of how to "refocus." I had learned to very carefully draw the shape of the pot before beginning to make it. Then when I had the ball of clay fixed on the wheel and it was spinning while I was shaping a bowl or a plate, I was completely involved, almost meditating.**

**But I learned that it's very important, part way through the process, to step back and look at the shape of the unfinished pot from somewhere else in the room. Then I would refer to my drawing to see how close in profile my pot was to the drawing. One style of working for the potter is to repeat as perfectly as possible the original shape and size of a particular pot. Repetition and noticing variation are what make it work. I would make fifteen or so copies and usually they would become more refined and interesting through the whole series.**

**The analogy to CoreSelf Journaling is this: first, it takes energy and focus to prepare the ingredients properly so that the clay on**

**the wheel can take the stress of the complete process; next [comes] refining the design through continuous and repeated observation of many versions; last [is] refining techniques of trimming the pot to create the desired product.**

**I think that when you are mapping or journaling, it is similar: first deciding what you want the pot to look like and then what in actual experience it does look like. So the first part of mapping is drawing as best you can the "shape that you want to have." That is your Bottom Circle. Then you move into the Top Circle and you try to physically create that shape. In comparison to your drawing, it has some variance or "deficiencies." Next, you do the Middle Circle exercise of asking: "What are my best next steps to do this?" If I have taken the time to create the detailed profile first, then my brain can gradually transform it into a three-dimensional object from the two-dimensional outline that's on the page.**

**When I turn the project over to the I/ON and continue practicing, "they" continue to develop it when I'm thinking about other things. Maybe it's overnight, maybe it's a couple of days later, but something that I have been trying to describe or to understand shows up in my imagination and my next series of pots is better defined and much closer to the original look and feel of what I was "inspired to create."**

Right. That's your brain doing work on its own when you're not engaged directly. In architectural design, a lot has been written about the creative process, which suggests "sketching" lots of possibilities, sifting through them, then experimenting with those that are most promising. The importance of giving your mind time and space to "incubate" new concepts has been well documented. Let it settle and then go back to it.

You sparked another thought when you were discussing what happens when doing a map. One of the big gifts of the map is slowing down and "just observing" to let the magic happen. Let a part of you talk to yourself. Let yourself know something you didn't know you knew. Have a conversation with the coaches you didn't even know you had. That "coaches comment" the other day was pretty insightful.

Journaling lets us slow down, observe, and relieve pressure in a stressful situation, and have a conversation with ourself. In Barrett's book, *How Emotions Are Made*, she posits that our experiences year-to-date create and impact our emotions; consequently, she suggests, "If one wants to increase how they experience the world, increase your experiences … learn a new language, visit a new country." And, I might add, "Do a new map; make a new pot."

*Journaling is a way to increase these experiences and its only cost is our time. It allows us the opportunity to experience our situations in new ways by observing and considering different options. CoreSelf Mapping allows us to create new experiences by contemplating alternate best next steps that leverage all of our emotions, beliefs, and thoughts. In my experience, it's hard to not grow if I am journaling on a daily basis during both good and bad times.*

I'm interested in how different people journal and ask questions. Regardless of one's initial method, the importance of creating the daily habit is key. Experiment with what works for you and what doesn't, but remain focused on learning about yourself. Here are a few prompts to get us started in the daily habit of journaling: What time of day works best for you? Is it early morning when the day starts or is it the end of the day before you retire? Do you prefer longhand or shorthand? Each of us has a preference and the question is important as it will reinforce our habit. Do prompts make it easier to start? Are they necessary later? There are many daily-journal formats that can be purchased that offer prompts in the form of questions, categories, and reminders.

**A lot of people talk about watching the flow between the mind and the heart and between feeling and breathing. I don't think there is a right or wrong answer. It's personal.**

I'm clearly biased, as I think our 4Ss makes journaling simple and scalable. Granted, there are no prompts, but my experience is that everyone has a top-of-mind situation they're thinking about without any prompting.

I wanted to touch on gratitude and the importance of adding it to one's journaling practice; the overall benefits of practicing gratitude are well documented. I thought: "What if there was a way to make journaling fun while also giving my functioning mind a break and still move forward toward a goal? That's a process for which I would certainly be grateful!" Never having journaled before, I wasn't sure whether it would work; it certainly wasn't a habit, and it didn't even feel natural. So originally, I designated Fridays as my "day of gratitude," which initially felt like a day off. It was a sort of game I played, but it was a way of giving myself a rest day from journaling, if you will. My entire Friday journal entry was, "I am grateful for____?"

However, as I became more proficient and my journaling became a daily habit, two things happened: I started having frequent double entries on Friday, which was the end of my week and I had a need to add more than just gratitude; I eventually changed my Gratitude Day to Sunday, which reduced my double entries on Friday. Next, and more importantly, gratitude started to appear in entries throughout the week, sort of creeping into daily life.

Starting the practice of gratitude has its benefits over time, which has been written about plenty. Inevitably it builds into each day, which can give each of us those natural dopamine or serotonin hits.

Is there anything else that stands out in your mind as we're going through this section on CoreSelf Journaling?

**There's something that I have been trying to describe about momentum that comes from practicing the CoreSelf Map: starting at the Bottom Circle, climbing to the top of the page, and then letting it roll down. I've always enjoyed that part of the way the map works. It's about coming to a new awareness of one's part in a situation, either an emotional or logical understanding that creates a positive momentum. That's what I think people are looking for when they undertake this kind of a practice; they want to either reverse the direction of certain circumstances or build momentum in a positive direction. That's what I see the CSM process being about in a certain way. If something good has come out of this work we have been doing, let's take advantage of this momentum.**

I'm curious: what's been your experience of when you've seen or suggested that people journal? Are they leaning towards paper? Leaning towards digital?

**They're "all over the map," pun intended. I think both media work as long as they take their mental process and transfer it into something "objective," something they can see and touch, no longer just a thought. The more one wields a pencil or a pen or a tool of some sort to do that, the better. But some people just don't operate that way. Maybe it's because of how their nervous system is set up, but they can dictate. One person I know just talks to me with his hands on the keyboard and he's looking at me. He's absolutely eye to eye with me the whole time. And he's relating in a very detailed, verbal way, but it's all going into the machine as though he doesn't have to think about it.**

Such a gift to be able to effortlessly type while talking.

So, I think it's best to have a physical activity that parallels whatever the thinking process is and whatever the discussion process is when words are flying through the air. Ideas are flying through people's minds that have to be captured in some way, like a butterfly or a nut. It's got to be available for continued study in "real life."

Let's expand on two other journaling topics: one's perception of journaling might be determined by how one is introduced to it and the frequency of one's practice. For example, journaling might be suggested by a professional advisor, which often happens in therapy. Or journaling may be self-initiated, perhaps just from curiosity. I surveyed a number of friends recently about this and I learned that most of the people I know that journal do so as a result of their therapist's suggestion. I also learned that they only took the time to journal when they felt badly and tended not to journal when they felt well. I can't help wanting to ask them what they are missing if journaling works just as well both times.

In sales there's an interesting and recurring dynamic with new salespeople; they work really hard to learn new sales skills and products, get comfortable calling people they don't know, and if all goes right, they experience some financial success and proceed to enjoy the fruits of their labor. Then for a variety of reasons, they stop doing what they did to become successful and wake up one day wondering why they're not successful anymore.

My point in sharing the story above, is that it sure seems that journaling has a similar narrative. If journaling can help us navigate bad times, then why stop journaling during good times? Could journaling in good times provide us with tools to navigate bad days? Is there some intrinsic value to knowing what a good day looks like, instead of just what bad days feel like?

So back to, "Is one's perception of journaling related to how they were introduced to it?" And the second question revolves around: "What is the benefit of journaling all the time, not only during challenging or bad times?"

**The question really is, "Does journaling give you a perspective**

**and a set of tools that are going to move your life in the direction you want it to go?" If it is, then intrinsically it's good for you and probably good for others too. That has been my experience.**

That was a lot. I appreciate your sharing. I remember your summary of our first year of work together: "I never minded being a walking stick. I just never wanted to be a crutch."

**Right.**

Those are two powerful words that paint powerful pictures. I had never discussed any of those thoughts before we started our work together. It was refreshing.

I love the work we're doing, too. Once someone turns on their Internal Observer "pilot light," it's accessible and they don't have to keep coming back to us to relight it. I want to be in the business of helping people be self-sufficient, grow, and become the best version of themselves.

**Yes.**

And if they need help along the way, then pick up the phone and let's talk. There's availability, but it's not a requirement.

It's interesting what you say about therapy and it's similar to how I think about business consultants and many types of coaches. Many share a concept I call the "financial umbilical cord," which is, "As long as you keep paying me, I will keep helping you; however, the moment we sever that financial umbilical cord, I will stop providing coaching. Hopefully if you continue the practices I suggested, you will continue to succeed at the same level." I think that some consultants and coaches have created such a complex model that only they can decipher it and share its value. I've often wondered, "Is their model's complexity intentional to prevent others from duplicating their performance?"

*I believe we're both less interested in making people feel better temporarily and more interested in helping them get somewhere that they want to be, that is good for them, and when they get there, we want them to know how they got there. The CoreSelf tools give people an amazing opportunity to be self-sufficient and to understand how their Internal Observer and Navigator helps them navigate to where they want to be.*

**Yes.**

You made a comment about journaling, ***"People tend to continue to do something that is good for them."***

It occurs to me that one of the biggest benefits of CoreSelf Journaling is that each of us only needs to ask and answer a few Real Questions in their lifetime to have a significant impact on the direction of their life, to determine where it's best to go. Then they have a better opportunity to understand the parts they can play to make meaning in their world.

**If one Real Question could change your life or its trajectory, why not search for it every day by journaling?**

I vividly remember very early on, probably in our first month or two, you invited a number of peers to your home and one gentleman agreed to have you walk him through the CoreSelf Map in front of us to observe how it works live. That was very courageous of him.

As I recall, he had spent decades working, had done well financially, and was on to his second or third career. Unfortunately, his health (Situation) had suffered and I remember him saying, *"My daughter would like me to walk her down the aisle one day, and my parents would like to see me walk her down the aisle one day."* Next, he shared resources available to him to get healthier and good-faith efforts he has made along the way. When he got to the final step (Strategies | Real Questions) of the Map, he said out loud, *"I realize I've spent my whole life taking care of other people, instead of myself."*

I was new to this material and only knew enough to be dangerous, so I raised my hand and asked, *"Didn't he just ask a Real Question?"* Suggesting, if he restates his last statement as a question, he would be asking *"Why do I always take care of other people, instead of myself?"*

**Yes.**

There's another Real Question, that always gives me goosebumps; it's a story you've shared about a daughter that's been in the hospital and coming home, and it's still unclear if she's going to get well. The mom is completing a CoreSelf Map and in the last step writes, *"How do I take care of the child that I have, instead of the child I wanted."*

**Yes.**

If journaling in this method, in this format, could deliver one or two Real Questions like those above, that could totally change the trajectory of somebody's life in all the best ways, why wouldn't they continue to do it?

**Right.**

So this is interesting. Let's go back to journaling in general; we were talking about how some people need structure and prompts. My bonus son was visiting, and his girlfriend had a journal she had purchased and was loving; I asked her what she liked about it and if I could leaf through the table of contents and some of the structure. It was divided into the twelve months of the year: the first three months were titled "self-awareness," April was "understanding your past," May's topic was "love," June was focused on "relationships," and by July, she gets to "self-care." Seriously! I'm being a little bit sarcastic. August was "happiness," September was "habits," October was "passion," in November she gets to "personal growth," and finally in December we have "goals."

I'm glad it was working for her, but to me there were so many things wrong with the structure. Like, should "self-care" really be halfway through the year? My point isn't to chastise or make fun of this particular journal because I'm sure someone put a lot of time and effort into it and many are getting benefit from it, and they're selling journals. My main point is that effective journaling should give the participant the ability to address their most important needs, while building on all these other areas of life.

Which is why I'm totally jazzed about the CoreSelf Map and CoreSelf Journaling; they both allow one to go to whichever one of these topics is front of mind and the most important to them at that specific moment of their life.

**Yes, something that I've been thinking about is how simply the CoreSelf's three circles plus one are structured. The structure can apply to any activity in any situation. So I think the structure matters, and the structure includes energy and emotion. It includes values and practices, and it includes thoughts and plans. So I think you can have a structure that helps order people's experience and leads them to take constructive action. That is simple enough that it applies to every person in every situation, because those are the main things that I think we do: we react to things; we have energy to spend, and we do it to improve our situation in one way or another. How and what we believe about why it works can have an extraordinarily wide range. So it's fascinating to me that there's this practice, this CoreSelf structure, that is so flexible that it can go into any corner of somebody's experience and still be relevant.**

It sure seems to address what needs to be addressed at the moment. If I go back to when we started and I was learning the map and I'd try to put myself in other's shoes: I assumed people might not want to start with a sensitive situation, or would feel the need to hold their cards close to their chest, as if to say, "I'm not going to share anything personal with you." So when prompting them to think of a situation, I'd offer a lay-up situation, like, "How can I be a better person—personally or professionally?"

However, 100 percent of the time, every single map I've done with others, every single time, bar none, no one has ever picked my lay-up situation. They always think of a situation of interest to them, in the moment, almost instantaneously.

Right.

It can be anything. How do I find a job? Or it can be something very personal. One individual was so impressed with his results that he shared his personal situation after, "I've been getting some slack from my wife because she doesn't think that I'm helping to bring up our kids the way that we talked about from a religious perspective." His simple strategy was to periodically just take the pulse of his activities.

**And some people say, well, that's just nagging on their mind. It's tugging at them because they value that relationship.**

Right. I shared the map with my bonus son, Sean, regarding a situation he wanted to consider. He kept saying the whole time that he was doing the map, "This is so accessible; this is incredibly accessible."

**Yes.**

I want to make note of Covey's eighth habit: "Find your voice and inspire others to find theirs." He wrote this book fifteen years after he wrote, *The Seven Habits of Highly Effective People*, which is so amazing. Someone was expanding on how do we employ the eighth habit? They wrote, "The key to learning the eighth habit is the whole-person paradigm. To achieve our potential, we should respect each of the four elements of ourselves—body, mind, heart, and spirit. To improve teamwork and get the most from our people [and self], we need to honor each of these aspects and respect each team member as a whole person."

**Yes.**

The reason this resonates with me is because I think it's exactly what journaling does. I'm respecting each of those four elements in myself. It reinforces our conversation the other day when we started talking about CoreSelf Journaling and kept referring to the components of the CoreSelf Map. It was incredible how new material was uncovered and said in a different way.

One of the most insightful comments, for me, was asking you to expand on where the second question, "Where do you want to be?" came from. Because the first question, "Where are you?" seemed logical and intuitive.

Your response was eye-opening. ***"I would ask, "Where are you?" and then we would talk about, "What are the things that you could do to be in a place better than where you are right now?" Then it made sense to ask, "And if you did those things, where would you be?"***

What I find incredibly insightful about where you ended with the map and where it is today is you streamlined the process and you did it much more effectively. And now we have the neuroscience research that explains why it works.

Today on the bottom circle, one simply points to their current location: "Here's where I am. Where do I want to be?" Then they move to that third step, values and practices, that has a question built in: "What are the things that I could do to get to a better place?" It's fascinating to see how you've changed the order of the questions and made the process more effective.

Moving up to values and practices: "What are the things that matter most to me?" Also meaning, "What are the things that center me?" A reminder of all the things that you know you already can do. Then counterbalance and tether that down to the bottom-circle questions: "Let's talk about things that you could do that would help you get there, that are in alignment with your values." Practicing zooming in and out of one's position on the CoreSelf Map to calm an emotionally charged situation is a good strategy.

**Yes. Thanks.**

It's very cool. I was always curious and never thought to ask, then you answered it. The CoreSelf Map makes the process go much smoother, faster, and better. All the pieces are in there. The ingredients mix themselves together in all the right ways. I think that's where you give yourself a high five.

**It's pretty cool how well it works. That's my high-five to myself.**

It's quite fascinating. So now a couple other things and I will just wrap up the interview in the next ten or so. There's been some really interesting components that came out in the conversation the other day. You mentioned Joan Didion saying, "I don't know what I think until I write it down."

Yes. A number of people have said something like that. I think those were her words. It shows up in terms of famous quotes from several people, but that one was hers.

Another one is from James Baldwin, a novelist, poet, essayist, playwright whose description is really interesting: "James Baldwin who read his way up." He writes, "When you're writing, you're trying to find out something which you don't know. The whole language of writing for me is finding out what you don't want to know. What you don't want to find out, but something forces you to do it anyway."

**Yes. It's interesting. When I read Didion and Baldwin saying such similar things about how our minds work that allow us to**

**write down "what we don't know," I think they are referring in their own terms to the way the Internal Observer/Navigator "surprises" us in all parts of the CoreSelf method.**

Do you think there's something in the human condition that makes writing help? That makes us resist something that's as simple, clear, and doable. Seems like so many people spend their lives all mired up in things that are complex, and perhaps they resist simple solutions like journaling.

**Well, I'm going to pick back up on Sean's comment about accessible. I think it is accessible. I think it is simple. You know, it's not a bad thing if the only not easy thing to do is, "Just Map It."**

Right, on a regular basis.

**Yes. Right.**

Didion goes on to say, "Had I been blessed with unlimited access to my mind, there would have been no reason to write, I write entirely to find out what I'm thinking, what I'm looking at and what I see and what it means, what I want and what I fear."

Combining her comments with your journaling sequence of a movie comments the other day, when the picture tells you how to arrange the words and the arrangement of the words begin to tell us what's going on in the situation.

**Yes.**

I'm reminded of Gawande's *The Checklist Manifesto*, a Harvard surgeon who showed that even experienced surgeons can improve the performance of their teams dramatically by using a simple checklist.

**Ah yes, I read about that a long time ago, and that's really good.**

He emphasizes that if surgeons could be better surgeons with checklists and experienced pilots continue to use checklists, imagine the power that checklists could bring to our everyday lives.

I think a powerful reminder from Gawande's *The Checklist Manifesto* directly applies to daily journaling. He writes, "After using the checklist for a few days, you will probably decide that you can run through it mentally. You'll reason that it's so simple, you already have it memorized. Resist that impulse. Without looking at the physical checklist as part of your daily routine and recording your thoughts, you'll be likely to stop doing it altogether. Next thing you know, daily progress, catalysts, and nourishers will have slipped off your mental agenda."

Change his word "checklist" to "journal," and it's profound how similar they are!

**Yes.**

So at the end of the day, journaling is similar. You'll probably think you can do it in your head. Journaling keeps us focused on important daily events and progress, including small wins. Small wins that add up over the week to let us know we're on track with our big picture, long-term plans that matters most.

**Yes, I think that's an essential, very essential piece to know towards the end, but maybe it shouldn't wait till the end. We could put in a note towards the beginning which says, "I don't know how you feel about checklists, but by the end of this book I hope that you're convinced that it's a good idea."**

Good point to move it closer to the start.

In closing, I've been looking forward to this chapter for a long time because there's so much good material waiting to get out on the page like: "Daily life can offer us warning signs of wrong turns or exceeding speed limits. However, we have to be alert to our surroundings and watch the signs along our journey. By recording day to day entries we provide ourselves with the ability to periodically step back and observe patterns, or holes in the pattern, that can provide both insight and powerful learning experiences.

Over time, these conversations with our inner core can lead to new courses of positive action that can increase both our emotional energy and self- esteem."

**Excellent.**

It's all there.

**It's exciting.**

This is good. I'll get this one down as well. Anything that we missed? History has shown, as we've been doing this project, we'll get the words down. And then as we start sharing examples of journaling, different types of journaling, I feel like the graphics will talk back and forth and complement each other like they've been doing.

**Yes. Did I tell you about the time period for me, which was a couple of years ago, when I was dictating my journal entry? I think of this with great fondness because I was getting out in the morning, especially at this time of year, and walking two and a half miles on the rail trail right near my house.**

I do remember that.

**Where I was walking, you know, it's parallel to Route 9. So, there's some traffic noises, but especially early in the morning, it's just incredibly peaceful and the trail goes across the bridge over the Connecticut River. So, I would just bring my phone and get started on my walk. And when I felt like it, spontaneously I turned on the machine and started dictating. What's my situation? And it came out with more coherence than I would have expected.**

That is an effective different medium in which to journal.

**Yes, and a different way to capture it. So, you know, when I finished, I could just print it out and see it in black and white. And that was a good way to do it. Yes, different mechanism,**

**different process, but the Observer switched on and I had the ability to review that moment.**

Very cool. The technology today, tools we didn't have before. They're so easy and accessible today. It's pretty amazing, right?

**Yes. I always wondered about the choice we were talking about earlier—the pencil, the pen, or the keyboard—is an integral part of how this works. I did an experiment, and I found out that speaking, when I began the paragraph with the date and "Situation," my Observer function "switched on." Even when I was walking and looking around at a beautiful farmland landscape, I could have been distracted, but the description of the "Situation" was there.**

Earlier I asked a question about should we journal every day and I got caught up on what's the best way. But it occurred to me as we were talking that the benefits of identifying and answering a few Real Questions in a lifetime can be have powerful impact. I guess the sheer fact that as long as you are Journaling every day, even if it's on a napkin, it keeps the process going. That reminds me of a conversation we had about a graphic of two concentric circles with a smaller circle outside them symbolizing the Internal Observer. A simple graphic reminder that either I want to get closer to my core or…

**Yes.**

…journaling can be done on a napkin. It can be done on a train on the way into New York City. I suspect in hindsight that as long as you're doing it on a daily basis in whatever format works for you at that time in life and at that time of day, consistent with your practice, you're going to receive the benefit from doing it.

**These small little pieces can turn into one big win and you don't need a lot of big wins in life.**

Right. It's not about winning and losing, but to live an amazing life.

Look at the project we're doing right now. This is an amazing win, you know? Very, very neat. Well, that's all I have for today.

That was plenty and thank you.

**Thank you.**

# PART FIVE

# *Mastering CoreSelf Agility*

# **Mastering CoreSelf Agility:** Putting—Pulling It All Together

"Putting it all together, you can stack the deck in your favor by playing to your strengths, living your values, and finding the best arena for your greatest results."

— JIM COLLINS

*Jim Collins has spent over 25 years rigorously researching Real Questions about what differentiates great companies and great leaders. He has looked at these questions from different vantage points and published his findings solo and with others. They include: Good to Great, which asks why some companies make the leap to great and others don't; Built to Last, which asks why some companies remain visionary for generations; Great by Choice, which asks which leadership behaviors thrive in chaos and uncertainty.*

*These are all questions we can explore when Getting on the Same Page with ourselves and others. Similar to Collins, we want to become a student and a teacher not of what makes companies tick, but of great relationships. What are the strategies that improve sustainable relationships from good to great? What arenas are best for practicing our CoreSelf skills?*

---

Practicing CoreSelf Agility is **simple**; this book provides the blueprint to build a strong foundation. CoreSelf Journaling provides the daily practice and opportunity to expand its power as needed. The entire CoreSelf Map is available to you whenever difficult situations arise and you choose to invest the time to navigate to where you want to be and to new Real Questions.

Mastering CoreSelf Agility requires significant effort and intention. Getting on the Same Page with another or others might *initially* feel **not easy**. Experimenting with new skills can feel challenging for all participants—especially if prior communication or collaboration has not gone smoothly.

There will come a day that, with practice and curiosity, you will find yourself *observing* who is involved in a triangle. Next, you will silently ask yourself, "Where am I in this conversation and where do I want to be?"

This is the beginning of CoreSelf mastery. This is your mind internalizing the material. This is what Bowen would refer to as *systems thinking*. This is not losing empathy for the conversation or relationship—it is learning to actively observe the situation.

What happens next is actively navigating the situation or conversation by asking Real Questions.

Watch and listen to what will happen next.

You will notice that another or others will engage in a different way. The building blocks of trust and respect are being laid. The conversation is different.

We are getting on the same page, at the same time, together!

### Building Blocks of Mastering CoreSelf Agility

Mastering anything usually requires years of dedication and practice. If mastery is synonymous with being an expert, it has been said that expertise requires 10,000 hours.

That equation might look like this:

**40 hours x 50 weeks = 2000 hours per year x 5 years = 10,000**

This might seem daunting until we put it in perspective. A college degree (a.k.a. new expertise or experience), years of work experience, completing an apprenticeship are all examples of putting in the time (hours).

Mastering CoreSelf Agility can be done in a few minutes every day in addition to any/ all of your current responsibilities or roles. It starts with daily journaling.

The more actively you practice, share, and teach others—the faster you will master it.

## A Roadmap to Mastering CoreSelf Agility

Just as there are different ways to get to the same destination, each of us can choose how we will embark on our journey to Mastering CoreSelf Agility.

Start by considering the skills, knowledge, and desire that you bring to your CoreSelf journey. Are you looking to better understand and center yourself? Are there important relationships in your life that you would like to strengthen? Perhaps you are at a stage in life where you are ready for a change and are simply looking for a new destination …

Consider your destination (and level of mastery desired) and the joy in arriving there.

**Q: What is the best way to get to the desired destination safely?**

You have taken the first steps to experience the CoreSelf journey. You have a new companion—your Internal Observer and Navigator—who carries additional resources in your backpack of life.

Enjoy the journey of *Getting on the Same Page* with yourself and others.

---

To share your CoreSelf Experiences with others, visit:

https://www.simplenoteasy.org/share-your-coreself-mapping-experience/

After sharing your CoreSelf 5**S** Experience, we will share 90 days of the **Core**Self + Portal with you for free; this area of the website is filled with tools and perspectives.

# Epilogue: **Work to Be Done and an Invitation**

"It often happens that scattered facts of a certain kind float around for a long time, but that nothing scientific or solid comes of them until some[one] writes just enough of a book to give them a possible body and meaning. Then they shoot together, as it were, from all directions, and that book becomes the center of crystallization of a rapid accumulation of new knowledge."

— WILLIAM JAMES

*Who will add to this new knowledge? You are invited. There is still much to be done.*

---

## *CoreSelf Applications*

William James began this investigation and Ernest Hilgard expanded on it; we believe that we have made it accessible without the need for hypnosis; there is more work to be done to expand on this knowledge and other possible applications. You are invited.

### Primary and Secondary Education

While we have initiated some research with younger children (K-12) and in college environments, there are many related areas to explore, such as the ability of the CoreSelf Framework to add value for guidance counselors or for the Zones of Regulation[71] curriculum work being done in school systems around the country.

### Professional Organizations

Ongoing research and application in the professional workplace will continue to refine practices in Getting on the Same Page with others; it will be of value to monitor how Getting on the Same Page with oneself (personally) can impact work/life integration.

## Psychology and Neuroscience

There is much to be researched and learned in both these fields, specifically around functional MRI (fMRI) of the brain; observing brain activity when completing an individual CoreSelf Map; or how group's brains mesh when CoreSelf Positioning.

# Appendix:
# **Glossary of Terms**

The following glossary of terms is offered and any trademarks after the beginning of the book were removed for readability; Simple Not Easy, LLC reserves all rights to these terms and many of them are in the process of being, or are, trademarked.

***CoreSelf Mapping™ (CSM)*** is a framework delivered in an eight-step worksheet for *Getting on the Same Page* with oneself. It is comprised of two main components: an observing component (left side) that builds *CoreSelf-Trust*, *CoreSelf-Respect*, and *CoreSelf-Certainty,* and a navigating component (right side) that utilizes language to explore/expand on the **S***ituation,* **S***trengths,* **S***truggles,* **S***trategies (4***S***).™*

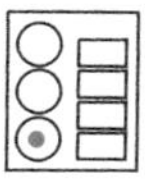

It is an effective and efficient tool for leveraging one's *Internal Observer/Navigator* to identify a *Best Next Step* or a *Real Question.* (Illustration to the left is used in the book with dots to show current step)

***CoreSelf-Respect™*** provides an opportunity to counterbalance heightened emotional energy (in bottom circle) of a single, specific situation by changing focus to an individual's important values and practices that one can count on to center themself; practicing these values increase one's self-respect. This portion of the CoreSelf Mapping worksheet represents Step 3 of 8 and is also referred to as the Top Circle.

***CoreSelf-Certainty™*** acts as a vantage point between heightened emotional energy of a single, specific situation and long-term values to allow individuals to consider thoughtful plans or options that might provide more certainty. This portion of the CoreSelf Mapping worksheet represents Step 4 of 8 and is also referred to as the Middle Circle.

***CoreSelf-Trust™*** focuses on observing and answering two important Real Questions to identify one's current and desired position; these questions capture one's Emotional Energy and Sensations (on a scale of 1-10) pertaining to a single, specific situation. Moving closer to where we want to be can increase one's self-trust. This portion of the CoreSelf Mapping worksheet represents Step 2 of 8 and is also referred to as the Bottom Circle.

***Situation, Strengths, Struggles, Strategies™ (4S)*** represent the navigating right side of the CoreSelf Map; one writes out a brief and concise explanation of the single, specific *Situation* (Step 5 of 8) being explored. Next one notes *Strengths* or resources available to call on or count on that could assist in moving this situation closer to where they want to be (Step 6 of 8). Following resources available, one makes note of any good-faith efforts they may have made to resolve *Struggles* (Step 7 of 8) with this situation; Struggles provide an opportunity to give oneself credit for investments made that have not paid off yet (this is the antithesis of listing all the things one has tried that have not worked). *Strategies* (Step 8 of 8) represents any potential solutions that could move one closer to where they want to be regarding the situation; one's *Internal Observer/Navigator* is actively participating in providing insight during this long-hand portion of the CoreSelf Map.

***Internal Observer/Navigator™ (I/ON)*** represents a conscious part of our brain that can be activated and accessed using the CoreSelf Map; the importance of this part of our individual brain is multifaceted and it is aware of our unique history and narrative, our current values and prior choices, has our best interests front of mind and is not judgmental, is available and accessible 24x7, and can provide insightful *Best Next Steps* or *Real Questions*.

***Best Next Step™ (BNS)*** refers to the best next action that I/we can take to move us closer to where I/we want to be regarding this Situation. The significance of a single BNS for an individual is that it represents a specific action in a sequence for which one will remain accountable. Completion of a BNS represents a single "small win" in a sequence of actions that can lead to significantly larger outcomes (wins).

***Real Questions™ (RQ)*** are defined as: 1) I do not know the answer, 2) I want to know the answer, 3) I am willing to courageously ask a Real Question, and 4) I am willing to listen to the reply and reflect before responding. RQs are the opposite of rhetorical questions, which are asked to see if others can answer correctly or arrive at the same answer the questioner has already determined.

***Getting on the Same Page™ (GoSP)*** with oneself. The CoreSelf Map provides a framework for individuals to inventory all of their positions regarding a specific Situation. An individual's Internal Observer/Navigator provides valuable insights, questions, and potential solutions for positive movement.

***CoreSelf Positioning™ (CSP)*** builds on the CoreSelf *Framework* to provide a methodology for *Getting on the Same Page* with others (two or more people). All of the skills learned in CoreSelf *Mapping* (CSM) are demonstrated and built upon during this exercise. Beginning with an agreed upon single, specific *Situation,* each individual involved completes a CSM to record their observation and written position on this challenge. Each participant's *Internal Observer/Navigator* has a positive multiplier effect on combined *Best Next Steps* and *Real Questions.*

Next all parties collaborate to create a joint *4S* (*Situation, Strengths, Struggles, Strategies)* document. The iterative process of asking, hearing, and recording, corroborates that all parties have actively participated in and now have a common understanding of their joint position going forward.

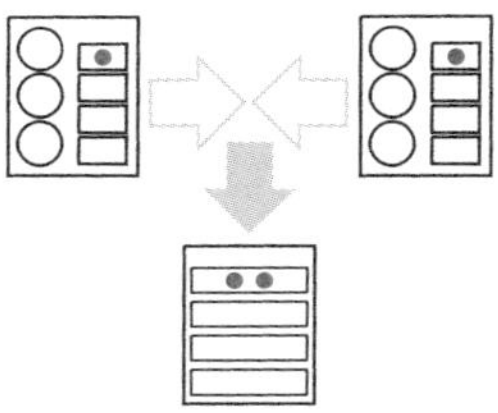

***Getting on the Same Page™*** with others occurs when all parties can move forward from a common understanding of where they (we) are and where they (we) want to be collectively. The magic of this approach is that it captures the framework of a *Same Page Partnership™* in a single document.

*CoreSelf Positioning* changes "We (you) Need to Get on the Same Page (with me)," to "We (all of us) want to be on the Same Page moving forward."

***Same Page Partnership™ (SPP)*** represents a formalized methodology of combining all of the CoreSelf tools into a cohesive workshop over time. The SPP Workshop builds on an individual's skill with CoreSelf *Mapping* and adds collaborative team building skills via CoreSelf *Positioning.* CoreSelf *Journaling* is introduced to practice and strengthen these new skills. A

CoreSelf Journaling practice strengthens these new skills on one's journey to Mastering CoreSelf Agility.

***CoreSelf Journaling™ (CSJ)*** is the practice of completing the 4**S**s (***S****itua-tion,* ***S****trengths,* ***S****truggles,* ***S****trategies)* of the CoreSelf Map on a daily basis.

The 4**S** format can be easily added to an existing journaling practice.

***Mastering CoreSelf Agility™*** represents a commitment to studying the concepts and integrating CoreSelf practice into one's daily conversations and relationships. It's about learning to actively observe our daily interactions and the triangles of people involved—being aware of who is on the inside and outside of the triangle; slowing down to ask ourselves where I am and where do I want to be in this important relationship; and being consciously aware of our internal dynamic responses to changing external conversations.

As with mastering any important skill, this is a lifelong commitment.

***CoreSelf Framework™ (CSF)*** is defined as a predetermined sequence that: identifies actions that need to be taken; functions as an algorithm which provides step-by-step input to produce reliable output; simplifies or explains a complex system.

***CoreSelf™*** is defined as one's most authentic or true self.

> Oneself (myself, ourselves, yourself ) refers to traditional ways we describe our everyday experience. This description includes all aspects of our reactions to internal and external stress, our wishes and intentions, our beliefs and actions, and any consequences of those actions. It's trying to deal with everything at once, day after day.
>
> CoreSelf refers to the key components of self that generate and increase *CoreSelf-Trust, CoreSelf-Respect,* and *CoreSelf-Certainty.*

***CoreSelf Certified Advisor™ (CSCA)*** has applied and completed a curriculum to become certified in utilizing the CoreSelf Framework in their current professional practice (e.g., coaching, legal, medical, therapy) or as an internal resource within their Company. They are committed to help others, and themselves, become their best CoreSelf.

# About the Authors

## JONATHAN THOMAS

Because he was born into a family of teachers and craftspeople, it is not surprising that Jonathan began his adult life working with clay and teaching children and adults how to make functional and beautiful objects on a potter's wheel. He spent ten years after college perfecting those two skills. Moving into an administrative role, he became the founding director of a large and successful regional community arts center in Northeastern Ohio.

Out of this experience, a new direction emerged when Jonathan undertook the challenge of coaching both individuals and teams to higher levels of accomplishment. A master's degree in Social Work at Columbia University in New York provided opportunities to develop expertise as a teacher and trainer of communication skills.

Coaching individuals and teams in the medical field occupied the next phase of his journey. In addition to directing an outpatient hospital team for twenty years, he developed a private counseling practice. Clipboard sketches created in the process of studying successful partnerships became the foundation of CoreSelf Mapping. Using the visual perspective learned during his earlier career opened up pathways to creative communication strategies for work with patients and colleagues. Empowering others to create their own mapping solutions as individuals and in teams became his central mission.

Over the years, professional associates in many fields saw possible applications of CoreSelf Mapping in their own disciplines and asked for more technical and practical information. The Simple. Not Easy. partnership was formed to respond to those requests. CoreSelf Mapping continues to evolve into a means of achieving breakthrough insights in response to challenges in many fields including executive coaching, legal mediation, wealth management, and fitness training.

## TIM PRESTON

Tim's why is to spark others to create, grow, and overcome with a reminder to Pay It Forward with gratitude. He lives with his lab in Scottsdale, AZ; enjoys red wine; and is an avid cyclist who's participated in the PanMass Challenge for over 20 years, which donates 100% of their fundraising to cancer research.

During his first ten years in the architectural industry, he learned that if you listen to building spaces, they will tell you what they want to be. Often a renovation solution is restoring a past flow to the space, with new designs tending to complement and unify the surrounding structures or spaces. Observing and asking those who experience these spaces can provide important feedback and insight.

Over the next twenty years, he built and grew a number of companies—some successful and others not so much. Creating a building or business from a blank piece of paper can be incredibly exciting; consequently, learning and growing at different stages of a building's or company's growth can be challenging.

Since co-founding Simple. Not Easy., LLC in 2017 with Jonathan, he has been able to share CoreSelf Mapping (CSM) with hundreds of individuals. Tim's passion for creating and working with businesses has evolved CSM into CoreSelf Positioning (CSP) and Same Page Partnership (SPP) for organizations, their vendors, and clients. CSP allows companies to grow and leverage their most important asset: their people. A unique benefit of the CoreSelf approach is that professional team members can utilize the same tool in their personal lives for growth and clarity.

Tim's learned that if you help people, professionally or personally, listen to themselves, they possess the ability to identify their best next steps and Real Questions. Practicing Getting on the Same Page with ourself and others is an absolute game changer.

# Notes

1 Ernest R. Hilgard, *Divided Consciousness: Multiple Controls in Human Thought and Action*, pg. 209-210, 212

2 Robert J. Ringer, *Looking Out for #1,* 1985

3 Joseph Deitch, *ELEVATE: An Essential Guide to Life,* 2018

4 https://www.goodtherapy.org/learn-about-therapy/types/family-systems-therapy

5 Bowen's concept of differentiation of self is a valuable tool, others, especially in close relationships. https://www.mypeoplepatterns.com/blog/differentiation

6 https://www.hbs.edu/ris/Publication%20Files/11-091.pdf

7 https://www.psychologytoday.com/us/blog/inside-the-box/201401/creativity-lesson-betty-crocker

8 "The Hidden Self," first published in *Scribner's Magazine,* Volume 7, Issue 3. March 1890

9 https://www.simplenoteasy.org/certainty-in-self-positioning/

10 Roger Trapp, *Harvard Business Review,* "Why Leaders Need To Learn To Be Able To Handle Ambiguity," August 2022

11 Available in our CoreSelf+ Portal at www.SimpleNotEasy.org

12 Hypnosis is a state of altered consciousness. The science of hypnosis began in the late 18th century with France Mesner (1734-1815), a German physician with an interest in astrology

13 Ernest R. Hilgard, *Divided Consciousness: Multiple Controls in Human Thought and Action*, 1977

14 Stephen Covey's 3rd Habit, in *The 7 Habits of Highly Effective People* is: "Put First Things First."

15 Stephen R. Covey, *The 7 Habits of Highly Effective People: Powerful Lessons in Personal Change,* pg. 18, 1989

16 https://www.franklincovey.com/the-7-habits/

17 Marshall Goldsmith and Mark Reiter, *The Earned Life: Lose Regret, Choose Fulfillment*, pg. 103, 202

18 https://www.newyorker.com/books/page-turner/what-dale-carnegies-how-to-win-friends-and-influence-people-can-teach-the-modern-worker

19 Ernest R. Hilgard, *Divided Consciousness: Multiple Controls in Human Thought and Action*, 1977

20 Matthew Schafer, Daniela Schiller

21 Excerpt, Steve Jobs's 2005 commencement speech at Stanford

22 https://s3.amazonaws.com/media.cloversites.com/ae/ae4d98d9-4f73-46c4-a095-c1a61c9a949a/documents/Triangles_-_The_Glue_of_the_BFST.pdf

23 https://www.thebowencenter.org/core-concepts-diagrams

24 https://www.ted.com/talks/brene_brown_the_power_of_vulnerability?language=en

25 https://brenebrown.com/about/

26 https://www.thebowencenter.org/introduction-eight-concepts

27 https://s3.amazonaws.com/media.cloversites.com/ae/ae4d98d9-4f73-46c4-a095-c1a61c9a949a/documents/Triangles_-_The_Glue_of_the_BFST.pdf

28 Robert K. Greenleaf, *Servant Leadership: A Journey into the Nature of Legitimate Power & Greatness.* 2002

29 https://www.thebowencenter.org/core-concepts-diagrams

30 https://www.sciencedirect.com/science/article/abs/pii/S0007681322001070

31 https://jamesclear.com/delayed-gratification

32 https://bio.libretexts.org/Bookshelves/Cell_and_Molecular_Biology/Book%3A_Cells_-_Molecules_and_Mechanisms_(Wong)/03%3A_Bioenergetics_-_Thermodynamics_and_Enzymes/3.01%3A_The_Laws_of_Thermodynamics

33 Geoffrey A. Moore, *The Infinite Staircase: What the Universe Tells Us About Life, Ethics, and Mortality.* 2021

34 https://www.rulerapproach.org/

35 https://ideas.ted.com/should-emotions-be-taught-in-schools/

36 https://www.nytimes.com/2014/03/23/opinion/sunday/the-lost-art-of-the-unsent-angry-letter.html

37 Stephen R. Covey, *The 7 Habits of Highly Effective People*, pg. 132

38 https://www.susandavid.com/search/values

39 https://www.ted.com/talks/simon_sinek_how_great_leaders_inspire_action/c

40 https://www.nirandfar.com/common-values/

41 Brené Brown, *Atlas of the Heart: Mapping Meaningful Connection and the Language of Human Experience.* 2021

42 Harris, Russ. *The Happiness Trap: How to Stop Struggling and Start Living.* 2022

43 https://www.business.com/articles/management-theory-of-stephen-covey/

44 Brianna Wiest, *101 Essays That Will Change the Way You Think*, Ch. 40, pg. 189

45 "Where am I? Where am I going? Scientists are discovering how the brain navigates," by May-Britt Moser and Edvard I. Moser, ScientificAmerican.com, January 2016, pages 26-33

46 https://mayfieldclinic.com/pe-anatbrain.htm

47 "The Brain's Social Road Maps" in *Scientific American* 322, 2, 30-35 (February 2020), Matthew Schafer, Daniela Schiller

48 https://vivekasrani.com/

49 https://vivekasrani.com/2021/07/31/it-is-okay-to-ask-for-help/

50 Lisa Feldman Barrett, *How Emotions Are Made: The Secret Life of the Brain.* 2018

51 https://mayfieldclinic.com/pe-anatbrain.htm

52 https://www.linkedin.com/posts/lynnemccarthyphd_in-his-book-thinking-fast-and-slow- daniel-activity-7090168849978802176-sXmt/?utm_source=share&utm_medium=member_ios

53 https://fisher.osu.edu/blogs/leadreadtoday/why-most-new-years-resolutions-fail#:~:text=Researchers

54 https://www.franklincovey.com/the-7-habits/

55 Stephen R. Covey, *The 7 Habits of Highly Effective People: Powerful Lessons in Personal Change*, pg. 18, 1989

56 https://medium.com/@nicksmoffatt/3-ways-to-break-the-bubble-youre-stuck-in-4e10793aa4a1

57 Ray Dalio, *Principles.* 2017

58 Steward D. Friedman, *Total Leadership: Be a Better Leader, Have a Richer Life.* 2014

59 *Harvard Business Review.* January 2005, https://hbr.org/2005/01/managing-oneself

60 Andrew S. Grove, *Only the Paranoid Survive: How to Exploit the Crisis Points That Challenge Every Company.* 1999

61 https://www.forbes.com/sites/georgebradt/2018/04/10/what-it-takes-to-accelerate-through-a-strategic-inflection-point/?sh=26efa2845cee

62 https://www.forbes.com/sites/georgebradt/2011/11/02/the-five-most-important-questions- for-brave-leader/?sh=39109bad66e3

63 Joseph S. Deitch, *Elevate: An Essential Guide to Live.* 2018

64 Ken Blanchard and Sheldon Bowles, *Raving Fans: A Revolutionary Approach to Customer Service.* 1993

65 https://www.thebowencenter.org/introduction-eight-concepts

65 https://www.thebowencenter.org/introduction-eight-concepts

66 Teresa Amabile and Steven Kramer, *The Progress Principle: Using Small Wins to Ignite Joy, Engagement, and Creativity at Work.* 2011

67 "Inner Work Life." *The Progress Principle: Using Small Wins to Ignite Key, Engagement, and Creativity at Work*, Amabile and Kramer, 2011. (Rf HBR May 2007), pg. 30-31

68 Hal Gregersen, *Questions Are the Answer: A Breakthrough Approach to Your Most Vexing Problems at Work and in Life.* 2018

69 Lisa Feldman Barrett, *How Emotions Are Made: The Secret Life of the Brain.* 2018

70 Atul Gawande, *The Checklist Manifesto: How to Get Things Right.* 2011

71 Leah M. Kuypers, MA Ed. OTR/L, *The Zones of Regulation: A Curriculum Designed to Foster Self-Regulation and Emotional Control.* 2011